Toward a
Meaningful Life

TOWARD A
MEANINGFUL
LIFE

THE WISDOM OF
THE REBBE MENACHEM
MENDEL SCHNEERSON

SIMON
JACOBSON

wm

WILLIAM MORROW
An Imprint of HarperCollinsPublishers

Dedicated to the Divine Creator,
Who gave us the Rebbe

HarperCollins books may be purchased for educational, business, or sales promotional use. For information please e-mail the Special Markets Department at SPsales@harpercollins.com.

First William Morrow hardcover edition published 1995.
First Perennial Currents edition published 2004.
Second William Morrow hardcover edition published 2017.
First William Morrow paperback edition published 2017.
Second William Morrow paperback edition published 2019.

Designed by Richard Oriolo

The Library of Congress has catalogued a previous edition as follows:

Jacobson, Simon.
Toward a meaningful life : the wisdom of the sages / Rebbe
    Menachem Mendel Schneerson ; adapted by Simon Jacobson.
    p. cm.
"Although this work is a product of contributions from many
    scholars, inevitably it is an adaptation as seen through the lens
    of my scholastic experience and understanding of the Rebbe,
    for which I assume responsibility."—Introd.
ISBN 0-688-14196-X
ISBN 0-06-051190-7 (new edition)
1. Hasidism 2. Habad 3. Judaism—Doctrines.
I. Schneerson. Menachem Mendel, 1902–1994. II. Title.

BM198.2.J33   1995   95–15865
296.8'3322—dc20
                                                              CIP
                                                              r95

ISBN 978-0-06-298876-8 (pbk.)

23 24 25 26 27 LBC 12 11 10 9 8

CONTENTS

II / SOCIETY

III / G-D

INTRODUCTION

N̲o matter how accomplished we may be, no matter how happy or wealthy or talented, at some point we all find ourselves seeking a deeper meaning in life. Never has this search been as intensely felt as it is today. We have searched in houses of worship and in our own hearts; we have read the works of every kind of philosopher, psychologist, and spiritualist imaginable.

How is this book different? *Toward a Meaningful Life* is a practical distillation of the philosophy of Rabbi Menachem Mendel Schneerson, a revered leader and teacher known throughout the world simply as "the Rebbe." Although he was a Jewish leader, the Rebbe taught—and embodied—a distinctly universal message, calling upon all humankind to lead productive and virtuous lives, and calling for unity between all people. His passing on June 12, 1994, was met with great sadness—not only by the hundreds of thousands of members of the Lubavitch movement of Chassidus, which he had led since 1950, but by heads of state, religious leaders, editorial writers, and the additional millions who recognized his selfless leadership and deep spirituality, his dedication to education and to the betterment of society.

Much of the media coverage in the later years of the Rebbe's life concentrated on the controversy over whether or not he was the Messiah; what was often overlooked was the fact that he was a brilliant and kindhearted leader and teacher, which accounted for the extent of his influence and the legendary devotion of his followers.

This is the first book to present the Rebbe's original teachings to a wide audience. Although it contains material about the Rebbe himself, it is not a biography; although it concerns theological matters, it is not a book on theology; although the Rebbe was a renowned scholar in matters both secular and spiritual, it is not a scholarly text. *Toward a Meaningful Life* is meant to give the modern reader, from the most devout to the most secular, a fresh perspective on every important aspect of his or her life, whether it is a trivial concern or the most profound matter of the soul. Above all, this book is meant to be practical, a blueprint for building a life of greater significance.

While the Rebbe's teachings and leadership were indeed revolutionary, his message is hardly new. In fact, its strength lies in the continuation of the generations-old tradition of Torah. The Torah (the word means "instruction") includes not only the Bible but the collective written and oral teachings, and their interpretation and application, passed down from master to pupil in an unbroken chain beginning with Moses. For every question that modern life raises, the Rebbe found its answer in the Torah—the same Torah that Moses was given at Mount Sinai, the same Torah whose unshakable truths have been embedded in the very makeup of humankind since its genesis.

The Rebbe applied these universal truths to real-life situations, from the wonder of birth to the sadness of death, from the technological revolution to the very definition of G-d. (Throughout this book, G-d is written with a hyphen instead of an "o," in keeping with the Rebbe's style, based on the belief that even while writing, we must feel a sense of awe, a sense that G-d is above and beyond all our words.)

Because of the comprehensive nature of the Rebbe's teachings, this book includes material that might already be familiar to some readers, particularly those acquainted with theology and Torah thought. While the Rebbe's presentation is firmly built on the teachings that preceded him, he reveals dimensions that go well beyond the initial understanding of any given idea. One of his great contributions was the capacity to consolidate the information and ideas of the past and present them in the most relevant of terms. He also revealed the underlying unity and truth in all disciplines of thought and all aspects of life. The greatest tribute one could pay the Rebbe would be to say, "I have not learned anything new from what you taught, for I have sensed it all along." This is the sign of the most profound truth emerging—a truth that resonates from within, not one that is imposed from outside.

The material in this book has been gleaned from a variety of sources. The Rebbe's literary output was formidable: a corpus of writing including hundreds of essays and over 200,000 letters to people of every conceivable background, occupation, and faith. The Rebbe spoke to groups and met with thousands of individuals who were seeking guidance on matters ranging from the personal to the political; he established many charitable and educational organizations, which he frequently addressed. His various activities and his daily interactions, even the seemingly simple ones, contain myriad lessons. But the Rebbe's main medium for teaching, and the primary source of material for this book, was the *farbrengen*, which means "gathering."

These gatherings were held several times a month in the central Lubavitch synagogue, at 770 Eastern Parkway in the Crown Heights section of Brooklyn, New York. They were attended by thousands of people, including the Rebbe's followers and visitors from all corners of the world. The Rebbe would be seated on a platform at the front of the great room; also on the platform were elderly followers and the dignitaries who were visiting on any given day. For several hours, as is traditional in Chassidic culture, there would be songs and toasts of *l'chaim*, which served to punctuate the Rebbe's intense discourses on matters that would span a variety of issues, from the personal to the societal to the theological.

The Rebbe would often begin a *farbrengen* by discussing the relevance of that particular day by relating it to the weekly Torah reading or an approaching holiday. The Rebbe would demonstrate the significance of the various currents of time that had converged to form the unique juncture occupied by the day of that *farbrengen*. Next, he might offer a commentary on a discourse of Chassidic teaching written by one of his predecessors. Over the next several hours, he might examine a debate in the Talmud (the vast anthology of Jewish law and lore, comprising the Mishnah and Gemara, which was compiled in the second and fifth centuries and includes commentary and analysis of the Torah). He would first explore it with the "conventional" tools of Talmudic logic and then move on to uncover its inner spiritual dimension; he might then do the same with a section of Rashi's classical commentary on the Bible, a saying in Ethics of the Fathers, a legal nuance in Maimonides' Code of Law, and a mystifying allegory in the Zohar. The *farbrengen* might also include an analysis of some historical event or a recent news story.

The Rebbe's style was unique. He would cite a Biblical verse or a Talmudic passage, then pose questions and counter-questions to reveal many levels of the same truth, drawing from many different disciplines of thought—from the literal and legal to the metaphorical, from the homiletic and mystical to the Chassidic tradition of Torah thought—always touching on both the philosophical and psychological implications of any given issue.

Regardless of the topic of the talk, the Rebbe always concluded with the same question: How can all this be concretely applied to our daily lives? For as the Rebbe stressed constantly, all the virtuous *thoughts* in the world do not produce a single virtuous act, a single gesture of help, a single dollar for charity. A fusion of thought and action, he taught, was vital.

After each *farbrengen*, in keeping with Chassidic tradition, a small group of individuals would gather to review and transcribe the Rebbe's discourse. This was an especially demanding task, since *farbrengens* were often held on the Sabbath or another holy day on which Jewish law prohibits writing or the use of electronic recording devices. These reviewers would literally memorize the entire *farbrengen*, becoming, in effect, "oral scribes." They would later commit the Rebbe's talks to paper, annotate them, and often present them to the Rebbe for final review before they were published and distributed worldwide. For over forty years, the contents of the *farbrengens* were compiled and disseminated in the original Yiddish, and translated into Hebrew, English, and other languages.

As anyone who ever attended even one *farbrengen* could attest, they were events of astounding impact—at once intellectually, spiritually, and emotionally fulfilling. Having grown up in a Chassidic family in Crown Heights, I had the good fortune of attending *farbrengens* since my early childhood. In 1977, I was privileged to become one of the "oral scribes," and in 1980, I was appointed chief editor of the committee that published the aforementioned transcripts. It was also my honor, therefore, to gain an intimate knowledge of the Rebbe's teachings and the Rebbe himself, communicating with him on a regular basis in order to clarify various points in his discussions, and to incorporate his exacting notes and revisions into the published version of his talks.

There is no one book or one person that could hope to do justice to a man of the Rebbe's stature and to teachings of such intensity. *Toward a Meaningful Life* represents a humble attempt to convey something of the tremendous depth and scope of the Rebbe's writings and talks, particularly as they pertain to living a truly meaningful life.

There were several serious challenges in compiling such a volume. Because the Rebbe incorporated so many different intellectual dimensions and idioms in his writings and discourses, it was difficult to summarize them in chapter form. A particular challenge lay in rendering into English concepts that were originally expounded upon in Yiddish and Hebrew, creating translational problems that were as much ideological as linguistic.

In addition, the Rebbe's message touched individuals in very different ways. Asking one hundred people what they took away from a particular *farbrengen* might well produce one hundred different replies. A discouraged teacher might have been inspired to continue his or her work. A man or woman in the midst of great suffering might have found solace and soothing. Another person might have gained the strength needed to commit to a deeper spirituality. And yet another might have come away with a new intellectual insight.

Most challenging was the task of trying to capture the Rebbe's personal spirit, a combination of gentleness and strength, of simplicity and profundity, of sheer accessibility and remarkable intellect. And finally, there was the challenge of trying to encapsulate in a single volume a lifetime of teaching based on the power of a tradition of Jewish scholarship that is over three thousand years old.

While the Rebbe's teachings carry a universal message, it must be remembered that he was primarily a Jewish leader. As such, he launched an unprecedented effort to encourage every Jew to embrace and deepen his or her connection to Judaism; his talks specifically addressed the means by which Jews should perform the *mitzvoth* ("obligations") that the Torah commands them. But all his teachings essentially revolved around one premise: that G-d created the universe with the intention that humankind would civilize and perfect it. And G-d gave a blueprint by which to fulfill that purpose: Torah. As the Rebbe constantly reminded us, observing Torah and its edicts is neither optional nor arbitrary. While utterly faithful to Jewish tradition and law, the Rebbe presented the Torah's universal truths in an accessible and relevant manner, providing instruction to people of all races and all beliefs. The Rebbe put special emphasis on the obligation to adhere to the Seven Noahide Laws, the universal code of morality and ethics that was given to all humankind at Sinai. (Given this shared foundation and given the fact that such words as "Torah" and *"mitzvoth"* may be foreign to some readers—however integral and morally imperative they are in the Rebbe's teachings—they were used in this book only when it was necessary to protect the integrity of a particular concept.)

No matter how diverse we may be as human beings, no matter how our individual backgrounds and destinies may differ, the Torah's message speaks to us all, saying that each of us was created in G-d's image, and that we must live up to that fact. That we must live in harmony with one another and transform this world through virtue, charity, and kindness into a home for G-d. Every person and every nation has a particular role—and their specific *mitzvoth*—through which this universal mission must be fulfilled.

As a true leader of his times, the Rebbe taught us how to lift the veil of modern life, to discover the essence of any issue and address it accordingly. This book is an attempt to show that the Rebbe's teachings are more relevant today than ever; to demonstrate how they can profoundly reshape the way we think and act, by introducing us to a higher level of consciousness and awareness; how he prepared us to enter the new millennium, with a fresh perspective in all areas of life and in all the sciences—political, social, and physical.

If this is the case, one might ask, why is it that relatively few people are fully aware of his message? The answer is quite simple. In part it is that the Rebbe's wisdom has never before been made accessible in English to the general reading public. But also, the modern world might have trouble relating to the message of an elderly rabbi dressed in Old World Chassidic garb. Yes, he might be a great Talmudic scholar, but can he teach us anything relevant to our modern lives? Can he relate to contemporary society and to the climate of desperate soul-searching?

Toward a Meaningful Life demonstrates that the Rebbe is not only a brilliant religious scholar but an unparalleled observer of the human condition. Just as the Rebbe's teachings unravel the layers of mystery surrounding a spiritual question, this book will hopefully unravel some of the layers of mystery or unfamiliarity surrounding the Rebbe. Perhaps you are well aware of his philosophy, or perhaps you have merely glimpsed his face one time in a newspaper. In either case, this book attempts to allow you the opportunity to feel as though you were attending a *farbrengen*, experiencing the Rebbe's insight and warmth.

The Rebbe's message, and the way he taught it, is the culmination of more than ninety generations of Torah scholarship, beginning with Moses. It is also the culmination of nine generations of the Chassidic tradition, going back to the founding of the movement in 1734 by Rabbi Israel Baal Shem Tov, who was followed by Rabbi Dovber of Mezeritch and Rabbi Schneur Zalman of Liadi. It was Rabbi Schneur Zalman who established the branch of Chabad Chassidus later known as Lubavitch.

Chabad Chassidus, in brief, is the study of the esoteric and spiritual dimension of Torah, which, when coupled with Jewish law and tradition, creates a synergy of body and soul, helping make G-d as real and relevant to us as the air we breathe and the food we eat. This inner dimension was always a part of tradition, but in previous generations it was studied only by a select few scholars. Chassidus ushered in a new era in which this mysticism was made more accessible to those who wished to study and be inspired by it, with the intention that disseminating these teachings would make G-d a reality in people's lives and bring redemption to the entire world. Each progressive generation of Chabad-Lubavitch leaders, of which the Rebbe was the seventh, further broadened the teachings of Chassidus.

One of the Rebbe's most important contributions was presenting Torah and Chassidic thought in language that was contemporary and timeless. This book is culled from the Rebbe's teachings of Judaism and Chassidism—which are so central to his approach—concentrating on the universal elements of his message, how all people must dedicate their lives to G-d.

When I wrote the first draft of this book, it was my intention, as a devoted student of the Rebbe, to present a thorough portrait of the Rebbe's wisdom and approach to life—to write a book, that is, *about* the Rebbe. Over time, though, it became apparent that the first widely published book about the Rebbe should not be an intellectual biography; I realized that a practical application of his teachings would be far more appropriate. After all, if the Rebbe's lifetime of teaching could be distilled into one thought, it would be that all humankind must learn to live a more meaningful life, in thought and in deed, leading to personal and universal redemption.

Toward a Meaningful Life, therefore, is not meant to be a definitive study of the Rebbe's work. Nor can any publication possibly capture the authenticity of his teachings in their original form. This book is meant to serve as an introduction to those teachings, to offer an overview and summary of the Rebbe and his message, removing much of its academic frame of discourse and omitting the numerous citations and references that so characterized the Rebbe's teachings. Above all, this book does not at all reflect on the Rebbe's enormous contributions as a Torah scholar to all areas of Jewish thought and Torah scholarship. The Rebbe's ideas are presented here in a simplified style by focusing on topics rather than an exposition on a particular verse or passage in Torah or Talmud.

Although this work is a product of contributions from many scholars, inevitably it is an adaptation as seen through the lens of my scholastic experience and understanding of the Rebbe, for which I assume responsibility.

I believe that as the Rebbe's scholarship is increasingly recognized by modern scholars, the true scope of his contributions will be realized. My hope is that this book will lead to continued interest in the Rebbe, inspiring others to study and write about his ideas in greater depth. Nothing would be more gratifying than for this book to be seen as an introduction to a wealth of information that could transform people's lives.

I must admit that I approached this book with great trepidation, for never before had such a project been undertaken. I also wondered whether the Rebbe would be pleased with a book of this nature. He had often expressed the need to make the Torah's spiritual wisdom accessible to everyone, but I was unsure of how best to accomplish this. After all, for generations, this wisdom had been very carefully taught, directly from teacher to student, in an oral tradition. Because of its divine nature and many intricate subtleties, there has always existed the concern that the material be transmitted in a manner in which its sublime essence was not compromised.

With the advent of Chassidus, Torah became more widely disseminated and its esoteric dimension became more accessible, which inevitably produced the concern that its message might be diluted or compromised. But Rabbi Schneur Zalman countered these concerns with the following story:

The young child of a great king fell so ill that the king's doctors could think of no way to save him. Finally, one doctor was found who thought he could save the child. The only hope, he claimed, was to take the most precious stone in the king's crown, crush it and mix it with water, and feed it to the child. Even though the entire crown would be ruined, and even though there was no guarantee the child would survive, the king agreed without any hesitation. After all, what good were his riches if his child died? "The same is true with the esoteric teachings of Torah, G-d's crown jewel," Rabbi Schneur Zalman concluded. "True, some of it may spill on the ground, but if even one drop enters the heart and soul of a person and saves his spiritual life, it is well worth it."

Still, with all the previous dissemination of Chassidic thought, it was always taught in controlled settings. A book such as this one is obviously a different matter, and is subject to various readings and interpretations. As the Rebbe often said, citing a Lubavitch adage, "A thought belongs to you, a word belongs to others, and how much more so the *published* word, which is forever."

It was the Rebbe's call for redemption that finally convinced me to write this book. He stressed that, after all the years of refining this material universe, the time had come to make G-d a reality in people's lives; he recognized that people everywhere are now receptive to a world that will be "filled with the knowledge of G-d as the waters cover the sea" (Isaiah 11:9). And what better means to help accomplish this objective than rendering the Rebbe's message in a book?

I first considered this project several years ago, but my schedule was already overloaded with transcribing the Rebbe's discourses and publishing his various works. Then, in February 1992, the Rebbe suffered a stroke that left him unable to speak. For more than forty years, he had been a wellspring of information and inspiration; the flow of his words suddenly ceased on that dark Monday evening. However, true to his nature, the Rebbe did not leave us unprepared.

Eight weeks earlier, he had delivered a talk—unusual and unnerving at the time—about his father-in-law, Rabbi Yosef Yitzchak Schneersohn, who was the previous Lubavitcher Rebbe. In 1942, Rabbi Yosef Yitzchak suffered a stroke, robbing him of the ability to speak. At the time, a doctor asked Rabbi Yosef Yitzchak why G-d would allow him, a great teacher and leader, to lose his most precious ability. The Rebbe, in his talk in 1992, pointed to the case of Moses, who was "not a man of words" and who found it "difficult to speak" (Exodus 4:10); but G-d told Moses, "Who gave man a mouth . . . Is it not I, G-d? Now go, and I will be your mouth" (4:11–12). "Just as G-d had sent along Aaron to be Moses' mouthpiece," the Rebbe explained, "so too must we, guided by my father-in-law, the [previous] Rebbe, be the mouthpiece that carries his words and teachings to all."

And now, barely two months after telling this story, the Rebbe himself suffered a debilitating stroke. It soon became clear to me that the Rebbe had tragically yet lucidly prepared us for what would be and, more important, for what we must do.

It was on the Rebbe's ninety-second birthday that I sat down and began to work on the outline for this book. Not quite three months later, on Sunday, June 12, 1994, his soul ascended on high.

It is my sincerest hope and prayer to G-d that this book serves as a genuine representation of the Rebbe's wisdom, unfiltered, without any extraneous interpretation or commentary. It is also my hope that, though the Rebbe is no longer speaking to us in a literal sense, his words continue to resonate and reach people everywhere. And so, with the help of G-d, and with a small measure of uncertainty and a large measure of satisfaction and joy, I invite you to begin a journey *Toward a Meaningful Life*.

(RABBI) SIMON JACOBSON
Crown Heights

I

MAN

1

⁓

BODY AND SOUL
One Person, Two Worlds

*The human spirit ascends on high; the spirit of the beast
descends down into the earth.*
—Ecclesiastes 3:21

*Man can never be happy if he does not nourish his soul
as he does his body.*
—The Rebbe

⁓

A man visiting the Rebbe complained of a lack of meaningful-
ness in his life. Yes, he had a successful career and healthy
family, but at the end of the day, he felt lonely and empty.

"Do you ever devote time to your soul?" the Rebbe asked him.

"How can I have time for my soul when I am so consumed
with work and family?"

"There is an old saying," the Rebbe replied, "that when two
people meet, it is two souls against one body. Because bodies are
self-centered by nature, they cannot join forces—each pursues its
own physical needs. Souls, however, are selfless by nature, so when
two people join forces, their souls converge. May I suggest that you
and I resolve here and now to designate a time each day to study

and pray, and do an additional good deed. This will nourish your soul and give focus and meaning to all that you do, rather than your being controlled by the random forces of your life."

WHAT IS A SOUL?

Have you ever just burst out in tears for no apparent reason, finding yourself in deep sadness? That is the soft voice of your soul, crying out for attention, asking to be nourished with at least as much care as you nourish your body.

Have you ever experienced a truly sacred moment, when, despite the constant turmoil of life, you felt a profound sense of awe and belonging? That, too, is the voice of your soul, expressing a deep satisfaction with its intrinsic connection to the forces of spirituality.

We use the words *body* and *soul* constantly, in different contexts. But do we know what they really mean? What is the nature of soul? What is its relationship to the body?

The soul manifests the very reason for our existence; it is the one part of our being that directly reflects our connection to G-d, our creator. Even though it is not tangible and is hidden within the body, the soul is the very fabric of who we are. While the body encompasses the material aspects of our lives, the soul encompasses the spiritual. The body is driven primarily by having its physical needs met. This does not imply that the body is inherently bad; it is not. It was created by G-d and is initially neutral, with great potential for good. But it is the soul that energizes and guides the body to do good deeds and connect to the divine. The soul is transcendent by nature, for "the flame of G-d is the soul of man."[1]

There is a built-in dichotomy, therefore, between the tangible nature of the body and the transcendent nature of the soul. Look closely at the flame of a candle, and you will see an approximation of your soul—the flame licking the air, reaching upward, as if toward G-d. And yet the wick pulls it back to earth. Similarly, your soul is constantly reaching upward, while your body holds you back with its insistent demands for physical sustenance or gratification. The question for each of us is, Do we choose to be the flame that rises upward or the wick that holds us down?

To be a wholesome and healthy person, your body and soul must work in harmony. We need not choose one over the other, indulgence or abstinence; we can and must merge body and soul. And this means uniting the body and soul to fulfill the mission for which we were all put on earth: to lead a meaningful, productive, and virtuous life by making this physical world a comfortable home for spirituality and G-dliness. Every one of us fulfills this mission using his or her unique abilities and talents, whether a person is a teacher or a parent, a businessperson or a scientist. We must all seek to become aware of our mission and actualize it by conducting our lives from minute to minute, from day to day, from year to year in accordance with G-d's laws.

The dichotomy of body and soul is everywhere we look, and there are many labels for it: form and function, matter and energy, materialism and spirituality. In a book, for instance, the words on the page are the body and the ideas behind them the soul. The same is true of every aspect of our universe, because the universe itself is composed of a body and a soul—its material components and the spiritual components that give it life. So the first step toward creating unity throughout the universe, the first step toward spiritualizing the material, is to first unite your own body and soul.

Leading a meaningful life means being able to pierce the outer, material layer and connect to the energy within. This is not an easy task, for the body operates with sensory tools (sight, hearing, smell, taste, and touch), while the soul traffics in the suprasensory (emotions, conscience, intelligence, and most important, the subliminal spiritual forces). And the energy within is not a quantifiable energy as defined by physics—there is an element of mystery to it that defies measurement. It is not just a force; it is the force we call *life*. And there are elements of life that we have just begun to discover.

Look around you today. It is obvious that many of us are searching for inner peace, happiness, or calm, searching for our *soul*. But are we using the right tools with which to search? Because we have grown so reliant on our sensory tools, we often feel as though they are the only ones at our disposal. But how difficult it is to try to grasp the meaning of our souls using only the five senses! It is like using your eyes to hear a piece of music. Still, because the call of the soul is so persistent, we never stop searching.

WHY IS IT IMPORTANT TO KNOW
THAT I HAVE A SOUL?

Because your sensory tools are so predominant, you almost need to turn them down in order to experience that which is within. If you were to suspend your senses of sight, hearing, smell, taste, and touch, what would you be left with? Initially, this may be a terrifying thought—that you would be left with nothing. But you are not left with nothing: you are left with yourself. We only need our senses to interact with the world *outside* ourselves. You don't need eyes to see yourself or ears to hear yourself. You know you are there, without using any sensory tools; it is simply an awareness, a totally separate sense.

So we are fully alive without our senses. Without the soul, though, there is no life. Yes, there is the bodily struggle to survive, but life as we understand it is all about the pursuit of meaning, the search for our soul, the quest for G-d. When a scientist explores the laws of nature, he feels compelled to lift the curtain and see what is going on beyond the limits of our external senses. When a young child pulls apart a toy, he is looking for the same thing: the secret that makes it work. This curiosity is a staple of human nature.

It is the same with our own beings. If we don't acknowledge all the forces that drive us, including the soul, we will never understand ourselves. And if we are not aware of how the soul works, we will be unable to nourish it. Fortunately, when the soul is starved for nourishment, it lets us know. No matter how much one may try to silence the soul, distracting it through material bliss, it will always cry out, letting you know that a part of your life is missing. This may take the guise of anxiety, aimlessness, an emptiness. A yearning for something more.

Without experiencing the soul, there can be no personal growth, because it is the soul that expresses dissatisfaction, which is the motivation for growth. The body, as long as its own selfish needs are being met, has no desire for transcendence. The soul gives your life direction and unity. The material world—that is, the world of the body—is fragmented; the soul is the hub around which all our physical activities unite. If you were to observe your body's material drives during the course of a day, you would see it going around in circles or in jagged bursts of desire, randomly picking the stimuli that attract it at that given moment. The soul connects all these fragments; it connects the trivial to the paramount, and the material to the spiritual.

The soul also teaches humility. Whereas the body is selfish, the soul is humble. It provides us with the capacity to rise above ourselves, to see others' needs and to respond with sensitivity. Without a soul, the body's selfish desires can enslave and ultimately destroy us. The soul is our transcendent side, always reaching upward like the candle flame, always trying to reconnect us with G-d. The body may try to keep us earthbound, but the soul has the power to lift us above and beyond.

༺ ༻

A beloved rabbi, when he was yet a young child, was playing with a group of other children who were climbing a ladder. All his friends were afraid to climb to the top, but he had no fear. Later, his grandfather asked him, "Why were you not afraid to climb and the others were?"

"Because as they climbed, they kept looking down," he replied. "They saw how high they were, and they were frightened. As I climbed, I kept looking upward. I saw how low I was, and it motivated me to climb higher."

WHY IS THERE SUCH CONFLICT BETWEEN BODY AND SOUL?

The body and soul are in perpetual battle; all human conflict stems from the dichotomy of body and soul, the tension between our corporeal selves and the need for transcendence. Why is this so?

Because G-d created the body and soul in two distinct phases, taking dust from the earth and then blowing into it the breath and soul of life.[2] Why did He create our body and soul separately, unlike all the other creatures? So that man would always recognize that there are two distinct forces in life, the material and the spiritual. The material side is lowly, like the dust of the earth, while the spiritual side comes from the deepest place possible—from G-d.

In the beginning, body and soul were united. The body recognized its role as a vehicle for the soul's expression, and the soul recognized its need for the body to actualize G-d's will. Adam and Eve, therefore, "were not ashamed" of their nakedness,[3] for it was as innocent as the nakedness of a newborn child.

The first sin, though, created a self-consciousness; the independent selfish ego was born, divorced from G-d's will and intentions. Adam and Eve's "eyes were opened" and they became ashamed of their nakedness,[4] because they experienced their bodies as a distinct entity and they sensed their sexuality as separate from their divine mission. One human agenda was split into two: our material desires and our spiritual desires. Since that moment, our mission includes restoring the harmony between body and soul.

So we are really composed of two distinct elements, like the twin brothers Jacob and Esau, battling within their mother's womb. Jacob was the innocent man, the scholar, while Esau was the warrior, the man of the field.[5] The body is the warrior within us, the aggressive force with the power to tame the elements of this world. In this material world, the body serves to protect the vulnerable soul. A body without a soul, on the other hand, would be a dangerous aggressor with neither focus nor conscience.

And yet the split persists. To the soul, the body is initially a hulking presence in constant need of indulgence. While the soul wants to reach for spiritual ecstasy, the body needs to eat and sleep. To the body, the soul is initially a nuisance, a conscience, that is always limiting the body's behavior.

Why would G-d create the potential for such a conflict? Because the soul needs to be challenged and the body refined, and the tension between them ultimately brings out the best in both. Ultimately, the body and the soul must realize that they are each stronger *with* each other than without. It is the very resistance of the body that brings out the creativity of the soul, while the soul's guidance allows the body to use its strength for the good. A rushing river has a certain amount of energy, but when the river is dammed and that energy is harnessed, it is multiplied many, many times over.

WHAT CAN WE DO ABOUT THIS CONFLICT?

The first step in dealing with the conflict between body and soul is to acknowledge that the struggle exists, and be aware of the two distinct forces. As long as we think we are a single entity, we are existentially confused, and that confusion causes paralysis. We shuttle between the demands of the soul and the body without ever recognizing the need to fuse the two. One day we are virtuous, the next we are selfish; one day we are motivated, the next we procrastinate.

We relieve the tension between the body and soul not by negating one of them but by integrating them toward fulfilling one objective: spiritualizing the material. All the body's strengths and experiences are directed to assist the noble and transcendent pursuits of the soul.

The only way to unite body and soul is to recognize that G-d is far higher than our limited selves, far greater than both body and soul. This requires a degree of humility, for a person tends to be self-serving by nature. The soul, because of its transcendent nature, can rise above selfishness more easily than the body, and can discipline the body, through study and deed, to recognize its true mission. Only then can the body rise to its true prominence—when it serves as a vehicle for the soul instead of acting under its own power, energized by its own needs. We can experience "spiritual arrogance" as well by insulating ourselves and neglecting the body and its needs. Asceticism, though, is not an option. G-d gave us a body to refine and elevate, to join the soul in its journey.

An important tool to address the conflict between body and soul is to allow the soul to yearn, to reach upward toward the sublime. What does this mean in practical terms? Always recognize that you are not totally a material person. Yes, we have to eat and sleep and pay our bills, but that is not why we are here—we are here to bring out the best of our soul and to refine the body. But because of our body's physical element, we may inevitably get mired in the muck of materialism. There is a certain sadness to that, which makes your soul cry out. So listen when your soul yearns for better nourishment than it is being given; listen to your inner voice that expresses doubt and sadness when you immerse yourself exclusively in material concerns. Trust your voices.

But even as your soul yearns to transcend, it must permeate your body and material needs. As the sages teach us, "Run like a gazelle . . . to do the will of your Father in heaven."[6] The soul must run, it must yearn, but it must run as a gazelle. Just as a gazelle even in flight "turns his head back to the place from which he is running,"[7] so too your yen for transcendence must always be with an eye to the material reality we are fleeing, with the awareness that the purpose of every escape to the heavens is a return to earth.

Once you acknowledge the soul, you must begin to learn how it functions. You realize that the soul comes from a greater spiritual place, and that it is trying to introduce G-dliness into your life. You learn that the soul is what leads you toward a meaningful life, and in order to nourish it, you must study and familiarize yourself with G-d's wisdom. Prayer is the emotional ladder that connects you from below; prayer, not materialism, provides you with a real home, a place within your body where the soul can find peace and perspective. That is why it is important to pray at the *beginning* of the day, to put our everyday, material world in proper perspective.

Finally, the body and soul converge by committing virtuous acts. It is not enough to encourage the soul and educate it; you must actualize the soul by partnering it with your body. To help a neighbor in need, to listen to a stranger in distress, to help provide food or clothing to someone who cannot afford it. These become more than simple good deeds; they become vital nourishment for your soul and a means of putting your physical body to appropriate spiritual use. When the soul is nurtured with awareness, warmheartedness, and refined behavior, it fully emerges in our lives with the heat and intensity of an actual flame, lifting the body with it.

◁~◇

A man once set out to visit a great sage. When he arrived, he asked where to find the man, and was shown to a decrepit shack at the edge of town. Inside, there was nothing but a broken-down bed and a table full of books, where an old man was studying. The traveler was shaken. "Where does the sage live?" he asked the old man.

"It is I to whom you refer," said the old man. "What is disturbing you so?"

"I don't understand. You are a great sage, with many disciples. Your name is known across the country. It doesn't seem fitting that you should be living in a room like this. You should be living in a palace."

"And where do you live?" the old man asked.

"I live in a mansion, a grand home with magnificent furnishings."

"And how do you make a living?"

The man explained that he was a businessman, traveling twice a year to a large city to buy materials that he brought back and sold to local merchants. The sage listening attentively asked him where he stayed when he was in the city.

"I stay in a small room in a small inn," he answered.

"If someone were to walk into that small room, might they not say, 'Why are you, a wealthy businessman, living in such a room?' And you might say, 'I am only on the road for a short time, so this is all I need. Come to my real home, and you will see that it is entirely different.'

"My friend, the same is true here," the old man continued. "I am also only on the road. This material world is just a road. In my home, too, it is very different. Come to my spiritual home, and you will see that I live in a palace."

HOW DO WE NOURISH
THE SOUL TODAY?

The battle between body and soul is greater now than it has ever been. The material world, to which our body is drawn, is in a period of unprecedented prosperity. Our standard of living is high and we have the technology to master many of the problems that once plagued us. But at the same time, our individual and collective soul is starving for nourishment.

We need to feed the soul more than ever, and education and virtue are the food of the soul. That is why it is so important to start teaching and modeling spiritual values as early as possible. Still, the challenge continues. The key is not to thwart the battle between body and soul, but to understand its purpose, to be at peace with the challenge. Once the body recognizes the soul's dominance, and makes peace with its twin brother, the tension can be properly harnessed. The body then becomes a force that propels the soul to a greater place than either one could ever reach on its own.

This harmony between your body and soul carries over to the world at large, helping unite the body and soul, the matter and spirit, of the entire universe. The key to meaning and happiness in your life, then, lies in your own hands: understanding the symmetry and rhythm of your own body and soul.

So the next time you look in the mirror, ask yourself: What have I before me? I recognize my body, but can I detect my soul within? I pay attention to all my bodily needs, but am I giving my tender soul equal attention?

And finally: I know what I need. But do I know what I am needed for?

⚬⚬⚬

The Rebbe once encouraged a gifted student to use his free time to inspire his fellow students to pursue not only their academic studies but their spiritual studies as well.

"My schedule is already so full, I don't know how I could possibly add anything more to it," the student said. And then, realizing that the Rebbe's own schedule was far more crowded, he said, "Frankly, I don't understand where you get the strength and stamina to work as you do."

"Every person has both a body and a soul," said the Rebbe. "It is like a bird and its wings. Imagine if a bird were unaware that its wings enabled it to fly; they would only add an extra burden of weight. But once it flaps its wings, it lifts itself skyward. We all have wings—our soul—that can lift us as high as we need go. All we have to do is learn to use them."

2

⧉

BIRTH
The Mission Begins

You are my child, I have given birth to you today.
—Psalms 2:7

Birth is G-d saying you matter.
—The Rebbe

⧉

At a gathering of family and friends celebrating a child's birth, the Rebbe explained three reasons to rejoice at such an occasion: the joy of the entire world for the birth of a new member, the joy of the parents for being blessed with a child, and the joy of the child for having been brought into the world.

"But how can we celebrate when we don't yet know how a child will turn out?" one man asked.

"Birth marks the moment when the soul enters the body," said the Rebbe. "And because the soul is connected directly to G-d, that is reason enough to rejoice."

WHY WERE WE BORN?

As we forge ahead in our busy lives and grow older and further away from the moment of our own birth, few of us pause to

14

appreciate just how miraculous that moment was. And yet in order to fully understand ourselves and live a meaningful life, we must return to the very beginning and look at the significance of our birth.

What your birth means is that you are G-d's child. Your birth was not an accident; G-d chooses each of us to fulfill a specific mission in this world, just as a composer arranges each musical note. Take away even one note, and the entire composition is affected. Each person matters; each person is irreplaceable. Your life is always leading you toward your destiny, and every single moment is meaningful and precious.

Many people seem to feel that because *we* didn't *choose* to enter the world, our birth is a stroke of coincidence or serendipity. This couldn't be further from the truth. Birth is G-d's way of saying that He has invested His will and energy in creating you; G-d feels great joy when you are born, the greatest pleasure imaginable, for the moment of birth realizes His intention in wanting you, which encompasses the potential for all your future achievements.

WHEN, EXACTLY, DOES LIFE BEGIN?

At birth, the soul enters the body, creating a life that sustains itself, an autonomous human being. A fetus, of course, is a living organism complete with functioning brain, heart, and limbs. But it is only an extension, albeit a living one, of its mother's being. It *contains* life but is not yet an independent life, sustained by its own force.[1]

The moment of birth marks the beginning of our mission on earth, which is to transform our material world into a vehicle of spiritual expression and G-dliness. The life process is much more than simple biology. It is about growth, development, and fulfilling our potential. A person is not fully alive unless he is attuned to his soul's higher purpose, unless he realizes its mission.

Many of us *sense* a spiritual side to our lives. Perhaps we even seek it out at times. But because we are so busy with our daily lives and so hungry for instant gratification, we forget—or never take the time to learn—why we are here in the first place.

Each of us has a choice. We can be merely biologically alive or we can be truly alive, *spiritually* alive. Even as adults, we can live the way a fetus does—eating, drinking, and sleeping, a complete person that is missing its most vital element: a soul. Or we can take advantage of our capacity to be spiritually sensitive, and participate in the world.

It is tempting to spend our lives in a fetuslike state. Even the sages admit this: "It is more pleasant not to be born than to be born."[2] Wouldn't it be easier to go through life warm and well fed, protected from the outside world, than to endure the harsh forces of life we have all come to know?

Indeed, many of us *do* try to insulate ourselves, reacting to life but never fully engaging it. In this light, we see that birth, above all else, is a *challenge*, the first and perhaps most difficult challenge we will ever face.

For a moment, think about the experiences of an infant. Now try to picture your own birth. What a monumental moment that was! What feelings did you have? What voices did you hear? Scientists and psychologists are only beginning to acknowledge what the Bible has been teaching for thousands of years: that our experiences as a newborn baby have a profound impact on our inner psyches. A newborn is as receptive as a dry sponge. He hears perhaps even more than an adult hears; precisely *because* his conscious mind is not yet at work, and *because* he doesn't understand the words, a newborn is much more impressionable. He absorbs everything in his environment in the purest form, unadulterated by the adult ego or intellect.

Education, therefore, begins the moment a child is born. This presents us with a profound responsibility as to how we behave in the presence of a child, and how we treat children from the moment of birth. Remember: the soul of a newborn child is fully alive, with open ears that hear everything.

ᘓᘙᘗᘙᘖ

A revered rabbi, when he was an infant, was often carried in
his bassinet to hear the sounds of study.[3] *He grew up to be a great*
scholar, and, in acknowledgment of how he was raised, he was greeted
with the blessing "Beloved is the one who gave birth to you."[4]

WHAT IS SO SPECIAL ABOUT BIRTH?

There is no greater blessing than the capacity to give birth, for it is the one opportunity we have to truly *create*, and to create something from our own flesh and blood. We spend our lives merely reshaping things. We invest money to make more money. We take words that already exist, reorder them, and produce a piece of writing. We take raw material and shape it into something more refined, more useful, more valuable.

But birth is not just reshaping one form of matter into another. It is an utterly mysterious act, the physical creation of something out of nothing. No matter how technologically advanced we become, the smartest men and women among us will never be able to replicate the mystery of birth. And because a new child will one day have the power to have children of his or her own, birth also gives us access to the infinite, to eternity.

Bearing children, therefore, is our one opportunity to act in a truly G-dlike way, as a true creator. And to touch eternity. The next time you see a newborn baby, observe the parents. They cannot help but feel immeasurably moved, experiencing a feeling of deep love, a sense of wonder that they were able to create something so awe-inspiring. A new parent instantly realizes that life is about much more than our narrow world of vanity. Suddenly, the things that give us such pride—the money we have accumulated, the businesses we have built—all pale in comparison to this simple, astounding accomplishment.

Why, then, don't we retain this awe throughout our lives? Because we are continually distracted by our daily struggle to survive. We don't create the time to appreciate the constant miracles of life—of which birth is just the first. Whenever a friend or family member has a baby, therefore, we should recognize the birth as an opportunity to think about our priorities and to appreciate the power of the eternal. And to exercise our responsibility to bring life into this world and to live fulfilling lives.

We need to properly appreciate the ability to create life. Birth is a gift from G-d. When you have been given this greatest of gifts, the ability to bear children, you must not suppress it; just look at all those people who would do anything to have a child.

Suppressing the ability to bear children can also have a negative psychological impact, for human health is dependent on using all our faculties, all our innate emotional and spiritual gifts, especially the power to create life.

HOW SHOULD WE CELEBRATE
OUR BIRTHDAYS?

It is good to be thankful for what you have in life and what you have accomplished. But open your eyes to the larger picture. If we are to appreciate the fruits of life, we must first appreciate the tree that bears the fruit: birth itself.

Birth is *your* beginning. It is a window to the chance of a lifetime, the chance to fulfill your unique mission. So a birthday is a momentous occasion, to be commemorated just as a nation commemorates *its* birth or as an organization celebrates its founding. Still, it is much more than an occasion to receive gifts. It is a chance to remember the day that a major event occurred, to celebrate and give thanks and to reflect upon how well we are fulfilling our calling.

Because time itself is like a spiral, something special happens on your birthday each year: The same energy that G-d invested in you at birth is present once again. It is our duty to be receptive to that force. How do we do so? By committing to a life guided by G-d's will, and by using the abilities and resources we were born with to perfect ourselves and society, and to make the world a good and sacred home for G-d.

A birthday is a time to celebrate birth itself, the joy of life. It is also an occasion to rethink your life: How great is the disparity between what I have accomplished and what I *can* accomplish? Am I spending my time properly or am I involved in things that distract me from my higher calling? How can I strengthen the thread that connects my outer life and my inner life?

A birthday can also teach us the concept of rebirth. To recall our birth is to recall a new beginning. No matter how things went yesterday, or last year, we always have the capacity to try again. Your birthday is a refresher, a chance for regeneration—not just materially, but spiritually.

On your birthday, gather with family and friends and study something meaningful together.

There is no better way to celebrate a birthday than to commit a special act of goodness. It is easy enough to *say* you are thankful; it is far better to *show* it by doing a kind deed, something that you did not do yesterday. Not because someone is forcing you. Not because someone suggests it. But simply because your inner goodness, your soul, wants to express its thanks for being born and alive.

Such an act of kindness gives G-d great pleasure, because He sees that the child in whom He invested, the particular child he wanted to be born on a particular day, is living up to its potential. And nothing, of course, gives a parent greater joy. This is the true experience of birth, the true beginning of a life of meaning.

◈

In 1992, a writer preparing a story about the Rebbe's upcoming ninetieth birthday asked the Rebbe what message he would like to convey in connection with his birthday.

"Ninety is the numerical equivalent of the Hebrew letter meaning 'righteous,'" the Rebbe explained. *"We must all constantly strive to be more righteous. Today we must be better than yesterday, and today we must prepare for a better tomorrow."*

3

CHILDHOOD
The Dawn of Life

The hearts of the parents will return through their children.
—Malachi 3:24

*The innocent faith of a child touches upon the utterly
simple essence of G-d.*
—The Rebbe

The Rebbe never had any children of his own. Yet all the children were his. During his entire leadership, he paid special attention to the needs and gifts of the young. As far back as 1943, he initiated a yearly children's parade to celebrate religious pride; he often gave special talks to groups of children, and in 1980 he established a worldwide program, with a membership now numbering in the hundreds of thousands, to encourage children to embrace their heritage and lead more spiritual lives.

In 1989, a young father in Brooklyn died of cancer, leaving behind a wife and children. Before he died, he had written to the Rebbe, asking him to keep the children in his prayers. Soon after the father's passing, some ten thousand people gathered in the synagogue to hear the Rebbe speak. Before he began, the Rebbe asked a *secretary to find the three young orphans, and he waited until they were brought forward. From that day on, those children were always given this special honor, the fatherly care that the Rebbe knew was vital to develop a child's spiritual well-being.*

WHAT IS A CHILD?

Is there any sight more uplifting, more joyous, than a child playing with a new toy? We have all seen the child's wonder as he shakes the toy back and forth, turns it upside down, maybe even tries to taste it. You may have witnessed this scene hundreds of times, but perhaps you've never really *seen* it. What is this child?

What you see before you is the most precious gift G-d has given us—a new life, as unmarked as fresh snow, whose parents have been blessed with the opportunity to nurture, protect, and teach so that the child becomes a productive and good human being. Every quality of a child is there for a reason, and must be cultivated. Every child carries great resources, the potential for the entire future. How you raise this child will not only influence the child's life, but his or her children's lives and their children's lives.

In our society, we may see childhood as a transitory stage and children merely as adults in the making. People sometimes look at childhood and education as pure investment—some statisticians have even calculated the age at which a person becomes worth more than the amount that was spent on his childhood care and education. How we see children very much reflects how we see ourselves. If we are overly concerned with our own material comforts, then a child may seem like a nuisance, interrupting the world we have carefully constructed for our gratification. But if we are in touch with the sacred in our lives, or at least seek it out, a child's curiosity and vivacity will enchant us to no end and be a source of the greatest pleasure.

It is extremely important to understand children for what they *are*, not for what we see them as. Whereas an adult is shaped by man and society, the child is shaped by G-d. Because of their innocence, their curiosity, and their purity, children stand closer to G-d than an adult. And so the great secret to childhood is not that our children have much to learn from us, but that we have much to learn from them.

⟨◦⟩

A young boy came home from school, ran into his grandfather's room, and began to cry. When his grandfather asked why he was crying, the boy replied that he had learned in school that G-d had revealed Himself to Abraham. "And so I am crying," said the boy, "because G-d has not revealed Himself to me."

WHY DO WE COME INTO THE WORLD AS CHILDREN?

Have you ever wondered if it might not be easier if we were all created as mature adults instead of children, fully functional and able to provide for ourselves?

But there is a beautiful lesson in childhood itself—above all, that a child is genuine and innocent, and that such innocence is the foundation of life. If we were born as adults, already prepared for the struggles of life, we would never experience the magic of childhood, the freedom to explore life with our eyes wide open, indiscriminately, unselectively. Childhood gives us the chance to soar through the sublime before we trudge through the mundane.

What do we think when we see a child reach for the hand of his mother and follow her wherever she goes? We surely don't need anyone leading *us* by the hand. But the child's receptivity and vulnerability, his simple faith, comes from a very deep, pure place—

from the very essence of the soul, which is receptive to that which is beyond itself.

As adults, we like to think that we are in control. After all, we have spent years developing our ideas and sharpening our minds. But which is truly more fundamental: an adult's intellect or a child's innocence and faith? Whereas an adult has narrowed his hopes and expectations, a child dreams and wonders. The same goes for education: a child's mind is not clouded by the self-interest of the adult, concerned only with how *he* will benefit from a certain idea.

While educating children, it is vital to cultivate this spirit, this faith, this genuine sense of curiosity. Otherwise, much of the information we impart will be misdirected; instead of allowing a child to experience a sense of awe at G-d and His world, we push him or her to analyze and categorize everything. Think of a child's first trip to the Grand Canyon. Which is more significant: to drink in the sight with awe and think about what it all means, or to boil it down to a pile of data and statistics?

We must be especially attentive to cultivating the G-dliness in children, the awe that comes through spirituality. Children have a glorious gift for realizing that the here and now, the visible world, is not always what is most important. Allow a child's imagination to wander, for it recognizes that we are all part of something greater than our selves. Children innately have a deep thirst for the ethereal and the natural sense of wonder and faith that is so receptive to spiritual matters.

Still, we must remember that a child is a vulnerable and impressionable young person who has been put in our care, entrusted to us for his or her well-being. We must take into account the two opposing elements of a child's nature: the curiosity and openness to learn versus a spirit of frivolity, a lack of seriousness. The key is to recognize both factors, and strive for a balance. A parent or educator who is too concerned with discipline might rob the child's free spirit; on the other hand, we cannot be so lenient as to let a child wander without direction.

The main ingredient in shaping good behavior is truth; these truths, especially those about G-d, and about right and wrong, should never be arbitrary. A child is naturally sincere, and compromising the truth is anathema to sincerity. A parent's tentativeness or ambivalence toward the truth will come back to haunt a child; it is vital that a child learn clarity and conviction, which are the roots of every decision a healthy adult will make. It is perhaps preferable to make an incorrect decision and learn from the experience than to be frozen by the fear of indecision.

Once you fully accept and understand that a child is a gift from G-d, the question of how to treat him or her becomes quite simple. The child does not belong to you; he or she belongs to G-d. And G-d entrusted you with the child, coupled with a commandment to protect and nurture. Children do not need to be taught fear; they have natural fear. So, for example, before punishing a child, you must take great care to think: Am I doing this in the best interest of the child, or because he or she made me angry? There is no place for ego in raising a child.

It is always better to encourage good behavior than to have to punish bad behavior. Even when discipline is necessary, it must be carried out with the utmost sensitivity and love—remember, if you hurt a child, you are hurting G-d. The intimidation of children that masquerades as discipline is an affront to G-d, who has asked us to care for these precious souls with sensitivity. In turn, a child should be taught to honor his parents not because they are authority figures, with controlling power over their children, but because it was they whom G-d chose to bring the child into the world.

ʘᴍᴍꙅ

An elderly rabbi was spending an evening speaking and studying with some of his followers, and they ran out of refreshments. They quickly took up a collection, but, after much debate, none of them would volunteer to leave and buy the food. "Give me the money," the rabbi finally said. "I

have a child waiting outside. He'll be happy to go to the
store for us."

When, in a few moments, the rabbi failed to return, they
all realized that he had gone himself. Shamefacedly, they
waited for him. "Why didn't you tell us the truth?" one of
them said when he returned. "Any one of us would gladly
have gone instead."

"I did tell you the truth," the rabbi answered. "As I
grew older, I resolved that I would never give up the child-
like aspects of my personality. Needless to say, it is not
always proper to act like a child, so when I study with all
of you, I leave the child within me outside. But he is al-
ways waiting for me."

WHAT CAN WE LEARN
FROM CHILDREN?

Beyond innocence, there are many other things about children
that we would do well to study, and learn from. Consider a
child's sense of pure amazement when he or she discovers something
new. The child may not yet have the sensory tools to fully comprehend this new experience, but do not be deceived: a child absorbs the experience far more deeply than an adult might. Why is
it that we can remember what we learned in nursery school while
we can hardly remember what we read yesterday? A child's mind is
extremely fertile, and must be treated with sensitivity and respect.

A child is also very single-minded; when a child is in the moment, he or she is completely immersed in the moment. An adult
will often anticipate and personalize: Where is this conversation
heading? What does it mean for *me?* A child can teach us to truly
focus, to fully absorb the moment as it exists.

There is another aspect to this single-mindedness. Since it seems to a child that his parents and the rest of the universe exist merely to cater to his needs, a child can easily begin to think that *he* is the main focus of life. The adverse effects of such an attitude are self-evident; indeed, in addition to enhancing our inherent positive qualities, weeding out the negative parts of our base behavior is a main focus of education. But the child's egocentric instinct also has a positive side: He is utterly convinced that his existence has meaning and that his deeds have consequence. This is one part of childhood that we especially need to cultivate—the conviction that every one of our thoughts and deeds is of real, even global, significance. Maimonides wrote that a person "should see the entire world as half good and half evil, so that with a single good deed, he will tip the scales for himself, and for the entire world, to the side of merit."[1]

It is easy to dismiss the simplicity of a child as a mere lack of knowledge. But such simplicity contains a certain power, an integrity and sincerity that may begin to erode as we rush to acquire wisdom and sophistication. We may get frustrated when a child cannot keep still, but this activity is a sign of healthy vitality; the external movement is reflective of the internal movement, it expresses a certain restlessness and spiritual angst. Consider how a child will look at one simple object and ask more questions than we could have ever imagined: Why is it that way? How did it get like that? What is it for?

This questioning, this movement that assumes the form of curiosity, should never be discouraged. Childhood is the one period in life when a person is free from the concerns of survival; it is the one opportunity to be totally dedicated to learning the value system through which all of life's experiences will be filtered. Therefore, we should never worry about taxing the mind of a child. We need to be realistic about how much a child can retain, but it is better to be taught more and retain less than to let a part of the mind remain unused. And, since we haven't yet discovered the true capacity of a child's mind to absorb information, a child should embark on a rigorous schedule of study. The first thing a child must be taught, of course, is the foundation of life—the distinction between good and evil, right and wrong. This gives direction to all his other studies and life choices.

As adults, we should try to re-create the cocoonlike state of child-hood. Take ten minutes out of your day and go back to the state of mind of a child, when you had no material worries, when your only concern was learning how to conduct your life in a productive, meaningful way. See how refreshing it is to substitute prayer, study, and good deeds for bill-paying, shopping, and running your business.

A child, through his innocence and curiosity, has many of the traits that we most crave. We have been so buffeted by life, and so conditioned to think only of ourselves, that we lose touch with these beautiful traits. As is written, "The hearts of the parents will return through their children." Once parents have resigned themselves to a certain way of life, they sometimes can't even consider the possibility of change. But, because they will do anything for their children in the course of teaching them to lead a meaningful life, parents do indeed stand a chance of changing. So childhood is not just for the child; it also allows parents to tap the purest part of themselves: their souls. Especially in our turbulent generation, it is often the children who end up teaching the most profound values to their parents.

So when you next spend time with your child—or any child—do not be casual about the experience. Look at the child intently and realize: G-d has given you this gift to nurture and care for, to teach good habits and the difference between right and wrong. Your attitude toward this child and the sensibilities you impart will be crucial to how his life develops and how he influences others. Now, how much time can you possibly devote to this enormous responsibility? And most important of all: Allow your child to be himself and to teach you how to live a more meaningful life.

❧

The holiday festival of Purim is an especially joyous
one for children. Each year, they come to synagogue with

noisemakers of every sort. At one point during the annual reading of the Purim scroll in the Rebbe's synagogue, the children got carried away in their enthusiasm; some of the adults grew distraught because they could not hear the reading, and went to great lengths to quiet down the children. Later, the Rebbe addressed these adults. "In their own innocence, the children were making a great racket and enjoying it so," he said. "You, of course, want to hear the reading, but we must also appreciate G-d's great joy in seeing these children celebrate."

4

✧

EDUCATION
What, Why, and How We Learn

*Educate the youngster according to his way; then, even when he
grows old, he shall not depart from it.*

—Proverbs 22:6

*We cannot rest until every child, boy and girl, receives a
proper moral education.*

—The Rebbe

✧

Throughout his four decades of leadership, the Rebbe established
more than two thousand new educational institutions across
the globe. In 1976, he launched a special education campaign, by
declaring the year as "education year," beginning dozens of new
schools, camps, and study programs. In 1978, the United States
government designated the Rebbe's birthday Education Day U.S.A.,
and did so on his birthday every year following.

WHY IS EDUCATION NECESSARY?

If there is one single factor within our control that can directly
influence who we are as people, it is education. Education is the

basis and sustenance of civilization. In order to produce healthy and wholesome adults, people who will lead selfless and meaningful lives, *we must educate our children.*

But what comes to mind when we see that word, *education*? Many of us may conjure up the same picture: twenty or thirty children, their faces scrubbed clean by loving parents, leaning over their desks or tapping into a computer.

There is nothing wrong with that picture—unless we come to think of it as the *only* picture of education we need to see. Education is not just learning the skills to make a living; it is learning to understand life itself. What is life? Life is the recognition of G-d and the mission that He has charged us with—refining ourselves and sanctifying our world.

True education is something that reaches deep inside a person, empowering us to use the information we absorb to be more productive from within. Education means sensitizing yourself, your friends, and your family to an entire world of truth, a commitment to a good greater than one's own desires.

Only once we have begun to instill these ideals in a child should we go on to teach the tools of survival; the *why* of education must precede the *how.* We teach children mathematics so they can think in an organized fashion and do business. We teach them languages so they can communicate their ideas. We teach them the sciences so they can understand the physical properties of the universe they live in. All this is well and good, and certainly important. But not a single one of these disciplines will necessarily affect the way a child will morally act in his daily life.

As we have seen throughout history, it is entirely possible for someone to become proficient in the sciences, for instance, and put his talents to destructive use. And when this person is confronted, and told that he should behave according to the will of his creator, he can often honestly say, "I was taught many things during all my years in school, but *never* was I taught why to behave!" Allowing a child to grow up and choose his or her own set of values—thinking that we must not infringe on individual liberties—is as ludicrous as a parent giving a child the choice of whether or not to get vaccinated.

So imparting information is but a single and rather simple component of education. A true education—an education for life—consists of teaching children that they have an uncompromising responsibility to G-d to live morally and ethically, which will sustain them individually and create a better world for their children and for generations to come.

Education also means dealing with the paradox of childhood. On one hand, a child lacks the ability to truly tell right from wrong, much less the maturity to choose good for its own sake and reject evil simply because it is evil. On the other hand, it is during childhood that a person's psyche and character are shaped. So children must be taught good habits, to know right from wrong, well before they ever set foot in a school. As a person grows older and his or her values and personality are formed, it becomes increasingly difficult to affect that person's outlook.

⚭

> A couple visited a rabbi to seek advice about how to
> educate their twelve-year-old son. The rabbi answered them:
> "You have come to me twelve years too late. A human being
> is like a tree. If you make a scratch on the branch of a full-
> grown tree, you affect only that branch. But if you make
> even a minuscule scratch on a seed, it affects the growth of
> the entire tree."

Since education is life itself, it never ends. While formal education may stop once we finish school, education itself should actually intensify as we become more experienced in life and gain a deeper understanding of our place in the universe. No matter how old we are, or how intellectually enlightened we become, we must always ask ourselves: How deep is my understanding of an inner meaningful life? How happy am I? Many of us might be surprised to discover how tenderly young we are in our spirituality, how much more we have to learn about our own soul and how we have yet to develop a mature relationship with G-d.

HOW SHOULD WE EDUCATE?

The question of how to educate is really the same as asking, How should we communicate? How should we do business? How should we *live*?

The answer is always the same: through love. Without love, education is at best incomplete and at worst destructive. Love means sensitivity—not to *your* ideas and *your* standards, but to your student's and, most important, to G-d's. This means that a child must be made aware of an existence that is greater than himself and far beyond his own drives and desires, his family and friends, his school and his play. Such an education is rigorous, demanding intellectual and emotional stamina. But as young people grow familiar with G-d and acquire an aptitude and intellectual taste for the spiritual, they become attuned to their higher purpose in life. They become children who relate to their parents with respect and affection. Children who will not take property that doesn't belong to them. Children who reach out to help others, and are generous with their time and love.

Education consists of several components, the most basic of which is the transfer of information. But we must remember that information is only a tool that we put in a child's hand; just as there is much more to constructing a house than having the right tools and materials, there is much more to education than having the right information.

The true educator is not one who simply teaches facts, but one who teaches a child to think for himself—to find answers to his own questions based on the principles he was taught, and not be solely dependent on a teacher or a parent to solve a dilemma. If your answers are constantly supplied by someone else, you may have the comfort of never having to take responsibility for a mistake. But if you learn to think for yourself, you receive the deep gratification of having acted on your own initiative. This is consistent with why G-d created the universe: not so puppets could play out a predetermined script, but so that each individual would have the desire, the *freedom*, to act honestly and virtuously.

Teaching also requires humility. Remember, a teacher is not the *source* of the information, but a vehicle for information that comes from a greater place. A teacher must never be arrogant in dispensing this knowledge, but should feel blessed with the opportunity to introduce the student to the knowledge.

Above all, remember this: Words that come from the heart enter the heart.[1] As a teacher, you must mean what you say, and you must be a living example of what you teach. Children often cannot distinguish between an *idea* and *behavior*, and if you show them that you can behave contrary to what you teach, you are undermining the entire process. Telling a child, in effect, "Do as I say and not as I do," is *also* education—of a negative sort.

It is written in Proverbs that we should "educate the youngster according to *his* way" so that, as he matures, "he shall not depart from it." But why the child's way? Isn't knowledge objective? How can we customize knowledge for each child? Will that not cause education to become, in a sense, arbitrary?

Of course there are absolutes in the value system that G-d has given us. But true education must be sensitive and apply these absolute values to each child individually, for each child has his own way and his own strengths.

This is especially true for those children who are deemed "handicapped." No matter what difficulties a child may possess, it is incumbent upon us to educate that child with as much care and sensitivity as any other child, if not more—for if there is ever a child who needs individual attention to achieve his or her potential, it is the "handicapped" child. When we lovingly apply ourselves to their education, we will be gratified to discover that they have far greater abilities than could have been imagined.

For any child, a teacher must pinpoint and draw out that child's strengths, not the strengths *we* think he should possess. The goal is for a child to grow into an adult who can stand on his own feet, not on *your* feet. We often think that if we teach absolute, dogmatic values, then a child will undoubtedly perpetuate that value system. That is only half the story. Yes, those values must be expressed, but in the child's language, so that they become a part of the child, integrated with his personality, instilled in his spirit.

A teacher who is too harsh, who thinks that he or she is in large part a disciplinarian, will never teach a child well, for the bedrock of education is love. Of course, education requires discipline, but even within the discipline, a child should feel a teacher's love. As the sages tell us, "With your right hand, draw close, and with your left, discipline."[2] The primary force, symbolized by the dominant right hand, should always be love.

If you feel that you are in competition with a child, do not be a teacher, because the child is not your equal. Whether you are a teacher or a parent, G-d has entrusted you to teach the child well and to treat the child well. The respect and awe we must have for a child is no different from the respect and awe we must have for G-dliness itself.

WHY BECOME AN EDUCATOR?

Isn't it difficult to deal with children, to patiently cope with their inattention, their discipline problems, and the chaos? Wouldn't it be more convenient to develop a career that would be more lucrative and lead to recognition by your peers? Or perhaps do something that involves personal growth, whether it be music or art or writing?

If education were nothing but the process of imparting information, the answer to these questions might be yes. But because education is far more than that, because education is life itself, the reason why we should teach extends directly from the reason why we should *live*. Because life is a continuous education for all of us, teaching is a lifelong obligation and responsibility for all of us. We should not look upon this as a burden, for the very act of teaching is a vital ingredient in our own education.

Your students—who really include anyone with whom you communicate—sharpen your tools of communication and introduce you to a new dimension beyond your own experience. In order to reach a student whose mind is less developed than your own, you must reach deeper into your own mind and heart—and the farther you want to reach out, the farther you must reach within yourself.

Even if there were not so many advantages to being an educator, it would be well worthwhile, for what greater gift is there, what greater act of love, than to have the opportunity to help shape a person for the rest of his or her life?

⚭

A great sage was once asked where he had learned so much. He replied, "I learned much from my teachers, I learned even more from my friends, and most of all, I learned from my students."[3]

HOW MUST THIS GENERATION BE EDUCATED?

Because a child is impressionable, he or she will be influenced by *whatever* is around him. Children today are inundated by many influences that are detrimental to a proper education. After fighting through all the modern-day distractions—whether it be television or the lure of crime and drugs—there is precious little time and energy left to cultivate our children's minds and hearts and souls. It is not enough to send your children off to school with a packed lunch; education is a full-time duty. We must always be as vigilant as when the child was a newborn—always on the alert, always ready to serve the child's spiritual needs.

Why do the Ten Commandments, which include moral laws, begin with "I am your G-d"? Because without the acceptance that morality is derived from G-d, morality—and, therefore, education—is guided by nothing more than human whim and conscience. History has shown us that a society can be extremely well educated and yet, if not guided by G-d's precepts, it may be steeped in malevolence.

Establishing a system of morally sound education is one of the primary responsibilities of society. To hand off such a responsibility to a group of administrators, no matter how qualified they may be, is both neglectful and ineffective. While there must be a certain group of people whose primary responsibility is to implement education, each member of society must take an active role. For parents of young children especially, the responsibility is clear. Think how disturbed we would be to learn about a parent who had a sick child but refused to take the child to a doctor. If that is the case for the child's body, shouldn't we feel the same concern for a child's mind, for his soul?

And yet, because of the heavy workload of so many parents now today, our schools have assumed much greater responsibility. There was a time when basic values were taught at home while schooling served primarily to give children the skills for a career. Many parents now depend on the schools to teach their children both skills *and* values. This underscores the great need for schools to establish moral curricula. Especially today, children as well as adults are longing to learn about higher values. We need to appreciate this receptivity and respond to it with the most effective and aggressive educational campaign possible.

Why has the moral fabric of this country deteriorated so badly? Because children are no longer taught about G-d. From its inception, the United States has been the refuge for millions of people of every religion who fled their homelands so they could worship freely. It was in such a spirit that we used to educate our children. Then a slow but devastating process began that often resulted in diluting and, ultimately, eliminating an education based on our personal responsibility to G-d. The old battle between G-d and science extended into one between G-d and education. That is one of the primary reasons for much of today's moral deterioration, and that is why there is no choice but to return to an educational philosophy in which we teach children not just the value of a mathematical equation, but the value of their souls.

Remember, it is children who can best relate to simplicity and the essence of G-d. Do not project your own skepticism onto children. Children, unlike adults, do not chew over every piece of new information until its essence is diluted or destroyed; they just listen and absorb—which is why they learn so well.

We must look at our children and tell ourselves again and again: Here is a fertile soul, an open heart and mind, that I have been given by G-d to nurture and teach. This child's life will affect many others, and I must teach him as best I can. Will G-d and society be pleased with the job I have done?

☙❧

One day, on his daily walk to work, the Rebbe met up with a community leader whom he knew. "Every day, I walk down this street and see young girls and boys passing by," the Rebbe said with great concern. "Now tell me, who is thinking about them? Who is making sure that their intellectual and spiritual needs are being met? You and everyone else who has influence must dedicate yourselves above all to the education of these young people."

Years later, the community leader recalled that he was so inspired by the Rebbe's heartfelt concern that he immediately conceived of and initiated a series of educational programs, which over the years grew to serve thousands of students.

5

oℳ℺

YOUTH
The Fire of Life

Youths will put the elderly to shame, and the old will rise
in the presence of the young.
—Talmud, Sotah 49b

The rebellion of youth must be directed against the
status quo and toward the sublime, toward G-d, and
toward a higher meaning.
—The Rebbe

oℳ℺

On the eve of Yom Kippur, the holiest moment of the Jewish
year, it is traditional for parents to bless their children.
Every year at this time, the Rebbe would bless the young adults of
the central Lubavitch school, often with a tremor in his voice and a
tear in his eye. It was an incredibly moving moment, and it inspired
the young people to rededicate themselves to their studies and to help
build communities and study centers all over the world. The Rebbe
clearly understood that youth is the engine that drives the human
machine.

An Israeli journalist once visited the Rebbe's synagogue during
the High Holidays. There were more than ten thousand people pres-

ent, *and the journalist was amazed to see that, as was untrue in many synagogues, most were in their teens. "Seventy percent, eighty percent of the people in that room were young people," he later wrote. "That a man eighty years old should be able to command the attention of so many young people coming from different backgrounds, and bring them to such a height of energy is a sure sign that there is a future."*

JUST WHAT IS THIS IN-BETWEEN TIME WE CALL YOUTH?

Think back to the time when you first understood the sheer power of fire: It both amazed and frightened you. When it is under control, fire betters our life in countless ways, many of which we have come to take for granted. But when we don't have it under control, a raging fire destroys everything in its path.

A young person is like fire. With direction and guidance, he or she can change the very shape of the world. Without direction, the fires of youth are wasted at best, while at worst, they can become a dangerous, destructive force. To lead a meaningful life means harnessing the fires of youth; to do so, we must first understand the purpose of youth itself.

The period of youth is an odd one by nature, nestled between childhood and adulthood. A teenager is no longer content to play like a child but doesn't yet have the knowledge and experience to be fully engaged in adult pursuits. Young people begin to experience many of the frustrations and yearnings of an adult, but may lack the maturity to deal with them. Teenagers have plenty of time on their hands, and yet contemporary society is far better at providing ways to *waste* this time than spend it productively. Youth is one of the most precious periods of a person's life, and yet one of the most difficult.

These various tensions within young people create a unique, untamed energy—the energy of life itself. Young people are not looking for comfort; they are searching for a meaningful cause. They are overflowing with a mixture of adrenaline and confidence—"I want to change the way the world works," young people often think. "I *can* change the world." Adults, burdened with the pressures of everyday life, may resign themselves that the world just *is* the way it is, but young people, untempered by the realities of adulthood, do not tolerate such resignation. This often causes conflict between the two groups: Young people abhor the status quo, while adults' lives revolve around it.

So what we have here, in the most general terms, is either energy without sufficient direction (youth) or direction without sufficient energy (adulthood). Many adults may simply throw up their hands, writing off youth as a rebellious period that a person must simply outgrow. Young people, meanwhile, often think that adults have forgotten how to appreciate the very meaning and thrill of life. Youths are rebellious, and adults see the rebellion as an aberration, or even one step shy of a crime.

But rebellion is not the crime; the crime occurs when the rebellion has no healthy outlet. Rebellion, in fact, can be the healthiest thing for a human being—an undiluted energy that inspires a person to not give up easily, to refuse to tolerate injustice, to not go along with an idea just because everyone else is thinking it. Depriving a young person of an outlet to release this energy can cause deep pain and anxiety. Think about the steam that builds up in a turbine—without a safety valve, it is bound to explode sooner or later. The worst thing we can do with a young person's spiritual or psychological energy is to bottle it up; in fact, we must do everything we can to tap this energy, to focus it, and channel it properly.

❧

*A very bright young man was constantly falling behind
in school, for no explicable reason. Finally, his parents took*

him to see a rabbi. "I hear you are very gifted at science," the rabbi said, "so tell me, what is the difference between a very bright electric light and a laser beam?"

"That's simple," the teenager said. "The laser amplifies and focuses light rays to make the beam more intense; the other light just disperses its rays every which way."

"But doesn't it take more energy to produce the laser beam?" the rabbi asked.

"Not really," the young man said, smiling as he realized where the rabbi was leading him. "It is just a matter of concentration and focus."

WHAT DOES THE REBELLION OF YOUTH REALLY MEAN?

Thus, the sound of youthful rebellion is the sound of a youthful energy crying out, searching for guidance. For adults, the challenge is to help turn the cry into a strong, sure voice. "Yes," we must tell our young people, "take that energy and do try to change the world for the better. Don't accept the status quo. Don't stand by and tolerate injustice."

Young people are searching for a reason that makes life meaningful. They may not articulate it so clearly, but that is why their souls cry out. They become seriously disillusioned with the hollowness they see in their parents' pursuits, and they sense that without a greater purpose, life is just an unconnected series of events. They are busy looking around the world, trying to figure out where they fit in, what they are supposed to accomplish with their own lives.

The answer is clear. Each of us was put on earth to accomplish G-d's mission by living a spiritually meaningful and productive life, and it is this message that we as adults must convey. Because this message is not being transmitted today, we are seeing an unprecedented level of rebellion and disillusion among our youth.

It is true, especially in this country, that youthful rebellion has led to extremes that were themselves unhealthy. But why did the rebellion come about in the first place? Because young people were saying to their parents, "No, we will *not* be happy with the creature comforts you are passing on to us. We want something deeper. We want a world with meaning and a value system. We want a G-d."

The cry of youth comes from a very pure place, and the idealism of a young person, no matter how outrageous it may seem to adult sensibilities, should be cherished. Just as the human body's immune system will reject a foreign substance, the soul of a youth will reject the hollow spirit of falseness. Adults must learn to listen to the cry of youth and give it a real and true answer. Think: When was the last time you had a heart-to-heart talk with a younger person about the real issues of life? A talk about our place in the world and what we are supposed to do with our lives. A talk that honestly looked at pain and failure and at joy and success. We need to all sit down calmly with our families, with our young people, and talk about our lives and aspirations.

For such communication to be effective, it must be sincere and it must be consistent; it cannot surface only in times of crisis. Instead of playing or languishing all weekend, designate an hour or two just to speak or take a walk together. Talk about values, about the difficult decisions that any young person must face. Talk about G-d, about morality, about how pure intellect is limited unless it is supported by a system of higher values. Talk about charity, about selflessness, about why we are here and where we are headed.

The relationship between an adult and a young person need not be an antagonistic one; by nature, in fact, it should be symbiotic. From the young person, an adult learns to reawaken himself to the raw power of the soul, and to access that power within himself. From the adult, a young person learns that there is no substitute for experience and the judgment it brings. Teenagers should be especially eager to partner their energy with the elderly, who have lived long enough to no longer be in competition with young people. As is written in Deuteronomy, "Ask your father and he will tell you. Ask your grandparent and he will relate to you."[1] In any case, the wisdom of an adult and the passion of a young person are an unbeatable combination.

HOW SHOULD THE ENERGY OF YOUTH BE CHANNELED?

Understanding this combination of youthful passion and adult wisdom goes a long way toward closing the so-called generation gap. Why is there a generation gap? Not because parents and children don't care for one another, but because they see themselves as distinct individuals divided by materialistic boundaries, with different attitudes and interests, different social groups, different priorities. There is no getting around the fact that a sixty-year-old person is sixty years old, perhaps on the verge of retirement, and that a twenty-year-old is only twenty, just about to embark on an adult life. They indeed seem to have little in common if we base our outlook on day-to-day materialistic activities. What they do have in common, though, is a soul, and a soul is not affected by age.

The key to solving the generation gap is learning to focus on a mission that will create continuity from generation to generation. It is not a matter of finding common ground to *talk* about; it is about finding common ground to *walk* upon. Adults and young people are in exactly the same situation: We all need to temper our materialistic pursuits and worries in order to pursue a meaningful life. We were put here together—you as a younger person and I as an older person—because G-d wanted me to learn from you and you from me.

Never before have we witnessed such a restlessness in our youth as today. Never before has the energy of youth, having no place to vent itself, exploded so loudly and so often. Never before have young people been so hungry for meaning —and many of today's adults have retained that hunger from their own youth. To satisfy this hunger, we must first recognize that it is not material but spiritual in nature, and that only spirituality can feed spiritual hunger.

If we truly desire a serious change in our youth, we must first enact a serious change in our adult attitudes. We need to find a new way of talking to our young people. In a relationship between an older person and a younger person, whether it is parent and child or teacher and student, a failure to communicate is always the fault of the one who knows *more*, not less. You didn't find the right words, or perhaps you weren't speaking from the heart. To blame a student for failing to learn is like blaming a baby for crying—the baby is crying out of need, and that need can only be satisfied by the more knowledgeable and experienced person.

No one is questioning the *intention* of parents who have trouble with their children; the problem lies in the weapons with which we arm our young people. To fight a spiritual war, they must be equipped with spiritual weapons. Remember, no person is ever lost; everyone can be reached. No matter how rebellious and disillusioned a young person may be, he has a soul and, connected to that individual soul, a distinct mission from G-d. This is the first lesson that young people must learn—that their lives include a higher purpose, that they must use their youthful energy for good and moral ends.

The fire of youth must be used not just to build careers but to build homes and communities based on love and giving. The hope for real change in this country and throughout the world rests on our youth, and today's leaders must recognize this fact. But we must also recognize that a young person is by nature restless and inexperienced. So it is the responsibility and privilege of adults to provide young people with a blueprint, a spiritual guide to life—which consists of G-d's wisdom and His instructions of how best to lead a meaningful life.

The timing is right to launch an all-out offensive against any complacency and indifference. It is not sufficient to wait for problems to arise, because no matter how valiantly we fight, we will only be attacking the symptom of the problem, and not the cause. The key is to take the offensive, to generate a spiritual revolution against the tide of material pursuits, to reintroduce G-d into our daily lives.

Today's youths should be encouraged to create a true revolution—a revolution of virtue and integrity. They should fight not simply out of duty, but with the zeal of someone in search of a truly significant life. In a positive way, the young should indeed "put the elderly to shame"—by storming the halls of vanity and selfishness. By rebelling against injustice and hypocrisy. By insisting that each one of us can and must make a difference. Young people should spread this message by publishing student newspapers, by establishing charitable groups, by taking advantage of modern technology to reach as many people as possible. With their combination of sincerity, conviction, and energy, they can influence countless hearts and minds with a message of hope and truth.

Should we extinguish the fires of youth because of their potency? Never! We should constantly encourage our young people: "You are our hope, our most precious natural resource." G-d gives us all a second chance through our offspring. Somewhere along the way, our society convinced us that prosperity would solve all of life's problems, but we have been bluntly reminded by our rebellious children that we need spirit more than we need matter, that we need meaning more than we need money. So we must say to our young men and women: "You are as alive as fire. If you complement your flame of youth with a sense of focus and urgency, you have the power to move worlds."

⟨∞⟩

In the 1950s, the Rebbe recognized that there was a
prevailing ignorance about higher spiritual values among
young people in many parts of this country. He established
the Lubavitch Youth Organization, with chapters around

the world, encouraging his students to share spiritual literature and other tools of education with the youth of other
communities.

In 1961, President John F. Kennedy initiated the Peace
Corps, calling on young American men and women to go
and help educate and develop underprivileged countries. The
President was convinced there would be hundreds of volun-
teers; there were, of course, far more.

The call of the President echoed the call of the Rebbe:
that young people should recognize the power they possess,
and should be encouraged to use that power for the good.

6

⚭

MARRIAGE
When Two Lives Unite as One

A man shall leave his father and mother and be united with his
wife, and they shall become one flesh.
—Genesis 2:24

A successful marriage is dependent on inviting
G-d into the relationship.
—The Rebbe

⚭

On November 27, 1928, in Warsaw, the Rebbe married
Chaya Mushka Schneersohn, the daughter of the previous
Lubavitcher Rebbe. On their twenty-fifth anniversary, the Rebbe
said to a gathering of his students and followers, "Today marks the
anniversary of the beginning of my public work. This day connected me with you. G-d should help that we all see fruit from our
labor." Many years later, a friend of the Rebbetzin (as the Rebbe's
wife is called) paid a visit on their wedding anniversary and saw
the many flowers and gifts that had been sent from all over the
world. On her way out, the friend noticed in another room the most
beautiful bouquet of all. As she moved closer, she realized that they
weren't actually flowers, but colorful dried fruits, arranged with ex-

quisite care and grace. "Who sent you these?" she asked. The Reb-betzin, smiling, replied, "Those were sent to me by my husband."

WHY GET MARRIED?

A wedding ceremony is indeed a joyous occasion. We see family members and old friends, we eat and drink, we dance and rejoice. We share in the happiness of the man and the woman who are committing their lives to each other. But why are they getting married in the first place?

Some might answer that a marriage is a contract that binds two people. But we know that if two people don't love each other, no contract is strong enough to hold them together. The real question comes one step before marriage: Why is there such a powerful attraction between man and woman?

Because G-d created them as one entity and then divided them into two. As it is written in the Bible, "G-d created man in His image . . . male and female He created them,"[1] as the sages explain, "a single individual with two faces."[2] As an independent individual, a person would be left without companionship, without challenge, without the potential for growth. Neither man nor woman would be able to transcend the individuality into which they were born. So G-d created them as one and clove them into two, two who can join with each other to become one. Man and woman are drawn to each other because individually, we feel incomplete; we are searching for our other half, through which we reunite with G-d.

So the key to a successful marriage is appreciating its sanctity. Beyond just uniting man and woman, marriage must introduce a third dimension: G-d. The Hebrew words for *man* and *woman* both contain the word *fire*.[3] They also each contain other letters that, when combined, make up G-d's name. Man and woman without G-d are like two fires that will consume each other. When they rise above their own self-contained limitations and introduce the G-dly and holy into their lives, they can become one, with an unseen hidden bond that makes their unity, their marriage, far greater than the sum of its parts.

Two people may love and care for each other, but without a divine force, what is to bond temporal human beings eternally? Such a bond is necessary, for, besides being two strangers with different personalities and backgrounds, a man and a woman differ biologically, emotionally, and psychologically and will undergo many transitions in their lives.

The single most important ingredient in creating this lifetime bond is the commitment of husband and wife to G-d and His timeless laws. Just as a home needs a foundation to stand on, a marriage needs to be built on an eternal foundation. Husband and wife need to invite G-d into their union by dedicating their lives to eternal values and connecting to a presence higher than their own, by acknowledging G-d who created them as two halves of one soul. This instills each spouse with a commitment to each other, to their families, to the world around them.

The unity created by marriage—the bond between man, woman, and G-d—enhances the unity and love in a family's home. It will determine how each child grows up and continues to love. And this unity is necessary for the well-being of each spouse, enabling them to grow both independently and together. Above all, our marriage—the way a man and woman unite with each other—reflects the way we unite with G-d.

☙❧

A great scholar was studying the concept of marriage and realized that because a successful marriage requires a divine energy that unites two opposites, this energy must constantly be renewed in order to keep the two together. When he shared this thought with a colleague, the other scholar said, "Congratulations!"

"Why are you congratulating me?" the scholar asked his friend.

"Because, according to what you just explained, your marriage is being renewed every moment. So mazel tov! You just got married anew!"

WHAT MAKES A MARRIAGE WORK?

Many raw materials go into building a healthy marriage. Love, of course, is necessary, and so is a sense of awe and respect—the respect that each spouse feels for the other, and the awe that both husband and wife feel for G-d. They must always acknowledge the divine force that brings them together, and the great responsibility of building a life and home together. Such awe will weave itself through every aspect of their lives, from the way they keep their home to the way they educate their children.

A successful marriage must have vitality. A union between two living people means that the union itself is alive, and must constantly be nurtured and encouraged to grow. A marriage must also abound in trust. Trust does not come overnight; it takes years to build. But once it is in place, it serves as a solid base that will support a marriage through crisis.

Trust does not come from perfect behavior; it comes from accountability. No one can be expected to be perfect, but a healthy person *can* be expected to be accountable, to acknowledge an error. Trust means that your attitude and conduct over time have demonstrated that your spouse can depend on you, that you have the integrity to act properly even when no one but G-d is watching. Otherwise, there will always be doubt: How can I know that my spouse is truly committed to this marriage?

A healthy marriage also means building a healthy home together—a home not just for your personal comfort, but one that will be a light unto others. From the outset, the priorities in a marriage must not be on the amount of money spent—for the wedding, or expensive furnishings in a house—but on the commitment to building a home that is guided by the divine principles of morality and virtue.

Sometimes it is the small things that matter, that demonstrate to your spouse and to G-d that you are committed. Going shopping. Cleaning up the house. Asking if there is anything you can do to help when your spouse's hands are full. When one spouse travels, he or she should bring back a gift for the other. Even when you are working on something independent of your home and marriage, you should try to involve your spouse as a constant partner in your life.

A crucial and central element in achieving a loving marriage is learning to cultivate peace at home, learning to communicate and handle the variables that will arise in any marriage. Learning how to get around an argument, how to reconcile, how to cope when things aren't going well. Whenever one spouse is having trouble, the other should remember that they are two halves of the same soul. Neglecting your spouse is the same as neglecting yourself, or neglecting G-d.

There are no magic formulas in handling problems within a marriage, of course. It depends on the mutual effort of both husband and wife. First of all, both spouses must understand that preserving the marriage, a sanctified union, is an absolute necessity for which they carry equal responsibility. We must also understand that a happy marriage cannot be built on one person's terms. Individuality is enhanced, not obliterated, by true love. It may be tempting to always have things your way, but love and respect are nurtured by acknowledging the wants and needs of a spouse. Such selflessness can only come from recognizing G-d in your life, which enables you to consider your spouse's space as sacred as your own.

A husband and wife must also have a mutual commitment to resolving problems by accepting their responsibility to make their sacred marriage work. This can only occur when both spouses learn to communicate openly and acknowledge their role in a problem. Each spouse must respect the other's concerns, no matter how minor they may seem. No problem should be allowed to linger unresolved.

Sometimes a conflict can be avoided by not responding in kind to a spouse's anger. When one spouse gets angry, the other often reciprocates without thinking, allowing a spark to flare into a raging fire. It is best to address the other's concerns patiently, or to avoid discussing them until the temporary state of anger passes. No one has the right to infringe in any way—psychologically, emotionally, or physically—on another person's space. Under no circumstances can such abuse be tolerated. An abusive person must be responsible for getting help; if necessary, those subject to the abuse must insist on it, and enlist others to ensure that the problem is dealt with.

Criticism does not work in a marriage. Invalidation of your spouse will only aggravate any problem. When you see something in your spouse that you feel needs correction, broach it gently, with love and concern. If your spouse has a blind spot in a certain area, you just might have to adjust and learn to smile at it. None of us are without our blind spots. It is not your job to determine what is best for your spouse; even though a husband and wife are constantly teaching each other, they are *not* each other's teacher or authority figure. They are each other's closest friends—equal friends.

If a dispute does arise between spouses, it is often better not to get family members involved. Relatives may mean well, but because of their subjectivity they tend to take sides and exacerbate the problem. A friend can often be more helpful, although it is sometimes a so-called friend who instigates a conflict, whether by exaggeration or just plain gossip. If this is the case, it might be best to distance yourself from the situation that incites such discord.

If you cannot reconcile differences no matter how hard you try, it is best to consult confidentially with a third party whom you both trust. Be sure that this person will not incite further bad feelings, that he is genuinely concerned with you and your marriage.

When dealing with a disagreement, it is important to compromise, to not allow your pride to stand in the way. Many of us feel we will look weak if we take the initiative to reconcile, but doing so is a sign of *true* strength.

Above all, a healthy marriage necessitates that the wife and husband must always remember their duty to their third partner, G-d. Their marriage is not a private affair; it affects the entire cosmic destiny. Both husband and wife must invite G-d into their marriage, not as a guest but as a constant partner.

This includes fulfilling the commandment and blessing that man was given upon his creation: "Be fruitful and multiply."[4] This is a critical component in a successful marriage. The ability to reproduce is part of our physiological and psychological makeup, and is necessary for our well-being. We should not tamper with or second-guess G-d, who blesses us with the ability to bear children; with every child to whom we give birth, G-d blesses us with the strength and resources to sustain, care for, and nurture this child. There may indeed be the fears that result from living in a dysfunctional environment, in which there are many ways for a child to be hurt. But one wrong does not justify another—the wrong of choosing not to bear children. Having children defines and crystallizes the priorities of a marriage—indeed, of life in general—and raising children is the most challenging, profound, and gratifying goal that a man and woman can hope to achieve together. It *eternally* bonds them to each other, to their family, and above all, to G-d.

HOW SHOULD WE PREPARE FOR MARRIAGE?

Why have we recently been experiencing such unprecedented levels of troubled marriages and of divorce? Because the G-dly dimension is missing from many marriages today. As many short-term solutions as there may be to keep a marriage together, it cannot be truly healthy unless its roots are solid.

Sages refer to marriage as man's second birth. First, the soul enters into the body and assumes a physical existence; when a person marries, the soul moves even deeper into the physical state. Although man's mission in life includes the positive development of the physical world, one must be equipped with the spiritual vision and fortitude to carry out such a mission with the proper perspective.

The implications are clear: In preparation for marriage, a person must devote special time to spiritual and G-dly pursuits, and to learning about the deeper significance of marriage. This period before marriage is crucial, for marriage itself demands that we immerse ourselves in the most material aspects of our physical world—providing for our family, caring for a home, building a career. By attuning ourselves spiritually *before* marriage, we lay a strong foundation for our home and family.

A successful marriage begins long before the ceremony; it begins with both the man and the woman individually recognizing G-d in their lives. And this means educating and preparing yourself in the formative years before marriage. For a marriage to be successful, we must first recognize who we are—that we are a soul within a body. When you are at peace with yourself, when your body and soul are attuned to each other in fulfilling your life's mission, you are then in a stronger position to find your proper soul mate. When you don't yet know who *you* are, how can you possibly know what sort of person will be best for you to marry?

The soul, feeling incomplete, demands that we go out and search for its other half. We may be confused and distracted by our physical and emotional attraction to the opposite sex. But this attraction should not be the sole *focus* of our search; it is only a manifestation of the soul's yearning to be complete. This attraction then becomes a positive force in cultivating a relationship. G-d blesses you in the endeavor of finding your mate. Still, as in all matters, you must take the initiative; it is your responsibility to seek out a person with whom you will be compatible in every way.

The emphasis in finding a mate cannot be only on external, superficial elements, which may well conflict with the search for the deeper compatibility that is necessary in a serious relationship. It is far more important to know how another person feels about G-d, to know how he or she feels about higher goals and objectives, things that will be truly important in your marriage and life.

It is only natural to have doubts and confusion when considering whom to marry. These doubts should be seen not as an obstacle, but as a healthy and open part of the process. Often, G-d waits to send you the blessing of an appropriate mate until you are ready to receive it by sincerely devoting yourself to spiritual growth, rather than just to your career or social life.

Preparing for marriage should be seen as a great opportunity for spiritual and personal growth. For a new beginning. It is a time to get to know your own soul and the soul of your future spouse, to build the proper spiritual foundation with which to go into marriage. We spend so much time planning the details of the marriage ceremony itself that we often overlook the spiritual preparation, even though it is far more important. Also, since marriage is such a comprehensive union, it is best that a man and woman get to know each other's families before deciding to marry, since it is our families who help build and define our value systems.

There is no need for the wedding itself to be so extravagant. Yes, it should be beautiful, but the sight of a man and woman committing their lives to each other and to G-d is in itself more beautiful than the most expensive trappings. It is also appropriate for the bride and groom to give some money to charity on their wedding day, and for their parents to do the same. This sets the tone of a giving and gracious relationship, and directs G-d's blessings to the new couple.

WHAT ABOUT DIVORCE?

G-d created the institution of marriage to allow a man and woman to unite eternally. Because of the demands of our physical world and because of the intricacies in any relationship between two people, there will surely be obstacles to overcome in a marriage. We must address these with the most vigor, patience, and fortitude that we can muster, for marriage is meant to be, in the words of the sages, "an eternal edifice." Divorce should only be considered an absolute last resort, if a couple has exhausted every possibility of reconciliation, and if they and those they trust have decided that it is the only remaining option.

We must see this time of rampant divorce as a signal from heaven to firmly address the root causes. Let us decide to acknowledge the need for G-d in our marriages. Let us commit to making our marriages divine, to making our family's home a place that helps fulfill our G-dly mission on earth.

Remember, how we marry and cultivate our marriage determines not just our own welfare, but the welfare of our children, our grandchildren, and generations well beyond them. Take your marriage seriously. It is not just a commitment between you and your spouse—it is a commitment between you, your spouse, and G-d. Such a unity gives off a light that shines throughout the world.

⟨⟩

A young unmarried woman was discussing with the Rebbe some prospective matches that had been suggested to her, and she explained why none of them appealed to her. The Rebbe smiled. "You have read too many romance novels," he replied. "Love is not the overwhelming, blinding emotion we find in the world of fiction. Real love is an emotion that intensifies throughout life. It is the small, everyday acts of being together that make love flourish. It is sharing and caring and respecting one another. It is building a life together, a family and a home. As two lives unite to form one, over time, there is a point where each partner feels a part of the other, where each partner can no longer visualize life without the other at his or her side."

7

───── ⌇⌇⌇ ─────

LOVE

The Purest Expression of the Soul

As water mirrors a face, a heart responds to another.
—Proverbs 27:1

Love is the transcendence of the soul over the body.
—The Rebbe

⌇⌇⌇

On Sunday afternoons, the Rebbe would stand outside the door of his office to greet and bestow a blessing upon anyone who came to see him. He would often stand for hours, as thousands of people filed by, many of them seeking a blessing or advice about a personal matter or a spiritual dilemma. The Rebbe was once asked how he had the strength to stand all day, sometimes for seven or eight hours, to accommodate everyone. "When I see all these people, it is like counting diamonds," he replied with a smile. "One doesn't grow weary or weak when counting something as beautiful as diamonds."

WHAT IS LOVE?

Love, one of our most-oft-used words, remains an enigma. There may have been more written about love than about any other subject, yet it remains intangible. We know that love is an integral part of human life, that we need it for our well-being, but there seems to be no guaranteed way to find it. So what is love?

Love is the single most necessary component in human life. It is both giving and receiving; it allows us to experience another person and lets that person experience us. Love is the origin and foundation of all human interaction. To live a meaningful life, we must learn more about love and how to bring it into our lives.

At first glance, we might think that we need love in the same way that we need to eat and drink, to breathe and sleep. We know that love fulfills our need to be cared for, our need for intimacy. So we pursue love in a manner that is often narcissistic and indulgent— we look for someone who will love us because we crave it; we may want to love someone so we can feel good about ourselves.

But if love is just another need like food or water, why is it so elusive? Why is attaining love difficult for so many people? And when we do find it, it doesn't come easily; it always comes with some pain and frustration. We may succeed at love for a time, but when we fail, the pain is intense.

These are the obstacles we face when we look at love as just another of our bodily needs. Yes, we do need love just as we need food and water, but there is a difference. Food and water are elements of the earth that sustain our physical bodies, whereas love is the language of G-d, which sustains our soul.

True love bears little resemblance to the love we read about in novels and hear about in songs. True love is transcendence, linking our physical selves to G-d and, therefore, to everyone else around us. All too often we look at love selfishly, as something we *want* and *need*; but true love, because it is integral to our relationship with G-d, is selfless.

One of our most fundamental principles is "Love your neighbor as yourself."[1] How can this be possible—don't we love ourselves more than we can love anything else? The answer lies in the fact that true, selfless love stems not from the body, but from the soul. Love is the dominance of spirit over matter.[2] By the definition of materialism, two objects cannot occupy the same space simultaneously. But the soul transcends time and space, and it also transcends narcissism, making it possible to truly share yourself with another person.

The sage Hillel says, "Do not do unto others that which you do not want done unto yourself. This is the entire Torah and the rest is commentary."[3] The wisdom of G-d is intended to do one thing: to teach us how to love, to transcend our material boundaries and reach a more spiritual place. Such a journey is only made through the soul, and love is the language that we must learn to speak along the way. Love is a way of talking to G-d. When you look into someone's eyes and love that person, you are transcending the physical world and connecting to G-d.

So love is much more than treating another person with compassion. It goes beyond exchanging feelings of warmth. It is much more than doing to others only as you would do unto yourself. Love is a G-dly act, the purest way to feed another person's soul as well as your own.

The deepest love is not merely human. It is a love infused with G-dliness, whereby a mortal kiss is transformed into an immortal one. True love is one soul greeting another.

WHY DO WE NEED LOVE?

In a sense, we have all wandered away from our true selves. Birth is the beginning of our soul's journey, sent off from its divine source to live in an unnatural state, a land of materialism. Throughout our lives, therefore, we crave to be reunited with our real selves. We search for our soul, for the G-dly spark within ourselves. We long to reconnect with our source.

Many of us don't realize that what we call love is actually a search for G-d. The urgent need we are expressing when we say "I need to be cared for" or "I need intimacy" is really the need to transcend our physical selves and connect to our souls. So in a sense, loving another person should be the same as loving G-d, and vice versa. A person who can love G-d but cannot love another human being is not really loving G-d. And a person who loves another person but has no love for G-d will ultimately discover that what he *calls* love is conditional and selfish, which means that it is not truly love at all.

The two types of love—selfish love and selfless love—are diametrically opposed. Selfish love is conditional love; you love on the condition that your needs will be met, and if the person you have chosen to love doesn't serve your needs, you reject that person and search elsewhere. Although it may seem beautiful for a time, such love is bound to be mercurial. When the person you love wants help, you may give it. But once the price becomes too high, if you feel you are giving more than you are receiving, you may simply stop loving. After all, there is only so much discomfort that you may be willing to tolerate for another person.

Selfless love, though, means rising above your own needs. It means going outside of yourself, truly connecting with another person's soul and, therefore, with G-d. When love is transcendent, you are reaching for a higher place; together, you are reaching for G-d. There are no conditions for such selfless love; when transcendence is the focus of our love, we do not constantly redefine our wants and needs.

Conditional, selfish love dissipates when its conditions are not met, but unconditional, selfless love is constant and eternal. Conditional love all too often means the obliteration or subjection of one individual; instead of two becoming one, the love of the more dominant person consumes the other. Unconditional love, though, the love of transcendence, enables you to put aside your selfish desires and love that person accordingly.

Conditional love does not encourage growth, for it is simply a temporary need being fulfilled. Just as you need to eat again a few hours after a meal, someone who loves conditionally will constantly need more helpings of assurance, caring, and acceptance. But unconditional love is the foundation of human growth. It is comprehensive—it spills over and affects not just your immediate needs but all of you. Whereas conditional love is compartmentalized in your life, unconditional love is an integral part of your entire existence. And finally, it is the tool by which we learn to experience the highest reality: G-d.

Love, therefore, is the foundation on which our entire world is built.[4] All our laws, all our attitudes, all our interactions stem from the same principle. Love is the root of all civility and morality. Without love, it would be impossible to live in peace with one another, to respect one another's needs, and to treat everyone with the same compassion that we would like to be given ourselves.

A young child once asked a rabbi why man was created with two eyes instead of one, like the nose and the mouth.

"With the left eye, you should look at yourself, to see how you can improve yourself. And with the right eye, you should look at others lovingly, always seeking out their best qualities."

How Do We Achieve Such Selfless Love?

Initially, it may seem terrifying to embrace selfless love. It is easier and safer to love on your own terms. Selfless love, on the other hand, creates risk and vulnerability. But we must learn to celebrate this newfound vulnerability, for that is precisely what makes true love so gratifying—the prospect of sharing your soul with another person.

Most of us are ready to love, but we have learned not to trust other people, sometimes with good reason. The only way to let go, to become vulnerable, to open yourself to the possibilities of true love, is to trust G-d and the G-dliness within the person that you love.

To achieve selfless love, you must first learn to love yourself, to create harmony between your own body and soul. This means understanding who you really are and what you have been put on this earth to accomplish. It means being comfortable with your calling and not looking for distractions. If you are in conflict with yourself, how can you expect to reach a comfortable love with another person?

Learning to love yourself can be difficult. Initially, the ego cannot coexist with G-d. You are either pursuing your own agenda or G-d's; you see yourself as either a self-made, self-contained being, or as a being created in the image of G-d. In order to grow, you must learn to suspend your ego, to empty yourself and make room for something greater than yourself.

If you don't find a way to love G-d, to love the G-d that resides in your soul, you will find yourself in a constant search for love. We may even turn to unhealthy forms of love to replace this lack on inner love. This is why we don't *begin* our lives searching for love. As children, we learn first to receive love from our parents, from our siblings, from our environment. Only when we mature can we begin to look for love from a stranger, someone who will become a lifelong partner in marriage.

The love between a married couple, the love among family members, and the love between friends are all different, of course. But they all have one thing in common: They reflect the love between man and G-d. And how do we learn such love? We learn it as children, by watching our parents, our families, our teachers. For a child to grow into a loving adult, he must receive love and see love constantly.

A child must also learn to appreciate every other human being and every aspect of our existence on earth. The sage Hillel says, "Love your fellow creatures"[5]; why "creatures" and not "human beings"? Because even if they are nothing but "creatures," they were created by G-d, which in itself is reason to love them. And each of

G-d's creatures has the potential to reach great heights.

Every single thing on earth is worthy of our awareness and respect, and every person is like a diamond. While a diamond may appear soiled, beneath the surface lies a beauty and grace that are unequaled. It is precious regardless of how it looks on the outside, regardless of its surroundings.

We should treat each person that we meet accordingly. We must respect his innate value and totally dedicate ourselves to helping him by whatever means necessary. If his outer layer appears soiled, we should encourage him to clean himself. If his edges seem rough, we should help educate and empower him to polish himself by accessing his inner resources.

This is the true idea of love—to appreciate each person no matter what or where he is, and to help that person become the best person possible. As the sages say, "The sins should be erased but not the sinners."[6] It is not important to love every single thing that a person does, but it *is* important to love the person unconditionally. You don't have to accept another person's choices, and you don't have to teach your children those choices, but you must still accept the person. Even if you reject the philosophy of a particular group of people, you must not reject the people.

Love is not smothering someone with what you think is good for him; love is appreciating a person's individuality. Love requires the ultimate sensitivity to every person, beginning with your own family and extending into the world at large. That means transcending our narrow vision and learning to love everyone, regardless of his or her background, education, personality, or temperament.

Such a selfless, healthy love must include a degree of education and discipline. This is true both on the personal level and on the community level, for both children and adults. It is not enough to love someone and then leave him alone when he is doing something harmful to himself or others. Love does not mean compromising higher standards. A parent is not truly loving his or her child when, out of so-called love, he does not want to discipline the child for doing something wrong or harmful.

Above all, love is a force for good. It is the means by which human beings achieve cosmic unity, the unity between one another, G-d, and the universe. So the next person you see, whether it is a stranger or your spouse, do something gracious in the name of love, even if you get nothing in return. Introduce love into your life not just on your own terms, but beyond your preset boundaries.

Learn to love your family in a new way. Love them not only because they are your flesh and blood, but because they are G-d's children. Before putting your children to sleep, give them a new kind of kiss, one filled with the fire of your G-dly soul. Talk to them about love, and how to care for one another. You will see how this new awareness of love carries over into everything that you do.

From a technological standpoint, we are now living in an age of unprecedented unity. And yet our personal connections are more frayed than ever. Let us embrace unconditional love and make it the call of our generation. Let us love one another to create unity between man and man, between man and G-d. Let us see our technological unity as an opportunity to introduce love to everyone—first within ourselves, then in our families, our communities, our nations, and finally the entire world. Let us usher in the day when there will be neither envy nor strife, when love and unity abound.

⟨∼∼∼⟩

After the riots in Crown Heights, in 1991, the Rebbe was visited by David Dinkins, the mayor of New York City, who asked for a blessing of peace between the two peoples, the Jews and the blacks. The Rebbe responded, "Not two peoples but one people, under one administration and under one G-d."

8

⁘

INTIMACY
The Sanctity of Sexuality

The dignity of the princess is within, more than the golden clothing which she wears.
—Psalms 45:14

If you are close when you should be distant, you will be distant when you should be close.
—The Rebbe

⁘

The Rebbe, in a conversation with a psychologist, once expressed the great need in society for an awareness of the proper guidelines and boundaries of intimacy. This was necessary, he said, in order to establish and preserve healthy marriages, which are the bedrock of a sound society. In 1975, the Rebbe called upon the worldwide chapters of the Lubavitch Women's Organization to establish committees to publish literature and organize classes dealing with intimacy.

WHAT ARE SEXUALITY AND INTIMACY?

In regard to intimacy, we live in a time of crisis. Everyone craves intimacy, and everyone is searching for intimacy, yet it has become an area of great conflict and confusion.

There are many forces at work. Society's standards of sexuality and intimacy have changed greatly since the so-called sexual revolution. Ours is now a society bombarded by sexual thought and imagery; sexual boundaries have been blurred.

It is obviously an appropriate time to review our attitude toward intimacy and sexuality. What is sexuality exactly, and what is the power behind its mystique? What deeper meaning does it have in our lives? Are intimacy and sexuality one and the same? The "sexual revolution" supposedly set people free; are *you* free, or are you enslaved more than ever to your desires, more confused than ever by shifting standards?

Sexuality is an internal, G-dly energy, a meeting of body and soul, that is nourished by true intimacy, by modesty and subtlety. It can only flourish in a healthy manner in the context of the sacred institution of marriage. Sexuality itself possesses both a body and a soul, a physical and spiritual dimension. Its body is the union of human bodies, accompanied by the deepest of physical pleasures. Its soul is the union with G-dliness, accompanied by the deepest of spiritual pleasures. When sexuality's spiritual nature is removed or ignored, it can become an irrational obsession that consumes an individual.

Sexuality is among the most potent forces in life. It can either lift us to the greatest heights of self-sacrifice and commitment or lower us into the depths of self-interest and demoralization. Sexuality is never neutral.

The irony is that focusing on sexuality is its undoing. Sexuality divorced of its intimate nature loses its true meaning, its dignity, its majesty. This is where sexuality and intimacy diverge. Intimacy does not equal sexuality; it is a special state, separate from all else in our lives, that must be approached with gentleness and awe. In the Bible, sexuality is called "knowledge," for it involves intimate knowledge shared by two people. When sexuality loses its intimacy and is seen in the same light as our other bodily needs, it becomes base hedonism, little more than a technical and biological function.

Because human beings tend to define things in physical terms, using only our sensory tools instead of our spiritual tools, we often ignore sexuality's spiritual component. Its powerful hold on man becomes a purely physical hold, defined individually by each person. Only by understanding the soul of sexuality, which is healthy intimacy, can we uncover the root of its power and passion.

⟨∞⟩

A young woman came to see a rabbi, saying she was having difficulty finding an appropriate spouse. The rabbi suggested that she concentrate on communicating verbally with her prospective mates, in order to see if they were truly compatible, and to avoid any intimacy. "But in today's society," the woman responded, "that is simply unrealistic."

The rabbi sighed and said quietly, "Intimacy is like fire. When you think you will quench it by indulging it, you quickly realize that you are pouring gasoline, not water, on the fire. However, when intimacy is experienced with discipline, within the context of a sanctified marriage, it becomes a fire that warms both people and illuminates their home and family."

WHY IS SEXUALITY SO POWERFUL?

When G-d created man and woman, they were one human in the image of one G-d; then they were separated into two distinct parts. "Therefore," as is written in Genesis, "a man shall leave his father and his mother and be united with his wife, and they shall become one flesh."[1]

Man and woman constantly feel this need to reunite. And sexuality is this union. Man and woman seek to "become one flesh," thereby uniting with G-d, in whose image they were created. No wonder intimacy is such a powerful force: It is the only experience in human life in which we come face to face with G-d.

Intimacy is also the only experience in life that allows us to become truly G-dlike, in that it empowers a husband and wife to create. Nothing else we do as human beings is as G-dlike as creating a new life, which in turn can create other lives, on and on, into eternity. This G-dly nature is what gives sexuality its mystique; it is the one opportunity man has to "taste" G-d—to think as He thinks, to create as He creates.

In addition, intimacy is a celebration of vulnerability; it touches the softest spot in each person, the most private and fragile part of a human being. Therefore, we must cultivate a healthy environment for our intimacy, one that allows us to appreciate and revel in this vulnerability, secure and protected.

Most of us desire true intimacy, but we are afraid to experience true vulnerability, to lose control. But this makes it difficult to ever experience true intimacy, for being comfortable with your vulnerability is the ultimate intimacy. The *illusion* of intimacy—where each person is getting what he or she needs—only makes people feel good at the moment, if at all. If they are still in control at the end, if they have not exposed their vulnerability, then their "intimacy" was just another form of exercising control over another person.

The question is, How can we really let go? Maybe we simply can't. Human beings are weak, we say; we simply don't have the ability to truly trust one another. That might be the case if we were animals, but we are not—we are G-dly, our souls infused with the spirit of G-d, who gave us the capacity to love as He does. When we learn to see the G-dliness in each other, we can begin to trust, and reach beyond our own self-contained distrusting selves and to experience real love and intimacy. We, then, can choose to let go and be vulnerable, to be ourselves without putting up our defenses, without fear of abuse.

As with all matters, we have been given a choice. We can be distracted and misled by the physical passion of intimacy, pursuing it only to satisfy our selfish needs, which then drives man and woman apart. Or we can understand sexuality and intimacy as the truly meaningful forces that they are, as the means to connect with G-d in the most powerful, sublime manner, which in turn unites man and woman as one.

How Do We Experience Healthy Intimacy?

Healthy intimacy requires two ingredients: discipline and sanctification. We must exercise self-control, and we must also see sexuality as sacred.

One must approach the sanctity of sexuality with awe, like entering into the Holy of Holies, where every action counts, where any blemish is intolerable. We must experience sexuality in a controlled environment with appropriate boundaries—not to dampen the expression of love, but to channel the powerful physical energies into healthy passion.

In modern society, sexuality often involves two people who are each interested only in satisfying their own needs. But sexuality is meant to be *transcendent*, not indulgent, allowing you to let another person inside your soul so you can build something greater together. Only by introducing G-d into the relationship can a man and woman overcome their individual desires, and marriage is the only perfect environment in which to do so. In all other environments, intimacy is unhealthy and harmful.

And yet, how often are we victims of our own sexuality, allowing our unchecked needs and desires to control our decisions? How often do we use sexuality to distract ourselves from existential pain, mistakenly believing we can remedy a deep-seated problem with a superficial solution?

The key to healthy intimacy is to stop the vicious cycle of untamed sexuality, for the more you feed it the hungrier it gets. Discipline and subtlety direct these into a healthy and growthful experience.

The argument that one must first try living with another person before deciding whether to marry is not valid. When sexuality is experienced in an inappropriate manner, it only hampers our ability to achieve true intimacy when the time is right; if you are close when you should be distant, you will be distant when you should be close. But when intimacy is experienced properly, we achieve a closeness that flows into the rest of our lives and introduces sanctity and unity into all that we do. Intimacy is an integral part of our lives and cannot be compartmentalized. It is part of building a home and family,[2] a full and complete life.

Healthy intimacy must also be modest. By definition, intimacy is quiet and discreet. Upon their creation, man and woman "were both naked but they were not ashamed."[3] They were as innocent as children, seeing sexuality only as a part of G-d's creation and designed to serve a sacred function. But after they transgressed and ate from the Tree of Knowledge, they lost their innocence: "The eyes of both of them were opened, and they realized that they were naked."[4] They experienced a healthy shame stemming from modesty, and they covered themselves.

The only members of our society today who are not self-conscious about their sexuality are children, for they are born with an innate sense of modesty. This modesty needs to be cultivated and nurtured by parents and educators. Ideally, we would all be as innocent as children. Sexuality would flow from a healthy spirit and soul. We would learn about healthy intimacy simply by being around our healthy parents and grandparents.

But in these turbulent times, such lessons are not so easily gained, and this concept of modesty must be articulated. Young people today are more than willing to be taught an alternative to our current standards, but they are caught in a whirlwind of peer pressure. It is the responsibility of teachers, parents, and every sort of leader to teach them about the sanctity of sexuality.

So we must strive to realize that true intimacy, the authentic dignity of a human being, shines from within. What kind of message is being sent by someone who dresses provocatively or who speaks of sexuality without the proper respect? Such overt sexuality only promotes sexist attitudes that further distort how we look at our fellow human beings. True beauty, one that commands both love and respect, is inner beauty.

It is true, especially in contemporary society, that people don't want anyone to impose restrictions on their sexuality. But not all forms of sexual behavior are acceptable. The sanctity of sexuality obviously requires behavior that follows the divine laws of our creator, laws that do not ask us to deny sexuality but to experience it in healthy and intimate forms that will enhance human growth and progress, and break the chains of enslavement to one's passions that ultimately leads to societal decadence.

The fact that we live in a society that is largely unfamiliar with healthy sexuality does not change this truth. And even if a particular aberrant sexual desire were thought to be genetic, for instance, it should still not be condoned, for much of our very existence is concerned with properly channeling our natural desires.

Still, we must distinguish between a person and a person's *behavior*. Establishing a standard of behavior should not be used to invalidate one who does not live by it; these standards—which are uncompromisable—are meant to give us clarity and the ability to improve our behavior. G-d's standard for human sexuality is what is best for each of us, and we must not be afraid to teach these ideals. As with communicating all serious matters of truth, we must do so sensitively, speaking with genuine love and concern but also with discipline, in a manner and language that emphasize the positive and motivate one to grow.

The current crisis surrounding sexuality in our society must be seen as an opportunity to explore its importance. During recent years, we have clearly witnessed that immodest sexual behavior does nothing to cultivate true intimacy. It only destroys the respect for the individual and for home and family. But we have also begun to see a growing consciousness that puts more emphasis on communication, both intellectually and emotionally, than on promiscuous sexual behavior, and that is clearly a step in the right direction.

The time has come to reclaim our sexuality and intimacy, to return them to the context of marriage, home, and family. The time has come to reintroduce G-d into our intimate lives, to populate and civilize the world, to "become one flesh," and to return to our original intimacy with our creator. This would be a true sexual revolution. Take this responsibility seriously. An entire world—beginning with your own small world—hangs in the balance.

⌘

The Rebbe was once asked his opinion concerning sex education in the schools. "Discussing such an issue does help resolve a problem," the Rebbe answered, "but as the sages tell us, the more you discuss sexuality, the more you instigate. Therefore, great care must be taken in this area. It should be done by sensitive professionals who will avoid any provocative expressions or associations. It should be discussed privately with a student, or at most with two or three students, and it should be discussed separately with boys and girls, to keep the boundaries clear."

9

---᮰᮰᮰---

HOME AND FAMILY
Building a Garden for Yourself and for G-d

A *person is not a person without a home.*
—Talmud, Yevamot 63a

Your *home should become a light that illuminates the entire
street and community.*
—The Rebbe

᮰᮰᮰

I*n the autumn of 1988, the Rebbe declared a "year of building."
He explained that a home is the most permanent of the three basic human necessities (food, clothing, and shelter), since it establishes
a fixed and secure place for man in this untamed world. Therefore,
by building or buying a home, or even adding on a room or simply dedicating one room to good deeds, you are establishing a presence of goodness in this world, a source of kindness that is both
tangible and permanent.*

WHY IS HOME LIFE SO IMPORTANT?

A fter many hours of looking for food, a bird returns to its nest,
taking supreme comfort in a place that is warm and safe, far
removed from the dangers and distractions of the world outside.

A human being should feel the same sense of warmth and security when he or she comes home. Your home and family are your nest, the center of your life, the hub from which all your daily experiences extend. Both as children and adults, our home and family are where we should feel most comfortable in the world. They determine how you make your life decisions; they shape your attitudes, your awareness, your self-esteem. A healthy home is obviously a vital ingredient in the pursuit of a meaningful life.

Home is where we learn to cope and to be productive, to work and play, to be comfortable with ourselves and with others. Most important, home is where we learn about happiness and wholesomeness. Think about the warmth you feel when you come home after being away for a few months or even a few days. How different that warmth is from what we experience in the world outside! Our home is a secure base that gives us the confidence to explore the terrain of an unpredictable and often dangerous world.

Just as a healthy person may take his health for granted, many of us fail to appreciate the beauty of a nurturing home. Our parents' attitudes and love provide us with a foundation from which we build our own lives. And like a foundation, it is invisible; it holds us up even though we never see it. To appreciate the strength of a truly loving home, we only need to see a situation where a home did *not* serve its function. Unfortunately, we don't need to look very far. Many people today never had a true home, a comfortable environment where they knew they were wanted, needed, and loved; where there was nothing to fear and where problems were dealt with directly rather than ignored or denied; where they could learn to love and be loved.

It is the parents' responsibility to build a happy and healthy home—not only for the sake of their children, but for themselves and for the guests who will enter their home. Especially in these troubled times, when so few people have healthy homes of their own, it is your duty to set an example.

Having a healthy home depends largely on your attitude toward it. Do you feel that your home is your true home, the most peaceful place in the world, or just another station along the way, where you do a few things before moving on? A true home must be the center of your life or it will inevitably become a liability and a burden. You must learn to respect your home, to see it as your partner. Part of respecting the home is respecting the commitment to build a family—the blessing that G-d has given us to have children, to fill the home with love and warmth.

We tend to compartmentalize our lives, seeing ourselves as distinct from our environment and our home. This separation only adds to the anxiety of dealing with a complicated world; it makes us feel that we have no place where we are truly safe and comfortable. Even when we are at home, we have one foot out the door.

It is important to remember: Your work may be important and necessary for survival, but the workplace is not your home. Neither is the restaurant where you eat, the museum you visit, or the foreign city you travel to. Many people today have replaced their homes with their careers or hobbies—perhaps because they, as children, never had comfortable homes, or because their parents put *their* careers and personal interests before home and family.

But why should your home be the center of your life when there are so many exciting things to do and learn outside the home? Because, in order to fully enjoy anything in life, you must feel entirely comfortable with yourself, and you learn to be this way at home, a place free from the distractions and struggles of the outside world.

What does it mean to be comfortable with yourself? It means being comfortable with your soul, the G-dliness within you. It means that the *outer* you, the part that deals with the material world, is at peace with the *inner* you, the real you. And that makes you a comfortable place for G-d to dwell in. When you radiate from within, you warm your entire home, filling it with a peace and gentleness that will be felt by all those who enter.

HOW DOES ONE BUILD A HEALTHY HOME?

Ο ne must do everything possible to ensure peace at home. There are three key elements in building a peaceful home life: the relationships between family members, the atmosphere of the home itself, and the way the home functions.

The tone of the relationships within the family is set by the parents—how they love and respect each other, how they go about their daily activities, how they communicate. A husband and wife must make their relationship their highest priority. They must spend time together, having meaningful talks and taking time to enjoy each other's company. Yes, they must share the household and financial responsibilities, but they must also share *themselves*—the personal and philosophical issues that are important to them.

Everyone recognizes the tragedy of the breakdown of the family and its devastating effects on children and parents alike. Now we are witnessing a return to more traditional beliefs. Greater efforts are being made toward lasting marriages; couples are deciding to have more children, and to spend more time with them.

But the desire to spend time together is not enough. Even when parents genuinely love their children, they may have trouble communicating. The reasons can be obvious: When a family's most important discussions concern where to take a vacation or what size television set to buy, a family will naturally grow apart. This is a product both of our materialistic society and of our natural self-interest. When every member of a family is concerned primarily with himself, the family is bound to suffer. When the father stays late at the office, when the mother is wrapped up in her career or community work, when the children care mainly about parties or school projects, they cannot maintain profound relationships within the family. They may sleep under the same roof and eat at the same table, yet be worlds apart.

When a family shares principles and values, though, they grow together. The home becomes a foundation for the family's shared sense of purpose while also providing a springboard for each member to pursue his or her own goals. In such homes, families stay up late talking heart to heart about what's on their minds. Children crowd around grandparents to hear stories. Teenagers debate meaningful issues with one another and with their parents. Children feel free to discuss their fears and pressures. The whole family gets together—and not just on holidays—for evenings of songs, games, and reminiscing. The home becomes *alive*, a source of energy and hope, of urgency and love and of tradition. It is not the quietude of a home that makes it peaceful; it is the life within.

⟨⟩

A young businessman worked hard and had great success, but he seemed very sad. His father noticed this and stopped by to talk to him; the young man was surprised when, instead of asking about work, his father asked how much time he was spending with his family.

"With all the demands of this job, I have very little time for that," he replied.

"That sounds like what my father used to say," his father said. "Every day I would wait by the window for him to come home, and every day I would fall asleep before he came. For the sake of your children, and for the sake of their children, no matter how much work you have, try to make it home every night in time to tuck them in. You cannot imagine how much you will be doing for them—and for yourself."

The second element of a healthy home is its atmosphere. A home must be warm and inviting for both the family and its visitors. Think about how displaced you feel when you are traveling, separated from all the things you know and the people you love. Your home should be a place where any guest can feel at peace.

A true home is more than simply a house; a true home is a beautiful home, a garden. A healthy family dynamic, of course, is the key ingredient in making a beautiful home, but the physical environment is also important—the spirit and look of the home. This does not mean that you must have a large and expensively furnished home, only that its furnishings should reflect the spirit of your family. A museum might have beautiful furnishings, but you would hardly want to live there.

A beautiful home must also be free from influences that can pollute its wholesomeness and spiritual grace. For instance: Everyone today recognizes the damaging effects that television has on impressionable children, and, for that matter, on teenagers and adults. Television must not be allowed to rule the home. While it may be very difficult for some to accept, it would be best to have no television set at all, rather than try to watch only positive programs.

The ultimate beauty in a home, of course, is its emotional and spiritual warmth. There are many ways to beautify your home spiritually, to invite G-d into your home. Place a charity box in each room. Talk with your family about G-d and our responsibilities as good-hearted people. Invite guests into your home, and allow it to be used as a place of study and prayer, or to hold charitable functions or community meetings.

These are the things that make your home *truly* beautiful—and they cost far less than expensive furniture or a television set. Think how children will react to such an atmosphere. They will grow up to remember their home as a place of warmth and kindness, where people felt comfortable to gather and talk about things that mattered to them. In all likelihood, these children will grow into adults who will create the same sort of home.

Finally, the way a home is run is very important. This includes all the "trivial" aspects of keeping a home—daily schedules and chores, cleaning and shopping, and so on. A healthy home must be smoothly run, not driven by hectic, independent interests. Everyone must share these responsibilities—not out of duty, but lovingly, because a healthy home is a quest for unity, and all members of the household are equal partners in its success.

WHAT HAPPENS WHEN PROBLEMS ARISE IN THE HOME?

Even in a home where the entire family is trying its best, there are bound to be problems. Each one must be handled with an eye toward both a short-term and a long-term solution, for the immediate problem is often an indication of deeper trouble. Whenever a problem arises, particularly a serious one, we should examine the dynamic between parents. A husband and wife must develop a healthy way of communicating with each other. This in turn sets a good example to their children. Also, a mother and father form a powerful problem-solving team.

It is important to remember that children's misbehavior is often the result of parental attitudes. Without changing these attitudes, we cannot hope for any serious change in our children. Parents must look beyond their own ego when dealing with their children. Only then can they truly assess the problem at hand and determine a plan of action. A parent must avoid getting into a battle with a child. In a relationship between a parent and child, the responsibility to communicate always lies with the parent, the one with more experience and knowledge. Perhaps you didn't speak sensitively enough. Perhaps you need to find a new way of talking, a new perspective.

It is often wise to seek the help of someone outside your family, someone who can judge the problem objectively, one who is spiritually sensitive and understands your family's goals and values.

Experience has shown that teenagers, especially today, are more likely to accept guidance from older friends and relatives than from their parents. Perhaps they feel that their parents are too determined to impose authority, too judgmental, or too quick to think of teenagers as immature. This is yet another reason for building a healthy home life—so it becomes a relaxed place for visiting friends and relatives, who can offer support to children in need of an older person's advice.

Above all, love is the most powerful tool with which to battle problems. Yes, a healthy home must be run with discipline, but even that discipline must contain love. This cannot be manufactured or superficial, for children are highly sensitive to honest emotions. On the other hand, they will react with pure joy when they receive the genuine love of their parents, and they will reciprocate. As is written in Proverbs, "As water mirrors a face, a heart responds to another."[1]

WHAT ARE THE ROLES OF DIFFERENT FAMILY MEMBERS?

Although a mother and father are equal partners, they each have unique qualities that complement each other in building a healthy home.

The mother is the foundation of the home. Although many women work today, they must never forget the fact that "the wisdom of women builds the home."[2] A mother has a unique sensitivity to human nature; she intrinsically knows what is healthy for the home and the family. While a man often battles the demons without, a woman cultivates the good within. She is the family's guardian of all that is pure and holy in G-d's world. When it came time for Abraham and Sarah to determine the fate of their son Isaac, G-d advised Abraham, "Heed all that Sarah tells you."[3] A mother has the fortitude and patience to deal with trying situations; she can communicate and get things done without confrontation. Any husband or father would do well to learn these ways from his wife.

The father, while he may often be the primary source of a family's income, must never forget that the center of his life is his home, not his career and friends. His career is just a means to earn the money necessary to build a healthy home and family. He must spend time with his children and discuss their education. He must exercise his masculinity to set a living example of strength and commitment. Every family member should look up to the father and feel confident that he will always protect them, standing up for them and responding to their needs.

A mother and father must respect each other's roles and be ready to help at a moment's notice. When a mother and father treat each other with such respect and cooperation, their children will inevitably learn to act the same. Children must be encouraged to participate in every aspect of family life. Older children should help care for their younger brothers and sisters; then, not only will they earn the appreciation and love of their parents, but they will learn to *give* love to someone younger and needier than they.

There is a natural love between child and parent. Still, we see how children take their parents for granted. We know that children tend to rebel when their parents *demand* love from them; it is better to teach them to love something far greater than themselves: G-d. The message children should be hearing from their parents is: "Respect me not because I am so great, but because of G-d. Just as G-d gave me life through your grandparents, G-d gave you life through me." Parents, of course, must examine how they treat *their* parents, especially in front of their children. We can hardly expect our children to listen to us when we behave contrary to what we teach them.

Parents' responsibilities are indeed manifold, and they must understand the gravity of these responsibilities. Building a true home is a job to be taken seriously—more seriously than the job we go to each day to earn a living. After all, there are many opportunities to make a living, but only one opportunity to build a healthy home.

Each healthy home is a microcosm of the entire universe, in turn making the entire world a home for G-d. Harmony at home, within a family, translates into harmony between families and communities and, ultimately, nations. When there is no harmony between people who are related by blood, how can we expect to create harmony between strangers?

After many centuries of exhausting journeys, it is time for all of us to come home—to ourselves, to our families, to G-d. After the thousands of years of civilizing this world, after the millions of spiritual seeds that human beings have planted through acts of kindness, the time has come for this world to sprout like a garden—G-d's garden, a universe filled with goodness and knowledge.

So the next time you are sitting in your living room or sharing a meal with your family, ask yourself: Do I truly feel at home? Am I doing everything possible to build a healthy family and household? Do guests feel welcome here? And, above all, does G-d feel comfortable in my home?

⌘

The Rebbe was separated from his parents in the late 1920s, when he was twenty-six years old, and did not reunite with his mother until 1947. His father had passed away three years earlier. The Rebbe often expressed his anguish at not having had the opportunity to fulfill his obligation of honoring his parents for so many years.

When the Rebbe first met his mother after all their years of separation, they embraced for twenty minutes without uttering a sound. Once he was reunited with his mother, he visited her every day, walking to her house in the late afternoons to serve her tea and to spend time talking.

Soon after his mother died in 1964, the Rebbe was visited by a teenage girl who wanted to discuss a conflict she was having with her mother. The girl was angry that her mother would not give her as much money as she felt she needed. The Rebbe replied with sadness: "I just lost my mother this year. Do you know how much money I would give to see her just once more? You have your mother with you, and yet you allow money to tear you apart."

10

HEALTH AND FITNESS
A Sound Soul in a Sound Body

*One has no right to harm his body, for it is not his property,
but G-d's.*
—Code of Jewish Law

*A sound and healthy body is dependent on a sound
and healthy soul.*
—The Rebbe

The Rebbe often spoke of how optimism, reinforced by a trust in
G-d, is just as important to the healing process as medicine
and doctors. In 1977, the Rebbe suffered a serious heart attack.
One day later, he insisted on giving a talk, as he had done on that
particular day for the previous thirty-eight years. A few days later,
the doctors asked the Rebbe how he was feeling. "Physically, thank
G-d, I feel fine," he replied, "but mentally, not so well." This, he
explained, was probably because he had not been able to visit the
grave site of his father-in-law, as he was accustomed to doing several times a month.

"You must take care of your health," the doctor insisted. "If
not, there is a twenty-five percent chance of a relapse." The doctor

asked if the Rebbe understood what he had said.

"Oh, yes," said the Rebbe with a smile. "You said that even if I don't take care of my health—which, I assure you, I will—there is a seventy-five percent chance that there won't be a relapse."

WHY IS IT IMPORTANT TO HAVE A HEALTHY BODY?

Look at a young child who has just begun to play with his fingers and toes. There is a sense of wonder and discovery. By the time we are adults, this sense has long passed. After many years of living in our bodies, we tend to take them for granted. You might assume that you can treat your body as you wish; some of us choose to take good care of our bodies and others do not.

The truth is that your body is *not* yours to treat as you wish. Your body belongs to G-d, who gave it to you to care for, as a vehicle to carry your soul through life. Just as you would not harm another person, just as you would not harm anything that G-d has created, you should not harm your own body. It is your duty to eat well, to rest, to stay in shape, and to treat your body with respect in every way. Physical fitness is not arbitrary or optional; it is part of your responsibility to G-d. On the other hand, *worshiping* the body is unacceptable. The body is a vehicle for the soul. This is its value; it is not an end unto itself.

Many people today are health-conscious; indeed, entire industries have sprung up around exercise and nutrition. We understand that being healthy makes us feel better, makes us more productive, and can ultimately lengthen our lives. We realize that when we are healthy, we can concentrate on family and work, and the other things that are important to us. But most significantly, a sound body allows you to concentrate on your *soul*, enabling you to fulfill your divine mission in this world and live a meaningful life.

WHAT IS GOOD HEALTH?

Good health is far more than a physical body that functions properly, much more than having a temperature of 98.6 degrees. Good health is a sound soul in a sound body. Modern medicine has begun to discover the dramatic effect that a person's spirit can have on the healing process. People with healthy, optimistic spirits, for example, have been shown to have stronger immune systems; psychologically, too, we are increasingly learning that a person's physical health is directly affected by his or her faith in G-d. Conversely, even a small weakness in the spirit can create a profound blemish in the body.

This is why it is imperative to instill the sick with hope and confidence in their recovery. Trust in G-d is a source of great comfort, especially when a patient must enter a hospital. This comfort is the best medicine to fight off the demoralization that accompanies illness, which is often as damaging as the illness itself.

This is also why we must visit the sick. Besides the fact that it is an obvious moral obligation, visiting a sick person shows him that he is cared for, which bolsters his confidence and hope. This, in turn, helps strengthen his determination to heal. Even though the physical environment of a hospital may depress a patient, awareness of the great potential help in medicine and doctors creates a certain peace of mind and a receptivity to healing.

So good health includes caring for the soul as much as the body. To do otherwise would be the equivalent of treating half a person, creating a split between a person's physical and spiritual needs.

Just as the body is nourished by certain foods, the soul needs spiritual nourishment. This nourishment includes an awareness of one's mission in life and an awareness of G-d, Who has empowered us with the abilities to fulfill that mission. A healthy soul connects to G-d through study, prayer, and virtuous acts; as you fulfill your moral and spiritual obligations, your soul is fed with divine energy, just as your body is fueled with material energy through the intake of food.

It is important to see that every aspect of your physical fitness has a spiritual component. When you eat, you should acknowledge that the food is not meant for simple indulgence, but to generate the vitality necessary to lead a meaningful life. When we go to bed with a humble recognition of G-d and a serious appraisal of our day's activities, the soul is allowed to drink from the regenerative spiritual waters during sleep.

WHAT IS THE ROLE OF A DOCTOR?

Sometimes, of course, it is impossible for us alone to heal our bodies, and we turn to a medical professional. One might wonder: Since it is G-d who gives life and heals, perhaps humans should not meddle in such affairs. But the sages tell us that G-d "gives permission and power for a doctor to heal."[1]

∞∞∞

A man who was very ill came to a rabbi for advice. He had the option of two doctors. One was a G-d-fearing man but was not considered an expert; the other was an expert but not particularly religious. "To whom should I go?" the sick man asked.

"Go to the better qualified doctor," the rabbi replied, "for G-d has given the doctor permission to heal with his medical knowledge, and the better expert is therefore better equipped to heal."

We must do everything within our power to care for ourselves, and we must be persistent in finding the best care. But one should turn to a doctor and not rely on one's own analysis or intuitions.

It is wise, particularly in serious situations, to get the advice of two independent doctors, preferably including one whom you know personally and who is sensitive to your individual situation.

The role of a doctor is obviously an important one—first, because he of all people appreciates the effect of the spirit on the body, and second, because he has earned the trust of a patient, and can therefore exert a strong influence.

A doctor should use this trust to motivate the patient to improve both his physical and spiritual health. He must recognize the great responsibility that G-d has vested in him; he cannot refuse someone in need. A doctor must also have the humility to know that, while he may be the one treating the patient, the power to *heal* comes from G-d. A doctor cannot be arrogant; he must be sensitive and concerned over his patients' welfare, because, after all, he is caring for G-d's property.

For all the authority that G-d has given a doctor, nowhere has a doctor been given the right to condemn a human being as incurable. A doctor has no right to weaken the hope of a patient, because, as is written in Exodus, "G-d is the healer,"[2] and we know not G-d's mysterious ways. So even if a doctor is pessimistic, we must remember that there are higher forces at work. Above all, a doctor must recognize that he has been chosen by G-d as an instrument of healing.

CARUS

A revered rabbi was sailing on a ship from Alexandria to Trieste when he received some sad news, which caused him to fall seriously ill. A doctor who happened to be on the boat attended the rabbi, and healed him. When the boat finally docked, the doctor approached the rabbi and begged his forgiveness. "How can I atone for being the cause of your illness?" he asked.

"You, the cause of my illness?" the rabbi replied in amazement.

"Yes," said the doctor. *"There is no doubt in my mind that if I had not been on the boat, you would not have fallen ill. You, rabbi, are a man upon whom many people depend. Surely, G-d would not have allowed a life-threatening illness to befall you unless the instrument of your cure was readily at hand."*

HOW DO WE ACHIEVE FITNESS OF BODY AND SOUL?

Although G-d in His kindness has given us doctors, the responsibility to care for our body and soul lies primarily within ourselves. Initially, of course, preventive medicine is the best option; this includes acknowledging the root of a problem and not just its symptoms. Identifying and attacking the root of a problem and explaining it to a person can help avoid the problem, or heal it at its source.

However, when we are struck with illness or by an accident, we must be in no way reluctant to use medicine. G-d has created certain substances with healing and regenerative powers. He has also given man the ability to mix these substances and to manipulate chemical structures to create various medicines. These substances must be appreciated for what they are: a means by which G-d enables us to care for our bodies and souls. To use such substances recklessly or needlessly is to violate the very reason for their existence.

Initially, the body and the soul are adversaries, each struggling for dominance. Eventually, though, they must learn to appreciate each other. The soul needs a sound body to express itself. The body needs to recognize the soul's authority. This recognition is a key to good health, for a strong soul lessens the body's selfish demands.

That is not to say that the body should be denied its material needs; the intention is not to weaken the body, but to discipline and refine it so it can serve as a proper vehicle for the soul's expression.

There are two phases to this process of self-refinement. The first is to recognize that without the direction of the soul, the body may indulge at will, often leading to destructive ends. The soul enables us to conquer and harness that pure physical energy, transferring the coarse expressions of our body into energy for the soul. The soul, once strengthened, will in turn feed the body with all the energy it needs to prosper.

So the next time you exercise and feel reenergized, realize that you have just reenergized a precious piece of G-d's property. As you breathe in deeply, or eat a healthy meal, realize that you are investing in a valuable commodity. But also remember that a healthy body is not an end in itself, only a means to achieve a healthy soul and spirit. Furthermore, the health of your body is dependent on the health of your soul. And it is your responsibility to nourish them both. When your body or soul cries out, recognize the symptoms for what they are: an urgent request for you to address their needs, be they spiritual or physical.

As much as we have learned about medicine, and the influence of the spirit on our physical well-being, we must continue to explore this influence and recognize it in our daily lives. We stand poised at the threshold of a new medicine—when body and spirit will live in complete harmony, eliminating illness and disease. Take advantage of this opportunity. Your health and well-being, your very *life*, depend on it.

⌒⊞⊞⊞⌒

A hospital administrator once came to the Rebbe for a blessing. When he mentioned that he worked in a beit cholim—Hebrew for "house of the sick"—the Rebbe suggested that hospitals should instead be called beit rofeim, "house of doctors" or "house of healing." When a patient enters a hospital, the Rebbe explained, and feels that he is entering a house of healing as opposed to a house of sickness, it lifts his morale and contributes to the healing process.

Another time, a woman came to the Rebbe for a blessing for her father, who was depressed that he had to spend the High Holidays in a hospital. The Rebbe smiled and said, "Tell your father that he should finish the mission he was sent to the hospital for, to inspire the others there to intensify their spiritual commitments. Then he will be released."

11

———❧———

WORK AND
PRODUCTIVITY

Your Contribution to Life

Man was born to toil.
—Job 5:7

Being human means being productive.
—The Rebbe

❧

A businessman once came to the Rebbe for advice. His appointment was late at night, and after his long day at work, he was exhausted; out of respect to the Rebbe, he apologized for his fatigue.

"Think of a large, powerful machine," said the Rebbe. "If you leave it idle for a long period of time, it begins to corrode and deteriorate. But when you do operate it, you must be very careful, for using it beyond its capacity will cause it to burn out. The same is true with a human being: idleness will certainly deplete a person, but one must also be aware of his capacity and work accordingly."

WHY MUST WE WORK?

You work hard to make ends meet, to provide for your family, and to enjoy the comforts of life. But do you ever stop to consider the deeper significance of all this work? And when your work is finally done, can you honestly say that you are happy? Why is it that when you are on vacation, you may suddenly yearn to get back to the world of achievement and productivity?

Most of us acknowledge and relate to the fact that we need to work, and yet we constantly agonize over our workload. Is this our destiny, or can we achieve some balance? More important, can we find a deeper meaning in this need to be productive without being overwhelmed by the need itself?

Let us take a closer look at work and productivity. We all occasionally ask ourselves, For what purpose am I here? What must I do to achieve happiness and perfection? Should I aspire to have the easiest, most comfortable life possible, or should I strive toward a life of work and accomplishment?

The drive to work and to accomplish is an integral part of human life. As the sages say, "Every person was created to toil."[1] A person cannot be satisfied if he or she is not productive. Human nature detests receiving something for nothing—"bread of shame" is how it is described by the sages.[2]

Remember: We were created to transform this material world into a more refined place and to introduce a higher dimension: G-dliness. So while the ultimate goal of our work may be spiritual growth, the fact that G-d placed us in a material world means that we reach that spiritual plane through physical labor.

But if we were created to toil, why do we so crave vacation and rest? Because man is composed of two dimensions, the body and the soul. The body, by its nature, grows weary, and needs to rest. The soul, on the other hand, never grows weary; it is the vibrant soul that pushes you to work even when your body itself would rather languish and be cared for by someone else.

᠙᠊ᠭ᠊᠙

A nobleman who enjoyed the aesthetics of life hired a
farmer to stand inside his castle and move back and forth

with a hand pick, just as he would do in the field. The nobleman took great pleasure in the simple elegance of the farmer's sway, and he paid the farmer well for his "work." Still, after entertaining the nobleman for several days, the farmer refused to continue. "But I pay you generously," said the surprised nobleman, "many times more than you would make by working in the field. And you don't have to exert yourself nearly as much."

"You don't seem to understand," the farmer replied. "I cannot continue doing something—even if it takes no toil and effort—that doesn't produce. I would rather work much harder and be productive than be paid well to do something that bears no fruit."

Why did G-d create man so that his satisfaction is linked to toil? Wouldn't we be even more thankful and indebted to Him if we received everything we needed with no effort at all?

The answer is that through work, a human being becomes a giver, a contributor to life. By creating man so that his deepest pleasure is derived from his own efforts, G-d bestowed the greatest gift of all: the capacity to become G-dly, an equal partner in the creation and development of the universe.

So work is not something that we do merely to make enough money to surround ourselves with material comforts; work is the natural expression of human life. Work is not a burden that must be wearily borne, but the very fabric of who we are and how we contribute to life. We must recognize and take advantage of this most precious innate tendency, and use it in a productive and divine manner.

No matter how much we may have accomplished, we can and must surpass our previous achievements. There are, of course, marked differences between each phase of human life, but we must be productive throughout them all. A child, unburdened by the need to earn a living, must be productive through education, study, and emotional growth in his formative years; the same is true for an older person who no longer needs to earn a living every day. Even a vacation should only be a pause from physical labor, not a vacation from personal and spiritual growth.

Each of us is born with tremendous resources and inestimable abilities; part of being productive is discovering these strengths. When we fully apply ourselves, we will accomplish far beyond our expectations. As the sages say, "If someone should tell you, 'I have toiled but not found,' do not believe him; if he says, 'I have not toiled but I have found,' do not believe him; but if he says, 'I have toiled and I have found,' believe him."[3]

TOWARD WHAT END
ARE WE WORKING?

It is well and good to say that we must be productive our entire lives, but what should our work consist of, and how should we go about it? Yes, man was created to toil, but to what end?

Work as an end unto itself cannot be fully satisfying or fulfilling. As more and more people are realizing, it is possible to have a hugely successful career and still feel empty; if you do not nourish your own emotional and spiritual needs, no amount of material success will satisfy you. We need to know that our work leads us to a higher purpose; we need to know that we are leaving a positive imprint on our world.

Does this mean that it is better to involve ourselves only in philanthropy and spiritual work, and put aside our business and career? Before answering that question, we must revisit the meaning of our existence, and the meaning of our work.

Remember, the underlying purpose of our work is to use our talents and abilities to improve the material world and make it a more G-dly place. To do so, we must recognize that spirituality is the primary force in our lives, while the material and physical are a vehicle for the soul's expression. So yes, you must do everything possible to ensure that your work is a success, using your physical *and* intellectual faculties to the utmost, but your primary objective should always be to make your work a channel for G-dliness, for noble and humane causes.

This requires a delicate balance. You must fully concentrate on your work, and yet not become so immersed as to lose sight of your higher objective; you must remember that the *real* bottom line is G-d and the virtuous results of your work, not the numbers written on the bottom of an accounting sheet.

How do you actualize your commitment to working toward a higher goal? By conducting your business ethically and honestly. By giving generously to charity. By recognizing that it is G-d who blesses you with prosperity. By understanding that every new business opportunity is really an opportunity to spread a spirit of G-dliness.

Similarly, we should always work as hard at serving G-d as we work on our own business. There are, in fact, many parallels between divine service and running a successful business. In our altruistic and spiritual pursuits, we should always try to return a profit, bearing more fruit than the original investment. We must be persistent: if one method doesn't succeed, try another. We must be totally immersed in our noble pursuits, even dreaming about them, not just acting as a hired hand. We must fully use all the resources available to us, and remember that accountability is crucial for success. And above all, wherever we go, we must look for new opportunities to perfect ourselves and society.

Initially, it might seem that such a strong commitment to G-d would detract from our work, but the exact opposite is true. For example, consider designating a part of your workday for study or prayer. Even if it is only a few minutes, you will achieve a specific focus within each day, which will carry over into your work. How often are we unproductive at work because we are unfocused? You may spend hours and hours at the office, but unless those hours are focused, you accomplish very little.

What about when we simply feel overwhelmed by our work burden? Again, the only way to meet this challenge is to connect with the divine. When you focus on and commit to fulfilling your higher mission, through generosity and kindness, your soul provides you with vast amounts of energy, far beyond your expectations. While the body constantly needs to be rested and refueled, there are no such limitations to our spiritual energy—nor, therefore, to our spiritual productivity.

We must set high standards for ourselves in our work. Just as the soul is limitless, so is our potential for growth.

HOW CAN WE OVERCOME THE CHALLENGE OF HARD WORK?

Since the whole point of life is for man to become an independent giver and creator, every obstacle must be seen as merely another challenge designed to bring out our best effort. Life itself is the greatest challenge of all—each of us is a vulnerable person in a brutal world, with no way of knowing what fate his or her destiny holds.

But life's challenges bring out the deepest dimensions of the soul. Every form of growth is preceded by frustration and pain. A mother must endure the difficulties of pregnancy and childbirth before she can experience the triumph of birth. An artist must endure the hours of confusion and frustration before his or her creativity yields fruit.

How do we access the inner strength to transform our work obstacles into challenges for growth? By seeing work for what it is—a means to fulfill our divine mission.

If we remember that we work not just for the monetary gain or the personal satisfaction, our commitment to work becomes that much stronger. And yet our work also becomes less all-consuming, for we are no longer totally controlled by the demands of the moment and by the subjective whims that are part of human nature. Instead of getting caught up in work at the expense of everything else, you see it as one more step in serving G-d, your family, and society.

We all know how it feels to be consumed by work. We can no longer see the world beyond our job; we feel overwhelmed and confused. But just acknowledging that our work has a higher purpose is the start of a healthier attitude. What once seemed like insurmountable obstacles will become challenges that spur you on to even greater accomplishments.

We especially encounter frustration at the start of a new project or a new job. As the sages say, "All beginnings are difficult."[4] If approached with the proper perspective, though, this frustration becomes an opportunity to start each new project with an added determination, an extra incentive to get off to a robust beginning.

The workplace is indeed a formidable challenge to our standards and values. We are inundated with demands and obligations, with complications and challenges that threaten to make us lose sight of why we are there in the first place. By focusing on your spiritual priorities, however, you can ensure that your work will keep moving toward productive and virtuous ends.

So when you go to work tomorrow, think about your goals in a new way. Transform your work environment into a place where kindness and goodwill flourish. Set an example of gracious conduct; greet everyone with an extra-pleasant "good morning." Instill your business with a commitment to higher values. Work hard to succeed, all the while knowing that you are working to fulfill G-d's will. At the end of every workday, you should be able to step back and see your work in this perspective. And this healthy perspective will benefit not only you and your family, but your business itself.

Modern technology enables us to spend far less time and energy on physical labor, freeing us to be more productive. Such freedom should not be squandered; it should be taken as a challenge to spur us on to greater spiritual growth and bring further harmony to the world. Until now, we have only known life in a world in which achievement was measured in terms of a wilderness tamed, a tyrant defeated, a disease cured. A world in which there is a Nobel Peace Prize only because there are wars, where there is learning only because there is ignorance, where there is philanthropy only because there is hunger and want.

But now we have the opportunity to go even further. We can do more than simply defeat evil; we can probe the infinite reaches of goodness. It is up to each of us to seek out and take advantage of these new opportunities, to exert ourselves and be more productive than ever. So at the end of every workday, ask yourself: Am I using all of my G-d-given resources and abilities to produce more than was given to me? If you can answer yes to this question, you will know that you are well on your way toward a meaningful life.

The Rebbe always demanded that he—and everyone else— be continuously productive. In the summer of 1956, he planned to visit a children's summer camp that he had established. Someone suggested that after the visit he stay in the mountains for a brief vacation. "The few hours that the trip will take, the few hours I spend there, and the few hours back is already an entire vacation," the Rebbe replied. In fact, in his more than forty years as leader of the Lubavitch movement, he took not a single vacation.

12

CHARITY AND WEALTH
The Need to Give

Happy are they who are charitable at all times.
—Psalms 106:3

Charity transforms matter to spirit; it turns a coin into fire.
—The Rebbe

Every Sunday morning, beginning on his birthday in April 1986, thousands of people would gather to receive the Rebbe's blessing. They ranged from the Rebbe's closest followers to heads of state to some of the most influential people in business and entertainment. Some were seeking spiritual inspiration, others advice on how to handle a particular problem. Along with the blessing, the Rebbe would hand each person a brand-new dollar bill, to be given to charity. Over the next several years, he handed out hundreds of thousands of dollar bills, always with the reminder of the need to give to those in need.

WHY DO WE GIVE CHARITY?

We all know that charity is considered a virtue. It has become part of the fabric of our lives, of our entire society. The United States in particular, with its humanitarian policies and its generosity in domestic and foreign aid, has done more to promote charity than any other nation in the world.

But why do we feel compelled to give charity? True, charity is the sign of a healthy and human society, but without understanding *why* we give charity, *why* we feel a need to share with others, we are left with a paradox that ultimately limits our generosity: Doesn't charity go against the very grain of human nature—that is, giving away what is rightfully ours?

And so, we must ask ourselves: Is generosity as much a part of human nature as selfishness? How do we balance the two? How can we teach our children to be more charitable? How often should one give charity, and in what manner? Should we give anonymously? And above all, what does charity truly accomplish—for ourselves, for those in need, and for society at large?

Perhaps it would be healthier to simply be charitable without analyzing why, as many people do. But the better you understand the true dynamic of charity, the more you can cultivate it within yourself, your family, and your friends. And greater charity can only lead to a more meaningful life. As is written in Proverbs, "One that pursues charity and generosity finds life, righteousness, and honor."[1]

The key to charity lies in understanding that it is not only a gift to the receiver, but to the giver as well. The need to be charitable is one of the most fundamental human needs; just as we need food and protection and love, we need to share what has been given to us. Charity is one of the simplest yet most profound ways to help refine the material world and unite with your fellow man and with G-d—and, therefore, to fulfill our cosmic mission. Through charity, we introduce unity into a diverse world.

Charity enables us to spiritualize the material, and to actualize our virtuous intentions. G-d could have easily distributed wealth evenly to all people. But, as the sages say, "If everyone were wealthy or poor, who would be generous?"[2] Just as G-d continues to give—every fraction of time, every day on earth—charity allows *us* to give, thus becoming G-dlike ourselves. Remember: The money you give away is not your own; G-d has lent it to you to allow you the gift of giving. Those who have been blessed with more money, then, are those who have been blessed by G-d with the opportunity and privilege to be more giving, to be more G-dlike.

So charity must be given with humility. If a wealthy person gives arrogantly, thinking that he is doing a great favor, he is sadly mistaken: The favor is being done to *him*. Recognizing this fact makes the act of giving charity that much more compelling.

After all, G-d created the universe as an intricate system of give and take; our entire existence revolves around this relationship. Just as plants, for instance, need the carbon dioxide that humans exhale, humans need the oxygen that plants produce. Charity is yet one more expression of this pattern: the giver and the receiver need one another. "More than the rich man does for the pauper," say the sages, "the pauper does for the rich man."[3]

Moreover, charity is an act of pure justice. It is true that responsibility for your own life comes first. But can your own comfort and pleasure be more valuable than your fellow man's most basic necessities? Can you pursue the highest levels of intellectual and spiritual achievement when your fellow man needs guidance in the most basic matters?

WHAT IS THE POWER OF MONEY?

Of the many forms of charity, the most powerful is monetary. Why is this so? Because money is how most people measure their self-worth. Because we invest so much time, energy, and labor into earning money, therefore, it represents the very energy of life itself. So contributing your money to charity expresses the deepest form of giving and refining this physical world,[4] which is self-oriented by nature.

Some people feel that they and they alone are responsible for their success, that their intelligence and abilities brought it about. This is the challenge of wealth, and a serious challenge it is: to not be deceived by your own ego. "You must remember that it is G-d who gives you the power to become prosperous."[5] Without this recognition, money becomes the ultimate symbol of the selfish ego, our contemporary "golden idol."

This is not to say that your success is not a result of your efforts; of course it is. And you must do everything possible to ensure success, not just sit back and wait for money to come your way. But you must acknowledge that it is G-d's blessing, and not your effort alone, that creates wealth. As any experienced businessperson knows, all the planning and hard work in the world are no guarantee for success.

The power of charity is such that it does not allow you to become immersed in self-interest. Virtuous acts are indeed good, and they elevate the soul, but giving money to charity is the most powerful way to spiritualize the material, for it means giving a piece of everything that we are—our abilities, our efforts, our ambitions, our compassion.

On its own, money can be a curse. Because it is the epitome of materialism, money—and wealth—are mercurial by nature. Money can therefore cause endless anxiety, for no matter how much you have, you are never sure whether you have enough or whether you will not somehow lose it all.

When you put money in perspective and recognize why it was given to you, it becomes a blessing instead of a curse. And by using your wealth for charitable and philanthropic purposes, which are for posterity, instead of spending it on the desire of the moment, your money becomes eternal.

❦

A rabbi once noticed that many of the people in his village had become obsessed with amassing wealth, often at the ex-

pense of the rest of the villagers. He called everyone together. "The fortunes of man are like a turning wheel," he said. "He who sits atop the wheel and laughs is a fool, for should the wheel turn, he may find himself lower than those at whom he was laughing. And he who lies beneath the wheel and bewails his fate is also a fool. Indeed, the very fact that he is now at the wheel's lowest point means that on its very next movement, his fortunes will improve. Both men should contemplate that fortune is nothing but a spinning wheel, with no enduring worth, but that a single virtuous act toward one's fellow man will endure forever."

HOW SHOULD ONE GIVE CHARITY?

It is important to financially assist those in need, since we live in a material world where only money can buy the necessities in life. But we must not forget that charity goes beyond the monetary. We can give our time, our counsel, our sympathy. We can invite a lonely person to dinner; we can give a teenager advice on how to handle a problem. Such spiritual charity is vital, for it sustains and resuscitates a person in need.

Even if a person has selfish motives when giving charity, or gives reluctantly, the objective has been reached, for a needy person has been sustained. Obviously, though, this is not optimal charity; it is far better to give graciously and wholeheartedly. It is even better to give anonymously when possible, especially if the donation would embarrass or shame the person in need.

The highest form of charity is something that we may not consider charity at all: providing a person with an opportunity so that he or she will no longer need to look to others for help. You may provide a family with food and necessities for an entire year, or ten years, or twenty. This is indeed a gracious and charitable act. But how much more gracious and charitable it would be to give the head of that family a job, or a loan, or another means to reestablish pride and self-respect, to be able to stand on his own feet.

Needless to say, charity must be given according to one's means; it would be inappropriate, for example, to take out a loan in order to give charity. However, everyone, even a poor person, is obligated to give according to his means. The traditional amount is one-tenth of one's income or, even better, one-fifth. And when one feels a special need for spiritual healing, he or she can give even more.[6]

One may argue that, from a pure business perspective, charity simply reduces one's financial resources. But when we recognize that G-d's blessing is the ultimate source of wealth, charity becomes the wisest investment there is. If someone is having financial difficulty in his business, he should increase the amount of his charitable contributions in order to increase G-d's blessing for wealth. As the sages say, "Tithe, so that you may prosper."[7] Charity opens up new channels of wealth from above. Indeed, before determining how much to bless a person in the future, G-d often watches to see how he gave of his previous wealth.

Beyond the financial aspect, charity enriches the mind and heart a thousandfold.[8] When you take time for a charitable act, even if it means setting aside an hour or an entire day that you thought you could not afford, you will find that you are rewarded many times over; with the added blessing from your charitable act, you will achieve well more than you could have if you had never lifted your attention—and your spirit—from your own affairs. Above all, it is important to be a generous person all around. Whatever the situation, you should give and help appropriately—not because you feel an obligation, but simply because you should strive to be a giver, to be G-dlike.

It is the call of our generation to increase charity in every way possible. We live in times that are more materially prosperous and yet more spiritually impoverished than ever before. Even the most secure among us are in dire need of love and friendship.

Especially because the United States is such a champion of charity, the citizens of this nation should all be inspired—and inspire others—to make charity a regular part of our lives. When you are blessed with good fortune, you must learn to recognize it as an opportunity for giving, not simply for personal gain.

There are many practical ways to encourage regular charity-giving, no matter how small it may be. Place a charity box in the various rooms of your home, in your office, in your car. Teach your children to give money and time to others. Companies should cultivate generosity by regularly distributing money and goods that their employees can pass on to those in need, and schools should do the same for their students—a token gesture of a few pennies will do.

We must all seek out new ways of giving and sharing. As long as there are needy people, we remain obligated to help them—not just for their sake, but for ours, because we are givers by nature. Even if there were not one person on earth in need of a meal or rent money, there will always be room to give encouragement, inspiration, and guidance.

So look around and ask yourself: What do I have to give that can help another person? Do not worry that you cannot be as generous as you would like, or that you don't have the time to spare. When it comes to giving of yourself, there is nothing too small, and nothing too great.

༄

A businessman came to see the Rebbe. He complained that his profits were far too low in every business venture he pursued, no matter how hard he or his partners worked. "And how much of these profits do you give to charity?" the Rebbe asked. The man shamefacedly replied that he had given none. "In your next venture," the Rebbe suggested, "make G-d your partner by contributing ten percent of your profits to charity. G-d, like any good business partner, will then do everything in His power to ensure that the business succeeds."

13

AGING AND RETIREMENT
Regeneration and Dignity

Many years add in wisdom.
—Job 32:7

The soul never ages; it only becomes more vibrant.
—The Rebbe

━━━━

I n the spring of 1972, when the Rebbe was about to turn seventy years old, he received many letters from well-wishers. Some of them suggested that he consider slowing his very active pace after his many fruitful decades as a leader and activist, that it might be time for him to rest, as do most people his age.

The Rebbe, of course, had no such intention. On his seventieth birthday, after a busy day receiving such luminaries as Yitzhak Rabin and Herman Wouk (who delivered a personal letter from President Nixon), the Rebbe convened a special gathering. His talk was long, emotional, and intense. True to his style, the Rebbe used a personal issue to deliver a universal message. He emphasized that the elderly must not succumb to conventional wisdom and cease *to pursue a productive life; on the contrary, they must use their added years of wisdom and experience to grow "from strength to strength."[1] To shunt the elderly aside is not only cruel, he added, but foolish; the faster our world changes, the more we need the experience and wisdom of our elderly friends and relatives.*

In 1982, the Rebbe presided over another huge gathering in honor of his birthday, this time his eightieth. He spoke passionately until 3:00 A.M., and still he wasn't through. In a striking testament to the strength of the elderly—and to the idea of exemplifying what one teaches—the Rebbe began distributing study books that had been printed especially for this occasion. There were several thousand men, women, and children present, and the Rebbe patiently handed a book to each one. By the time he finished, the light of dawn was trickling through the windows.

RETIREMENT FROM WHAT?

You have worked very hard for many years. As your physical faculties weaken, shouldn't you be slowing down? Hasn't the time come to reap the rewards of life? Society's solution, of course, is retirement. But have we considered the effects of retirement on our spirits? Why are so many of our elderly so unhappy? Why do they experience such emptiness in their lives? All of us, if we are fortunate, will grow old. Should we look toward that time with enthusiasm or with dread?

Before contemplating the later years of your life, you must ask yourself a basic question about life itself. Why am I here? Your attitude toward aging and retirement will depend on how you answer that question.

You may believe that the primary objective of life is to take advantage of its material possibilities and live as comfortably as you can. If so, you might think that you will be content to live out your later years in as much comfort as you can afford. You might see the last years of your life as a time to enjoy the just deserts of a long life of labor.

But why, then, do you often have a nagging feeling of dissatisfaction about spending your days in leisure? Because you were *not* put on earth to live a purely material existence; you were created to refine this material world with truth and virtue, introducing G-dliness into your every moment. This is our life's mission, and it lasts our *entire* life.

If we were to measure life solely in terms of material gain and productivity, then we would inevitably see the physical weakening of old age as a liability. But because man is primarily a spiritual being, whose true wealth is measured in intellectual, emotional, and spiritual gains, we recognize that the *soul* is the primary force in life. And the soul, unlike the body, never ages; it only grows.

As one ages, therefore, he should *not* decrease his level of activity, for spiritually, he is growing ever stronger. Unfortunately, society has taught us to see success in material terms—to think that a millionaire, regardless of his spiritual wealth, is somehow superior to a poor man who is truly wise. We must retrain the way we think, to define success in the more sublime terms of ability and competence, wisdom and experience.

Because man was created to spiritualize the material world, the only way to reach true happiness is through spiritual growth and achievement. And that means giving to others, loving and sharing, finding a deeper meaning in everything you do, and recognizing G-d in all your ways.

Recognizing the prominence of your timeless soul: This is the key to understanding the aging process, the key with which we open the door of opportunity in our twilight years. Human productivity is a direct result of human creativity, and human creativity is a direct result of the spiritual energies of the soul. "Every person was created to toil," as the sages say. However, this toil takes on different forms in our life cycles. As one ages and his physical strength wanes, his toil and productivity need to be expressed through spiritual achieve-ments. So if a human being reaches a certain age, whether it is fifty-five or sixty-five or seventy-five, and suddenly announces, "I'm going to retire," the question must be asked: Retire from what? Ambition? Creativity? From your soul? Such an attitude means that you are simply preparing to die, which is unacceptable for a person who comes into this world with a mission to produce. One does not retire from life.

The argument for retirement is an erroneous one. It assumes that our goal in life is to amass the right amount of wealth so that we can shut down our productivity at a certain age and revel in our material success and free time. This is not to say that we should not enjoy the fruits of our labor—only that we should never forget the reason that the labor has been done in the first place. Nor must we devote our entire lives to earning a living. But we should never abandon the world of work and productivity for a world of inactiv-ity, a world that doesn't challenge us, a world that isolates us from our spiritual quest.

WHERE DO OUR ATTITUDES ON AGING COME FROM?

Each phase of life, of course, has a unique set of characteristics and needs. That is why we must take great care in educating a child, for his mind is so impressionable; that is why we must prop-erly channel the fiery spirit of young people, for it is so strong; that is why we develop careers and raise families during middle age, because we have by then achieved the necessary blend of maturity and ability.

So too does the twilight of our lives have its inherent strengths. Sometimes, of course, modern society makes us forget this. Think about how we constantly celebrate the image of youth, how it has come to stand for everything that is energetic and desirable. This has an obvious demoralizing effect on the elderly and, by extension, on society in general. If we value the physical vitality of youth more than intelligence and wisdom, more than the *spiritual* vitality of an experienced soul, what does that tell us about *all* our standards?

So there are two vastly divergent views on aging—that is, "You are old and worn out, thus useless" versus "You are wise and experienced, thus indispensable."

The Bible assures us that old age is a virtue and a blessing. We are told to respect all the elderly, regardless of their scholarship and piety,[2] because each year of life yields wisdom and experience that the most accomplished young person cannot possibly yet possess.

But in many societies today, old age has come to be a liability. Youth, meanwhile, is considered the highest credential in every field from business to government, where a younger generation insists on learning from its own mistakes instead of standing on the shoulders of their elders. At fifty, a person is considered "over the hill," and is already enduring insinuations that his job might be better filled by someone twenty-five years younger. Society, in effect, is dictating that one's later years be marked by inactivity and decline. The aged are encouraged to move to retirement villages and nursing homes; after decades of achievement, they are thought to be of little use, their knowledge and talent suddenly deemed worthless.

On the surface, this modern attitude may seem at least partially justified. Is it not a fact that a person physically weakens as he or she advances in years? Is it not an inescapable fact that the physical body of a seventy-year-old is not the physical body of a thirty-year-old?

But is a person's worth to be measured by his physical prowess? This question goes beyond the issue of how we *treat* the elderly; our attitude toward them reflects our very concept of "value." If a person's physical strength has waned while his wisdom and insight have grown, do we consider this an improvement or a decline?

Certainly, if a person's priorities in life are material, then the body's physical weakening means a deterioration of spirit as well—a descent into boredom, futility, and despair. But when one regards the body as an accessory to the soul, the very opposite is true: The spiritual growth of old age invigorates the body. And the later years allow us to positively reorder our priorities, which is difficult to do during middle age, when the quest for material gains is at its peak.

The idea of retirement is rooted in society's notion that life is composed of productive and nonproductive periods. The first twenty to thirty years of life are seen as a time when a person is training for a productive life. The next thirty to forty years are when his creative energies are realized; he begins to return what has been invested in him by his now passive elders, and, in turn, begins investing in the still passive younger generation. Finally, as he enters his later years, he puts his period of "real" achievement behind him. If a creative urge still strikes, he is advised to find some harmless hobby to fill his time. Indeed, time has become something to be *filled*. In a sense, he has come full circle to childhood—once again, he is a passive recipient in a world shaped by the initiative of others.

The time to passively enjoy the fruits of one's labor does indeed have its time and place—in the world to come. The very fact that G-d has granted a person a single additional day of bodily life means that he or she has not yet concluded his or her mission in life, that there is still much to achieve in this world.

A hardworking adult may nostalgically remember childhood as a time of freedom from responsibility and toil. As we grow, however, we disdain such "freedom," wanting to do something real and creative. Similarly, the promise of a "happy retirement" is a cruel myth, for we know true happiness only when we are creatively contributing to our world. The weakened physical state of old age, therefore, is not a sentence of inactivity, but a challenge to find new—and superior—means of achievement.

ᏬᎧᏠᎧ

An aged man who could barely walk asked a group of
young men to help carry his packages. Instead, they began to
mock him. "Old people like you need to stay home," one of
them said. "You are useless and just a burden to the rest of us."
The young men were musicians, and a few days later,

*they went off into the woods to find a quiet place to play.
As they were walking, they heard from a far-off clearing a
rich, beautiful voice singing a haunting melody. From a distance, they finally saw the singer, sitting alone on a rock,
singing into the heavens. As they drew closer, they saw that
it was none other than the old man.*

WHAT STEPS SHOULD THE ELDERLY
TAKE FOR THEMSELVES?

We must always remember that, *spiritually*, we are all united.
The soul of a seventy-year-old shares the same spiritual space
as that of a seven-year-old or a twenty-seven-year-old. And so, just
as the seven-year-old must learn to respect his elders, and just as
the twenty-seven-year-old must learn that his decisions greatly affect
the elderly, the elderly themselves must recognize their role. That
role is not a passive one; in fact, the later years of life are filled with
opportunities that may have totally escaped our sight until we are
upon them.

Just because we stop going to work every day does not mean that
we stop using our body and soul to fulfill our G-dly mission. The
same energy that you once spent worrying about your competition
or planning your business can now be devoted to projects that you
never had time for, projects that shine a light of goodness on those
around you. Remember, the experience of an older man or woman—
whether in business, in civic matters, or in the home—is priceless.

Even before society begins to appreciate the value of age, the
elderly must take their lives into their own hands. The elderly must
learn to exercise their own convictions as strongly as modern society
exerts its own considerable force. *Do not*, therefore, feel defeated by
your age and its physical effects. *Do not* heed those who say that
you are less useful because you are less physically strong than you
once were. *Do not* listen to those who claim that nothing more is

expected of you than leisurely walks and playing golf, than spending your days and years doing nothing.

Our twilight years are just what the name implies—the beautiful culmination of a day well spent. In childhood, we peek into an uncertain future, eager to learn but inexperienced and dependent on others. In the twilight years, we look back at what we have learned, confident and eager to impart this wisdom unto others. Just as you may need a younger person's helping hand in your physical life, that person needs *your* helping hand in his spiritual life.

Yet retirement, mandatory or otherwise, is a fact of modern life. Year after year, it condemns valuable human resources—indeed, our *most* valuable human resources—to a state of stagnation. What is one to do in the face of such human and social tragedy? Should one embark on a campaign to change this practice and the value system behind it, or should one look for the brighter side of retirement?

Indeed, we must do both. We must change the attitudes of society's leaders, but we must also change the elderly's perception of themselves. We must tell them: Not only are you not useless, but you are a greater asset to society than ever before. At the same time, we must exploit the opportunities of retirement. For those men and women seeking to fill their time constructively, let us establish study centers in every community, and let us set up classes and workshops in every nursing home and retirement village. Education, like productivity, is a lifelong endeavor. Such an intensive pursuit of prayer and study will illuminate the elderly's self-worth and potential, transforming them from cast-asides into beacons of light for their families and communities. Indeed, if properly utilized, retirement can become one of the most productive periods in a long life.

How Can the Elderly Access the Fire of Their Young Souls?

We must remember that no matter how weak our bodies may become, the soul remains strong, constantly yearning for nourishment. You should nourish your soul by setting aside a special time each day to study and pray, to feed your mind and heart. You should also designate time to share your experiences with younger people, and encourage others to do the same. If you are sincere in your effort to communicate, a younger person will recognize the validity of what you have to say, and make a genuine effort to respond. Spend time with your grandchildren and share your life with them. Gently educate them in the priorities of life that only you can impart. Simply love and enjoy them, and allow them to love and enjoy you.

Look upon these activities not merely as a way to fill your spare time, but as a means to feed your soul, to rejuvenate your spirit. More and more, medicine is teaching us that our physical health is dependent on our spiritual health. So do not succumb to your body's voice, or to the discouraging voices of those around you. Remember that age is dignity, that age is wisdom. Physical strength may be ephemeral, but good deeds are eternal. And every good deed ultimately affects the entire world.

It is time to take a new look at the elderly. To take a new look at retirement. To take a new look at the very essence of life. Of all people, it is perhaps the elderly who most need—and who can best teach us all—to lead a meaningful life.

ᕮᜭᜲᎧ

In the summer of 1980, when the Rebbe was seventy-eight, he called for the establishment of study centers for the aged. Hundreds of such centers—named, at the Rebbe's suggestion, Tiferet Zkeinim ("Glory of the Aged")—have since been founded in every corner of the globe. Here, the elderly revel in each other's wisdom and face new intellectual challenges daily.

14

∽∾∽∾∾

DEATH AND GRIEVING
Life's Ultimate Transition

And the living shall take to heart.
—Ecclesiastes 7:2

The soul never dies.
—The Rebbe

∽∾∽∾∾

In 1950, after the passing of his predecessor and father-in-law, the Rebbe emphasized that the best way to eulogize the deceased is to let their good deeds speak for them. Citing a letter that his father-in-law wrote in 1920, after the passing of his own father, the Rebbe explained that a true leader is like a shepherd who never abandons his flock. Indeed, he explained, "He is even more present than during his lifetime, since his soul is freed from the physical constraints of time and space." The Rebbe suggested that a leader's followers should intensify their bond with him by studying his teachings, fulfilling his directives, and perpetuating his activities.

WHAT DOES DEATH REALLY MEAN?

Death: The very word strikes fear in people's hearts. They consider death as unfathomable as it is inevitable. They are barely able to

117

talk about it, to peer beyond the word itself and allow themselves to contemplate its true implications. This is an understandable reaction, given the fact that so many people think of *life* as nothing more than a state in which the human body is biologically active. But we must ask ourselves: What happens after death, if anything? What does death really mean? How should the surviving loved ones react?

The mystery of death is part of the enigma of the soul and of life itself; understanding death really means understanding life. During life as we know it, the body is vitalized by the soul; upon death, there is a separation between body and soul. But the soul continues to live on as it always has, now unfettered by the physical constraints of the body. And since a person's true character—his goodness, virtue, and selflessness—lies in the soul, he will ascend to a higher state after fulfilling his responsibilities on earth.

Modern physics has taught us that no substance truly disappears, that it only changes form, that matter is another form of energy. A tree, for instance, might be cut down and used to build a house, or a table, or a chair. Regardless of how the form changes, the wood remains wood. And when that same wood is burned in a furnace, it again changes form, becoming an energy that gives off heat and gas. The tree, the chair, and the fire are all merely different forms of the same substance.

If this is the case with a material substance, it is even more so with a spiritual substance. The spiritual life force in man, the soul, never disappears; upon death, it changes from one form to another, higher form. This may be difficult to comprehend at first, since we are so dependent on using our sensory tools to get through life. With wood, for example, it is easier to hold a chair in our hands than to grasp the heat and energy released from burning wood; and yet, the heat is no less real than the wooden chair.

As we become more attuned to spiritual thinking, we learn to relate to the reality of the spirit, and its elevation upon death and release from the body to a purer form of spiritual energy.

No matter what physical ailments might befall a person, they are just that: *physical* ailments. Nothing that happens to the flesh and blood diminishes in any way the soul's power, which is purely spiritual. It is inappropriate, therefore, to use the term "afterlife" to define what happens after death. "Afterlife" implies that we have entered another, separate place, whereas death is actually a continuation of life as we know it, only in a new, higher form. The chapter in Genesis discussing the death of Sarah, for instance, is called "The Life of Sarah." The chapter discussing the death of Jacob is called "And Jacob Lived."

So before we can truly answer the question "What is death?" we must first ask, "What is life?" By medical definition, life takes place when one's brain and heart are functioning. Yet a person can be biologically alive but not alive at all; breathing and walking and talking are only the *manifestations* of what we call life. The true source of life, the energy that allows the body to function, is the soul. And the soul, because it is connected to G-d, the giver of life, is immortal. While the manifestations of life may cease upon death, the soul lives on, only in a different form.

How can a mortal human being connect to eternal life? By living a material life that fuses body and soul, thereby connecting to G-d. A person who transforms his or her body into a vehicle for love and generosity is a person who nurtures his or her eternal soul. It is by giving life to others that one becomes truly alive.

To a person for whom life consists of material gains, death indeed represents "the end." It is the time when all fleeting achievements come to a halt. But to a person for whom life consists of spiritual gains, life never ends. The soul is fueled by the inexhaustible energy of the good deeds a person performed on earth, and it lives on materially through his or her children and the others who perpetuate his or her spiritual vitality. As the sages say, "Just as his descendants are alive, he, too, is alive."[1]

We often have a difficult time distinguishing between biological life and spiritual life, or true life. We are distracted by the many material trappings of biological life. Once the soul leaves the body, though, we can clearly see how it lives on, how that soul continues to inspire people to perform good deeds, to educate and help others,

to live G-dly and spiritual lives. It is when a righteous person physically departs the earth that he or she begins to exert the most
profound influence.

◦↝↜◦

*A revered rabbi, when he was very near death, asked
that he be moved into the study hall where he delivered his
discourses. "I am going to heaven," he told his followers,
"but I am leaving you my writings," the writings that carry
his spirit.*

*When his son heard these words, he began to weep. His
father, weak with illness, turned to him and said, "Emotions?
Emotions? No. Intellect, intellect." From that moment on,
his son remained steadfast, thinking only of the life of his
father's eternal soul.*

WHAT DOES DEATH MEAN
FOR THE SURVIVORS?

While death represents the soul's elevation to a higher level, it
nevertheless remains a painful experience for the survivors.
At the same time, it must serve—as must all experiences in life—as
a lesson; as a move forward. We must see death not as a negative
force, but as an opportunity for growth.

Since death provokes such strong emotions, we must have a
clear channel through which to express them, to go about healing
in a constructive way. When a loved one dies, powerful and conflicting emotions are aroused: sadness over the loss and confusion
about the future. The sages teach us that it would be barbaric not
to mourn at all, but that we should not mourn longer than necessary.[2] A week of mourning is sufficient; otherwise, a person's death

becomes a presence unto itself, continuously saddening us and impeding our progress in life.

But why should we restrain our natural pain and sadness over a loved one's death? Grief is a feeling, after all, and feelings cannot be controlled, can they? Isn't it wrong to set limits and repress our grief, or to try to channel it in a certain direction?

True, feelings are feelings, but we *can* choose whether to experience them in a destructive or productive light. The key in this case is to understand death for what it is, to celebrate its positive element. A mourner must ultimately come to realize that the soul of his or her loved one has now reached an even greater place than it occupied during its time on earth, and that it will continue to rise. It is the act of reconciling this positive realization with our grief that can turn death from a traumatic experience into a cathartic one.

To diminish our expression of grief is unhealthy and inappropriate, but to allow our grief to overwhelm us is to selfishly overlook the true meaning of death—the fact that a person's righteous soul has found an even more righteous home.

What Should We Learn from Death?

Besides celebrating the elevation of a loved one's soul and expressing our own grief, there is another purpose to mourning: Death is also an opportunity to examine our own lives and evaluate how we are fulfilling our divine mission. As Maimonides writes, a mourner should be "anxious and concerned and evaluate his behavior and repent."[3]

So remembering the soul of a loved one is a most appropriate occasion to gaze into your own soul. We all know how difficult it can be to assess one's own behavior, and we often aren't compelled to do so until a friend or family member has passed on. At that point, we remember the things he accomplished during his life, how he treated his family and friends, how he went out of his way to help strangers. Unfortunately, it is often the blow of a death that shakes us out of our complacency and makes us rethink our own priorities.

Because the true bond between a parent and child or a husband and wife is a spiritual one, it remains intact and strong after death. Mourning also helps us retain this bond, for the soul of a departed person, eternal and intact, watches over the people with whom she was close. Every gracious act gives her great pleasure and satisfaction, particularly when such acts are committed in a manner that she taught, whether by instruction or example.

Her soul is fully aware of what is happening to the friends and relatives she has left behind. The soul is distressed when they experience undue grief or depression, and it rejoices when they move beyond their initial pain and continue to build their lives and inspire those around them.

There is no way to replace a departed loved one, for each person is a complete world. But there is a way to help partially fill the void. When family and friends supplement their customary good deeds with further virtuous acts on behalf of the departed, they continue the work of his or her soul. By performing such acts in the memory of a loved one, we can truly build a living memorial.

Where does one find this extra energy, especially while we are experiencing grief over the death itself? Just as the body reaches into its reservoir of strength when it is under attack, the soul is able to exert hidden strength during times of great trauma, strength that we may not even have been aware of.

What are we to make of all this, this rethinking of the way we look at death? What implications are there for those of us who inhabit a reality defined by our five senses and the laws of nature, a reality in which physical life inevitably yields to a physical death?

For those who continue to look at only the outer layer of life, the physical component as circumscribed by the human body, death indeed seems to be the end of life. But we must learn to peer inside this outer layer and see the human soul, our connection to G-d and to eternity.

Deep in our hearts, we are all aware of this connection. Any thinking person who contemplates the solar system, for example, or the complexities of an atom, must come to the conclusion that our universe did not come about by some freak accident. Nor is it composed merely of physical matter; every fiber of being is pulsating with energy. Wherever we turn, we see design and purpose—the hallmark of our creator. It would follow, therefore, that each human being, too, has a purpose, as does every single event in our lives.

So even death has a purpose in our lives; even death becomes a tool for leading a more meaningful life; and even death is another form of energy.

But after all is said and done, death is still an incomprehensible, devastating experience to those who are left behind. After all the rationalizations, all the explanations, the heart still cries. And it *should* cry.

When friends or relatives are grieving for a loved one, do not try to explain; just be there with them. Soothe and console them, and weep with them. There is nothing one can really say, for no matter how we might try, we must accept that we often do not understand G-d's mysterious ways.

But we should ask of G-d to finally bring the day when death shall be no more, when "death shall be swallowed up forever and G-d shall wipe the tears from every face."[4]

⌒⨪⨪⨪⌒

Over his lifetime, the Rebbe experienced the passing of his entire family: his father, mother, two brothers, his father-in-law, and his wife. Each time, he transformed his grief into a catalyst to establish new educational and charitable institutions in their spirit. On the anniversary of their deaths each year, he would deliver talks dedicated to the goodness that they had accomplished in their lives, and initiating further activities in their memories.

He was particularly affected and inspired by the death of Rabbi Yosef Yitzchak Schneersohn, his father-in-law and predecessor. The Rebbe often visited his father-in-law's grave site several times a week, spending time in silent prayer and reading some of the thousands of letters he received seeking guidance. Indeed, the Rebbe concluded every piece of correspondence he answered with the words "I will mention it at the grave site."

15

PAIN AND
SUFFERING
Seeds for Growth

Those who sow in tears will reap with songs of joy.
—Psalms 126:6

We must translate pain into action, and tears into growth.
—The Rebbe

I t was the Rebbe's nature to see the positive where conventional
wisdom saw only the negative. In his own way, he was able to
bring hope and comfort even to those who were suffering the most
acute emotional or spiritual pain.

In 1973, the widow of the renowned sculptor Jacques Lipchitz
visited the Rebbe after her husband's sudden death. Besides being
broken by his passing, she was in a quandary because when he
died, he was nearing completion of a massive sculpture, a phoenix
in abstract, that had been commissioned for Mount Scopus in
Jerusalem. A sculptor herself, she would have liked to complete
her husband's work, but some people had begun to suggest
that perhaps the phoenix was an inappropriate symbol for

the holy city of Jerusalem. This conundrum left her doubly saddened.

The Rebbe opened the Book of Job and read, "And I shall multiply my days like the chol."[1] He proceeded to explain that the chol was a bird that lived for a thousand years and then died and was later resurrected from its ashes; clearly, the phoenix was an appropriate symbol. And one of hope and renewal in the face of pain. The Rebbe told her that she should proceed with the project with a full heart. She was comforted and delighted.

WHY DO WE FEEL SUCH PAIN?

There are certain questions that we all ask during our lifetime: Why is there so much suffering in the world? How do we deal with emotional, spiritual, and psychological pain? Why does G-d sometimes allow righteous people to suffer such extreme pain?

These questions pose a paradox. The very fact that we are naturally upset by suffering testifies to our belief in a fair and righteous G-d, whom we expect to rule the world justly. And yet, we see that pain and suffering cause many people to question the very existence of G-d, or at least His effectiveness.

No matter how vigorously we may challenge G-d, we never accept pain as our "natural" state; we recognize it as a suffocating and unacceptable experience, and we will do anything to relieve ourselves of the pain. Still, pain can break our will and prevent us from thinking clearly and finding help. So how do we resolve this dilemma and escape the clutches of pain?

One must take great care in discussing pain and suffering. Even though they stem from very real, sometimes devastating experiences—the loss of a loved one, a serious setback—they are manifested as *emotions*, and are therefore impervious to rational scrutiny.

How then can we discuss such matters without insulting the sufferer? By recognizing that emotional, spiritual, or psychological pain is real, and that no amount of talk can truly relieve it. Yet pain and suffering must be dealt with effectively and compassionately in order to forge ahead and live a truly meaningful life.

Any emotion clouds our rationale, and when it is as powerful as pain, it can consume us, distorting the way we look at ourselves and the world. Emotions are in themselves a paradox: they are natural feelings, yet they cause us to see things in an unnatural light. Acknowledging this paradox is the key to unlocking the mystery of pain and suffering. There are those who try to *explain* these emotions. Some people of faith try to minimize pain by explaining that this is what G-d wants for us. Others use pain as an excuse to justify bitterness or even malicious behavior.

But no explanation is sufficient. The greatest thinker, the firmest believer, the harshest skeptic—they are all left groping for answers when *they* are in pain. A person who is suffering stands in a class by himself. His pain gives him the prerogative to question and challenge G-d, or to remain silent and allow the pain to seep through his being. For those who haven't suffered, trying to explain away someone else's pain—or, in the other extreme, questioning the faith of the sufferer despite G-d's silence—is vulgar and arrogant.

We must challenge our own intentions in questioning G-d during times of pain. Are these questions coming out of anger? Are we using the pain to justify our response? No matter how difficult it may be, we must do everything possible to not let our emotions overwhelm us; we must remember that pain is an aberration, not a norm, and so we shouldn't allow our aberrational thoughts and doubts in response to pain to become the new norm.

Perhaps you have been tempted at some point to resign yourself to your pain, to give up your spirit. Your pain may even lead you to turn away from G-d. But turning away from G-d means turning away from the very answer to your pain and suffering, thus allowing the pain to victimize you.

Even in the deepest moments of despair, we must realize that our absolute faith in G-d is what gives us the capacity to somehow reconcile and deal with our grief. In a world without G-d, pain and suffering would indeed be fruitless. But with G-d at the helm, even though the pain may not subside, we can accept it as part of the challenge of life; it motivates us to seek answers, to explore our relationship with G-d, and to grow from the experience.

This is the great challenge of pain: Will you allow it to debilitate you or will you see it as a catalyst to delve deeper into yourself and your beliefs? Will you allow the emotions to distort your inner sense of the truth, or will you recognize pain as a crucible from which you will emerge stronger then ever?

We can truly relate to the meaning of pain only before or after the experience. During pain and suffering, there is little that can be said. So during the "years of plenty," we must prepare for the "years of famine." The better we truly understand our lives when things are going well, the better we will deal with pain when it strikes. While a tree with strong roots can withstand a harsh storm, it can hardly hope to grow them once the storm is on the horizon.

WHAT CAN WE LEARN FROM PAIN AND SUFFERING?

Pain and suffering are opportunities to challenge the way we look at life. When things are going well, we tend to take life for granted, but trauma brings us to the edges of life, allowing us to review it from a new, revealing angle.

So the real question we must ask is not just why we sometimes feel such acute pain, but what we are meant to learn from it.

When you see life as being limited to the here and now, to the immediacy of a bodily existence, you are bound to be frightened and hurt by anything that attacks that existence. When you are aware of a larger picture, though, of a spiritual reality besides a physical one, pain is only one component. Whereas pain is ultimately ephemeral—whether it is physical, emotional, or spiritual—life is eternal, and what matters most is the long-term contributions you make. To this end, you need to look for the positive energy that your suffering produces. Like the precious few drops of oil that can be extracted only when olives are crushed, suffering can lead us to reconsider the meaning of our existence, to commit more fully to our spiritual development.

In and of itself, your pain is often a sign that something else is wrong. It is a symptom of a cause that may not be readily visible, and you must look at life from a sharper angle to find this cause. Someone who leads a materialistic life is bound to misconstrue pain, for materialism is by nature transient, fragmented into many isolated moments. So when you feel pain, you concentrate on it and can feel nothing else. You may weigh the pain you are feeling at the moment against the joy you felt yesterday, and decide that perhaps life is not worth the trouble.

But when you see beyond a one-dimensional life, beyond the moment, when you realize that you are composed of not just a body but a body and a soul, you recognize that there is a far higher purpose to your life. And that there is a far deeper meaning to your pain.

To the naked eye, our goal in life may be to pursue momentary happiness through material comfort. But we ultimately discover this to be a shallow and meaningless objective. The true goal of life is to challenge ourselves in order to refine this material world. Life is synonymous with challenge, and challenge is synonymous with the potential for good *and* evil, and our ability to choose between the two. Without the possibility that we may fall temporarily, there would be no independence to life, and therefore no meaning.

Pain and suffering are consequences of this independence, and of the dichotomy between body and soul. By creating a harmony between body and soul, by moving from a physical, one-dimensional life into a spiritual, two-dimensional life, you begin to transform your pain into a learning experience and a positive energy.

Realigning your perspective on life necessitates a serious commitment, and it cannot be done easily. It takes discipline and the concentrated effort of study, prayer, and good deeds; it means introducing a higher value system into your life. But it is the only worthy response to pain—and even this may not lift the pain, which is just a short-term symptom of the long-term cause that you have now set out to address.

There is no true explanation for pain; the only way *we* can understand pain and suffering is by recognizing that the world itself is intrinsically good and that pain and suffering are somehow part of the larger good. This is not to suggest that pain *itself* is good, nor that we should peacefully accept it. In fact, we must express our feelings of pain to the fullest, and do everything in our power to alleviate suffering in ourselves and in others.

At the same time, we must recognize pain and suffering as part of the mystery of life, a larger picture that human eyes cannot always initially see but that becomes apparent over time. As the sages say, "Everything G-d does, He does for the best."[2] In no way does this justify any person inflicting pain or punishment on another— no one has a right to play G-d.

It is your duty to discover how pain may be a blessing in disguise and to overcome the pain and restore harmony to your body and soul. Consider the inevitable frustration that precedes any creative growth, or the intense pain that a woman feels while giving birth. No matter how great such pain may be, it is ultimately absorbed by the goodness it produces.

⟨∞∞∞⟩

A perplexed man once visited a rabbi. "The sages tell us to 'bless G-d for the bad just as one blesses Him for the good,'"[3] he said, "but how is this humanly possible?"

"That is a good question. For an answer, you must visit a farmer I know," the rabbi replied.

The man found the farmer. He had never before seen anyone who suffered such hardship. The farmer lived like a pauper.

There was no food in the house, and his entire family was beset with illness. Yet he was cheerful, constantly expressing his gratitude to G-d.

The man wanted to know the farmer's secret, and he finally asked him the same question he had asked the rabbi.

"That is a very good question," said the farmer. "But why did the rabbi send you to me? How would I know? He should have sent you to someone who has experienced suffering."

How Do We Relieve Our Pain?

Pain is a lonely experience. Still, we must strive to recognize that our pain is, in some form, G-d's way of communicating with us.

Breaking out of pain's vicious grip is very difficult to do alone, for the pain itself can hold us hostage, limiting our activity and vision to the point where we are nearly helpless. It is critical, therefore, to reach out to family or friends who can offer a wider perspective.

Freeing yourself from pain begins through movement—moving away and distracting yourself from the painful situation, moving away from the cause that produced such painful symptoms so that you can begin to heal. This movement may be as simple as finding a new friend, reading a new book, getting involved in a project, or taking a class—anything to help alter your solitary, myopic perspective on yourself and the world.

For some, starting the climb out of pain requires a strong push. One should try not to wait until he hits rock bottom. This is where true friends play a vital role. When someone you love and care for is in pain, you must be there for him, no matter what he needs. He may say he wants to be alone, that he wants to work through his problems by himself, and this must be respected. But you must help him also recognize that he needs to broaden his perspective, not further limit it. Find a way to spend time with him, to talk with him, to share your thoughts with each other. Most important, love him and help him to help himself.

Another component in easing pain is, paradoxically, accepting it with joy. You must be willing to release its inner good by making peace with your soul and with G-d. And you must remember that pain is an opportunity for growth—a chance to review your conduct, to pause and examine your busy life for the source of such pain. You must recognize that pain can cleanse you, just as a mother swabs her child's cut with alcohol. Surely she does not wish to cause further pain, but she knows it is necessary to properly heal the wound.

It is important that you see pain as a test that examines how consumed you are with material comfort as opposed to spiritual growth. When we recognize our true objective in life, and pursue it with a firm will, our obstacles turn into challenges; instead of being stymied, we draw upon our reservoirs of strength and determination. In this way, pain and suffering test our true commitment to G-d.

Still, we cannot help but ask: Why must there be such suffering? Couldn't G-d have allowed us to grow without such pain?

Our faith in G-d dictates that the very fact that there is no answer to this question is in itself proof that we do not need to answer the question in order to fulfill our purpose in life. The key to dealing with pain and suffering is to stop searching for an answer to satisfy our minds. After all, it was G-d who created us, not vice versa. How can we presume to fully understand His ways? So when we ask ourselves, Why does G-d allow such suffering? or Why does G-d permit tragedy and destruction?, ultimately our only true answer is: Only G-d knows.

Such trust should not be confused with resignation. Instead, we must look upon pain as an impetus to redouble our efforts to behave righteously, to encourage others to do the same, and to alleviate the suffering of our fellow man at every opportunity. By recognizing that pain serves a deeper purpose, we expose it for what it is—a challenge to be met with intense determination.

Instead of being broken by pain, you must demonstrate your

complete trust in G-d by continuing your life with an intense commitment to goodness, thereby challenging G-d to live up to His promises of being righteous and fair. Trust in G-d is our way of turning pain around. It proves to G-d that, although we may not fully understand our pain, we recognize it as part of a greater good. And despite our setbacks, despite our confusion, despite our pain, we remain absolutely confident that goodness will prevail.

True faith does not waver. A time of crisis or great pain is the time for prayer and absolute faith. By resigning yourself to your pain, you are basically giving up on G-d's goodness. By abandoning Him, you are only abandoning yourself, for the soul—your lifeline to G-d—is the one eternal element of your life. No matter how much pain you may feel in your body, the soul remains intact and dynamic, always ready to strengthen its connection to G-d. But you must do your part by strengthening yourself and your commitment to living a G-dly life. Ultimately, the best answer to pain and suffering is action.

Pain and suffering reflect the unfathomable mystery of G-d. And it is the suffering man or woman who has been given the right, like no other, to stand before G-d, to challenge G-d and to grow through the process.

⚬〰〰〰⚬

A teacher who was close to the Rebbe once came to him for advice. His deep emotional pain as a Holocaust survivor was preventing him from fulfilling his teaching responsibilities. "There are no words to console you," the Rebbe said, "but you cannot allow the Holocaust to continue in your life." He counseled the man with words he had learned from his father-in-law, the previous Rebbe: "We are day workers, and our task is to shed light. We need not expend our energies in battling darkness. We need only create day, and night will fade away."

16

FEAR AND ANXIETY
The Enemies Within

I am confident and shall not fear, for G-d is my strength and song,
and He has been a help to me.
—Isaiah 12:1

Think good and it will be good.
—The Rebbe

The Rebbe often told a story about his father-in-law, Rabbi Yosef Yitzchak Schneersohn, the previous Lubavitcher Rebbe. In 1927, Rabbi Yosef Yitzchak was summoned by the Communist authorities in Moscow. When he refused to cooperate, one of them lifted a revolver and pointed it at him. "This toy makes people cooperate," he said. "Fear of it has opened many a mouth."

"That toy frightens only someone who has but a single world and many gods," Rabbi Yosef Yitzchak replied. "But not one who has but a single G-d and two worlds."

WHAT ARE WE SO AFRAID OF?

We fear many things. We fear illness and death. We fear losing a job or falling into poverty. We fear change—a new career, a new home, a new marriage. We may fear being alone, or we may fear other people. And then there is the fear of not being accepted by others—by our families and friends, our colleagues and neighbors, by society at large.

Fear, anxiety, and depression are the underlying factors that drive much of human behavior today, yet they are among the most misunderstood forces in people's lives. In their most acute form, they paralyze us. How can we deal with these forces? Why are we afraid and what are we afraid of?

These are not simple questions to answer, for fear is a tremendous and complicated power. It is silent yet devastating, leading to anxiety and, ultimately, depression. When you are consumed by fear, your judgment is distorted; you become frozen by doubt, unable to make the simplest decision.

There is a natural, healthy fear of the unknown that often protects us from danger. But the cause of this fear is right out in the open, and serves a valuable purpose. The more common fear, and a more formidable fear, is one that doesn't allow us to identify it; lurking in the shadows, it thrives on our ignorance. Think of a child who is afraid of the dark. There is no rationale behind such a fear, and yet no words can explain it away. The only thing you can do is assure him that you are there to protect him. You can take him by the hand and turn on the light, showing that there is nothing to be afraid of.

It is the same with adults. There is often no basis to our fear, and even when there is, we may exaggerate its power to the point where it holds us hostage. Fear is born of doubt and confusion. Should I accept this job or shouldn't I? Will I be able to handle this problem or won't I? What will my family and friends think if I make this change in my life? Such confusion is anathema to a human being; the emotional strain can be debilitating.

Clarity is one of our greatest blessings. When you resolve doubts, you feel as though a heavy weight has been lifted from your heart. Even if you think you may have made a mistake in your decision, you can at least see clearly what lies ahead of you, and you gain the strength and confidence to move ahead. A person who does not have a clear objective in life remains confused. And confusion breeds more confusion; once we get entangled in the web of fear and anxiety, we only become more enmeshed in confusion and discouragement.

If you are to lead a meaningful and productive life, your heart must be free from the oppressive forces of anxiety and sadness. Despair dulls the heart and weakens the spirit. It lowers your resistance to the true challenges that are bound to arise. Surely we meet enough obstacles during a lifetime without the need to create our own inner obstacles!

The key is to patiently untie these doubts that bind you. While fear thrives in the darkness of confusion, it dissipates in the light of clarity. You must introduce clarity into your life by acknowledging your life's purpose and directing all your energies toward it.

WHERE DOES OUR FEAR COME FROM?

Fear has many parents. Perhaps your trust was abused as a child. Perhaps trauma left an indelible impression. Perhaps you were simply never taught a purpose and direction in life; and fear can take root when we believe that life is some random, rambling existence.

Most human anxiety springs from a fear of annihilation: you fear losing the world around you, the world to which you are so accustomed. Think of a child who has but one toy—take it away, and the child will surely cry. Similarly, when people perceive the material world as the only world that exists, they are bound to fear losing it, because it is all they know.

Let us look at how limited this attitude is. By its nature, materialism is fleeting. The food you ate yesterday is gone today. The money you make today will be spent tomorrow. The status and power you have worked so hard to achieve can be wiped away in a moment. When your life is built on such a temporary foundation, how can you expect to feel secure?

Making the material world your priority is the ultimate cause of fear and anxiety. Even as you shed the many fears of childhood, you develop an entirely new set of fears. Instead of being scared of the dark, you become frightened of not making enough money. Or of losing your job. Or of not being successful enough.

When you allow your life to be defined by money, by your job, by society, you become intensely afraid of not being accepted by others. Thus the cardinal dictate "Do not be ashamed before those that ridicule."[1] Still, we yearn to conform. We are afraid to stand out, and we worry incessantly about how others perceive us. We fear that people will mock us or won't respect our choices.

Think for a moment how empty that fear is. Human beings are inherently mercurial. Their moods change, their attitudes change, their values change. So when you are worried about being accepted by others, you are placing your happiness and security in the hands of unpredictable people—a moody boss, a difficult client. You are constantly investing great amounts of energy into pleasing first one person and then another. You are trying to be one person in the morning, another during the day, and yet another at night. No wonder your life is driven by anxiety; no wonder you have no peace of mind.

You must not compromise your values and standards out of fear of how others will perceive you. This is one of the most difficult challenges in life, for we all want to be loved and accepted. But accepted by whom? By people whose own standards are ever shifting? By people who themselves are worried about being accepted by yet others?

The only person on earth you need to be accepted by is *yourself*. You achieve this by integrating G-d into your life, which means devoting yourself to the purpose for which you were created. By following the divine laws of morality, you introduce sanctity and serenity into you life—and a sense of order. Only then will you discover the clarity that demolishes fear. Only then will you stop cowering in the face of the unexpected unknown. G-d has given each of us the abilities and resources to overcome the challenges that life provides. When you place absolute trust in G-d and acknowledge the true purpose of your life, even your most serious fears—of sickness or poverty or death—will begin to dissipate in the crisp light of clarity.

⌘

A young girl from a very poor family was having terrifying dreams. Her parents consulted their rabbi about this problem. He said, "The sages say that we dream at night what we think about during the day.² Ask your daughter what she is afraid of."

When they asked her, she replied, "I often see how you both sit and worry over the poverty we live in. Of everything, I am most afraid of your fear."

HOW CAN WE BATTLE FEAR?

Connecting to G-d is the only way to truly free yourself from fear. By recognizing that you are an integral part of G-d's plan, that your existence is significant and your participation is vital, you can wean yourself of the doubts that feed your fears.

As long as you place the highest premium on the material world, you will continue to be fearful and anxious. You will remain a victim of circumstance, subjecting yourself to the mercurial nature of materialism.

We have nothing to fear except G-d, because nothing is as real as G-d. As the sages say, "May you fear G-d as much as you fear man."[3] "Fear of G-d" is not actually fear at all, but an awe and respect for a higher presence in your life—and a recognition that G-d chose you to fill a specific role in refining this world. When you feel despondent or afraid, contemplate this point; when you fear that you won't be able to handle a particular challenge or a setback, think about what G-d wants of you.

When you have but one G-d and two worlds, the material and the spiritual, there is nothing to fear. The problems that loomed so large just a moment ago begin to seem eminently manageable. When you realize that money, status, and acceptance should not be the primary forces that drive your life, your confusion starts to melt away. You gain confidence in the knowledge that you are working toward a higher purpose, and that G-d would not ask you to do so if you were not capable of it.[4] There will be no room in your life for despair and anxiety, only for joy and celebration in the fact that you are fully alive.

Such confidence spills over into your entire life. And when you have learned to focus on the real matters of life, you will no longer need to worry about meeting the standards of those around you. G-d's standards are higher than man's, but they are actually easier to meet. While man's values are ephemeral, constantly shifting, spiritual values are eternal. When you connect to them, the trivial matters of life no longer frighten you, just as an adult is no longer scared of the dark. You no longer see fear and anxiety as distracting or crippling forces, but as challenges that must be overcome to lead a meaningful life. Half of winning any battle is understanding the enemy, and once you understand the root of your fears, you are well on the way to conquering them.

This is not to say that you will be freed of all fear and anxiety. They are a part of life. But they must be seen as a sign that something is out of sync in your life, that something is holding you back from achieving your goals. So when you become aware of fear or anxiety, do not give way to depression; instead, attack and improve the situation.

Depression is not a sin, but what depression does, no sin can do. There are two types of depression—one constructive, one destructive. The first is the despair of humility, of a person who not only recognizes his failings but cares enough to address them. It is the despair of a person who agonizes over his shortcomings and missed opportunities, but who refuses to become indifferent to his problems and those of the world. The second despair is that of a person who has given up on himself and his fellow man, who has allowed his melancholy to drain him of hope. The first despair is a springboard for self-improvement; the second is a bottomless pit.

How does one distinguish between the two? The first person weeps, the second person's eyes are dry and blank. The first person's mind and heart are in turmoil, the second person's mind and heart are silent with apathy and heavy as lead. And what happens when each person emerges from his mood of despair? The first person springs to action, taking his first faltering steps to escape his depression. The second person remains paralyzed, for his path is still no easier.

To defeat depression, you must introduce a fresh perspective to your thinking. You must begin to replace troubling, destructive thoughts with positive, constructive ones. Think good and it will be good. This is not foolish optimism; this is recognizing the goodness within even a seemingly bad situation, recognizing that battling your fear means overcoming a challenge.

Get rid of the confusion in your life. You must untie the knots that bind you, but you must also remember you can only untie one knot at a time. Do not be discouraged by the prospect; even the highest mountain must be climbed step by single step. Just as confusion breeds confusion, clarity breeds clarity, so as you take one step in a positive direction, you gain the momentum to travel whatever distance is necessary.

Write down and examine the five highest priorities in your life.

Are they ephemeral goals or eternal ones? Are money and status more important than your family and helping other people? If so, then it is obvious why you have great fear in your life. You know full well that you could always fall short of these goals.

You can distract yourself from your material cycle by focusing on the positive—your achievements, your abilities, the people you love. Better yet, share your anxiety[5] with friends or family members who will give you support, a fresh perspective, and positive suggestions. Get involved in projects that are profoundly gratifying. Soon enough, your life will be so full of meaningful activity that there will be no time for fear and anxiety.

Finally, introduce G-d into your life. Realize that you are here for a purpose that is greater than all the greatest experiences in life. The higher you set your values, the less you will fear the mundane anxieties that can dominate daily life. Recognize that G-d within you protects your soul; even someone who has been battered and abused by life has a pure soul. You must remember that there is nothing on this earth to fear, for G-d is always with you, and by following His instructions, you open the channels for His blessings.

No matter how overwhelming your fears may seem, give your soul time to speak to you. Initially, fear may prevent you from hearing your soul. But be patient, and be persistent. There is only one condition—that you address your fears truthfully and sincerely, for fear and anxiety will not respond to hollow statements.

Imagine coming to a place where money and power and vanity have no value. That place is here and now. The moment you look fear in the eye, it begins to crumble. Use your intellect to harness your emotions, and use your spirit to conquer your fear. Above all, let joy and enthusiasm—and G-d—come into your life, and let the brilliant light of your soul shine into every dark corner where fear might flourish.

An artist, after suffering a personal tragedy, wrote to the Rebbe about his depression and despair. The Rebbe wrote

back: "The genius of the artist is his ability to detach himself from the externality of the object he is portraying, to
look deeply into the object and see its essence. He must then
be able to express that essence so that whoever views the
painting sees a new dimension that he, the viewer, would
never have noticed in the object itself. The same applies to
each individual; his inner essence is his G-dliness. One must
take great care so that the external matters of his life should
not obscure his essence. The tragedies of life must be seen for
what they really are: part of the cosmic system of challenge
and endeavor, which enables us to achieve the highest levels
of happiness and goodness."

17

A DAY
OF LIFE

Toward a Meaningful Day

*The day is short, the work is much, the workmen are lazy, the
reward is great, and the Master is pressing.*
— Ethics of the Fathers 2:15

The world says that time is money; I say that time is life.
— The Rebbe

❧

The Rebbe's daily schedule, which did not change in over forty
years, was formidable. Besides reading and answering hundreds of
letters a day, reviewing and editing publications, fulfilling appointments
well into the evening, and praying and studying, he also delivered talks
that often lasted into the early morning hours. One morning, he asked
what time a particular prayer was to begin, and was told it would be
either 9:10 or 9:15. "Which one is it?" the Rebbe asked. "In five
minutes, so much can be accomplished."

WHAT WAS YOUR DAY LIKE?

I f you were to make a list of all the things you did today, it might look like this: You woke up, exercised, showered, ate breakfast, made a phone call, read the newspaper, checked the weather forecast, got dressed, went to work, had pleasant moments with some colleagues and unpleasant ones with others, took a lunch break, had some productive meetings and some unproductive ones, went home, ate dinner, did a little paperwork, talked with your family, read a magazine, and went to sleep. Along the way, you had hundreds of trivial encounters and perhaps one or two meaningful ones.

Your life is made up of countless such bits and pieces. One day's worth may not seem like much, but add up the pieces day after day, year after year, and you end up with an entire life split into millions of fragments, with no connecting thread. What is wrong with that? Human beings naturally abhor fragmentation; it rattles our peace of mind, creating untold tension and anxiety. What's worse, these trivial activities are bound to overwhelm the very few truly significant events in our lives. Over time, the fragments pile up and begin to suffocate your soul. While your inner self craves focus, purpose, and direction, any stray experiences disturb its steady course. Is it any wonder that after forty or fifty years of slogging through such disjointed days, we wake up and suddenly wonder, "What have I done with my life?"

We all want to live a meaningful life, and we all consider our lives to be precious. Would it not follow, then, that each day is precious as well, and each minute? After all, we constantly strive to make our mark on humanity, to contribute something worthwhile to our world. We never know when an opportunity to do so might present itself; shouldn't we be prepared at any moment?

You may have the best intentions and the greatest aspirations to accomplish great things, but when your day is filled with quotidian activity, you simply don't have room for anything else. With so many hours devoted to earning a living, to eating and sleeping, to meeting your social obligations, how much time do you have left to satisfy your true needs, to pursue your higher goals? Amidst the clamor of your chaotic life, how can you hear the voice of your soul?

Obviously, it is impossible to eliminate your basic daily needs—you have to eat and sleep and make a living. So the only option is to find a thread that unites all your daily activities and sews all the fragments together.

This thread is the mission that G-d has asked you to fulfill: to refine yourself and every aspect of your life, from your intellect and emotions all the way down to the most mundane activities. Such focus has a twofold result: Everything in your life becomes united toward one end, eliminating the fragmentation; and even the smallest activity becomes infused with real meaning, since everything you do has a G-dly purpose.

How do you become G-dly? By connecting to your soul. And how do you connect to your soul? By giving it time. Instead of acknowledging your soul sporadically, at certain times and in certain places, you acknowledge it all the time, everyplace. You sanctify every moment of your life—not only while you are studying or praying or doing charitable deeds, but while you are eating and sleeping, at home or at work, while traveling or on vacation. Instead of carrying out your daily activities by rote, you discover the G-dliness within each of them.

⟨෴⟩

A workman had taken a break and was reading a book of psalms when his employer approached him. "Why are you reading all of a sudden, right in the middle of work?" he asked.

"It doesn't seem to bother anyone that in the middle of praying, I can think about work," the man replied. "Why is it that, in the middle of work, I can't think for a minute about prayer?"

HOW DO YOU LIVE A MEANINGFUL DAY?

When you awake in the morning, while you are still lying in bed, think for a moment: What does it mean to be awake and alive? Begin each day with a prayer; thank G-d for the new day. Acknowledge your soul and the vibrancy and fortitude it provides. Think about what you would like to accomplish that would make today a meaningful day. Train yourself to do this every morning and you will begin to see your life in a new, sharper focus.

But concentrating on your soul is a daylong activity, not to be confined to those first waking moments. Create spaces during the day when you can be alone with your soul and with G-d. Study something meaningful, using your intellect to think about G-d, and contemplate the purpose of your existence. As your day grows increasingly hectic, look back to that calm moment when you awoke, when your thoughts and desires were crystallized. Try to recapture that focus, and apply it to the moment at hand, creating an island of purpose in a sea of randomness.

You should end your day just as you began it. As you prepare for sleep, review the day and how you used its opportunities. Recognize that G-d has put you here for a purpose, and that all your activities should express that purpose. Go to sleep with the resolve that no matter how good—or not so good—today was, tomorrow will be better. If you do so, your sleep will be more peaceful and your waking more meaningful.

By connecting with your soul first thing in the morning and last thing at night, you instill new meaning into every activity that falls in between. Instead of being pushed around by the myriad trivial events in any one day, you begin to control *them*. Instead of seeing hundreds of isolated fragments, you see one big picture and the many pieces of which it is composed.

You discover sanctity and holiness in everything you do. When you eat, you are not just satisfying your hunger or fulfilling your desires, but giving your body and soul the nourishment to help you become a better person. When you conduct business, you are not just working to survive, but using your skills to help refine the world by teaching others and setting a virtuous example. When you visit with family and friends, you are not just passing the time, but trying to inspire one another to take full advantage of their various abilities. Even sleep takes on a new dimension; instead of seeing it as one more fragment of your life, a regrettably large portion of the day that you must surrender, sleep becomes an opportunity to rejuvenate your soul by sending it back to a place that is detached from your material worries, returning refreshed for a new meaningful day.

HOW SHOULD YOU MANAGE TIME WITHIN THE DAY?

Without question, the material world and your everyday needs distract you from living meaningfully. This is why it is so important to connect with your soul in the morning. Before the day begins, you are not yet engaged in any physical activities. And it is only physically that you are constrained by the limits of time and place; mentally, there are no such boundaries. So during those first moments of the day, which are yours and yours alone, you can circumvent these boundaries and concentrate fully on spiritual matters. And this gives you the opportunity to plan the time management of your entire day.

We have been conditioned to see the passing of time as an adversary. We are always rushing to an appointment or trying to meet a deadline. But time is yet another of G-d's creations, and as such, it has a life of its own. When you waste a moment, you have killed it in a sense, squandering an irreplaceable opportunity. But when you use the moment properly, filling it with purpose and productivity, it lives on forever.

A father, concerned that his son was wasting his youth, took him for a walk. It was a bright, windless day, and they came upon a lake. "Look how the entire landscape—the sky, the sun, and the mountains—is reflected in the water," he said. Then he dipped his hand into the lake and flicked his fingers toward the ground. He encouraged his son to look closely at one of the drops of water that had landed on the earth. In that one drop, the entire reflection of the same landscape was visible.

"The same is true with time," said the father. "One minute has all the properties of your entire life. It is a microcosm of your entire day, just as one day is a microcosm of your life. And so you should treat each minute accordingly."

This is the key to time management—to see the value of every moment. Not only will this make you treat each moment more preciously, but you will be more patient with yourself and with others, recognizing that there are millions of moments on the path to any worthwhile achievement.

You cannot add more minutes to the day, but you *can* utilize each one to the fullest. How do you do this? By totally investing yourself in the one activity you are engaged in at any moment, ignoring everything that came before it and that will come after it. And how can you achieve such concentration? By recognizing that everything you do is important to G-d, and is one vital piece of the larger picture of your life.

HOW DO YOU LEARN TO RETHINK YOUR DAY?

To live a meaningful life—day by day, minute by minute—may seem daunting. How can one possibly focus amidst all the distractions, problems, and emotions? Even when you are satisfied with your past accomplishments, how can you continue to grow? How can you break out of old patterns and learn to look at life anew?

By isolating your problems and addressing them one at a time. As the sages say, "When you grasp for everything, you end up grasping nothing."[1] Since each day is a lifetime, you must focus on the day before you, not on yesterday or tomorrow, and utilize its opportunities to the fullest.

But at the same time, make each day a routine; start with concentrating on the purpose of your life at the beginning and end of the day. It may be tempting to change your life all at once, but slow, steady progress is always more effective than a "crash course." Make each day meaningful, and the days will begin to add up. Remember, even the longest journey can only be completed one step at a time.

Many of us have learned to look at each step—at each day in our life—as an almost inconsequential side trip that is disconnected from any larger journey. But the secret to any journey is to fix your eye on the destination and to keep traveling steadily toward it. Veering off, even for a short while, is at best a loss of time; at worst, we get confused and find it difficult to return on course.

Remember that in the journey of life, your body is the vehicle but your soul is the compass. By following its voice, you remain focused on your destination, and each step—each day—brings you closer. How you live today determines how you will live tomorrow. The very next thing you do, no matter how small, will determine the rest of your day and, ultimately, the rest of your life.

It is never too late to start living your life meaningfully.

ᏫᎲᎵᎧ

In 1970, thousands of visitors came from many different countries to participate in the celebration of two decades of the Rebbe's leadership. On the day that many of them were scheduled to return home, the Rebbe held a special gathering.

As it progressed, he sensed their tension about getting to the airport on time, and he began to tell a story about himself and his father-in-law, the previous Rebbe.

"He was living in Leningrad at the time, and had planned a trip to Moscow," the Rebbe recalled. "His train was set to leave in a half hour. This was during the period when the Communists had declared open war on religion, particularly against my father-in-law's efforts to promote Judaism. He was followed wherever he went, and word had arrived that the government was ready to stop him at any cost. When I entered his room, I was surprised to see that although his train was scheduled to leave shortly, he was perfectly composed, working at his desk, totally unconcerned with the impending danger. I asked him: 'How can you have such self-control at a time like this?'

"He told me that his father had once spoken of something called 'success with time.' 'What does that mean?' I asked. He explained: 'You cannot add more hours to the day, so when you are involved in an activity, you must be totally immersed in it, as if nothing before it or after it exists at all.'"

The Rebbe smiled after telling the story. "I realize it is difficult to expect that people who have a flight in a short while, and who still need to pack and say their goodbyes, will be able to totally focus on the present moment, to be oblivious to the fact that there exist airplane tickets, an airplane, a Kennedy Airport! So I will attempt to keep this gathering as brief as possible, and G-d should help that we all have 'success with time' in the future."

II

SOCIETY

18

RESPONSIBILITY
The Need to Share

*If I am not for myself, who is for me? And if I am only for myself,
what am I? And if not now, when?*
—Ethics of the Fathers 1:14

*We live in a state of emergency, where the fires of
confusion are raging. When a fire is burning, everyone is responsible
for helping his fellow man.*
—The Rebbe

When the Rebbe was a child in Russia, a pogrom broke out
in his hometown, Nikolayev. His mother took him and his
brothers to hide in a shelter. There were many other women and
children there, and some of the young children were so terrified that
they began crying loudly. The mothers grew very anxious, for if
the children's cries were heard, they would all be discovered. The
Rebbe, who was only five years old at the time, calmly soothed the
crying children, one by one, with a pat on the cheek or a gentle
whisper.

WHY DO WE FEEL THE NEED
TO BE RESPONSIBLE?

We all reach a point in our lives when we realize that if we don't take responsibility for ourselves, no one will. We also learn to be responsible to our families and friends, and to those in society who are less fortunate. But how far should these responsibilities go, and how should we prioritize them? Even more important, why do we feel the need to be responsible in the first place?

The answers lie in the fact that G-d created us for a reason—to actively pursue a virtuous life and perfect this imperfect world. To that end, responsibility is a basic human need, just like food or oxygen; we cannot fulfill or justify our existence without it.

So responsibility is not something that we should accept reluctantly out of guilt or duty; it is a necessary and healthy component in our lives. We may choose to ignore the inner need for personal responsibility, wandering off to satisfy our own agendas. But, just like hunger, it will haunt us. It will speak to us through our conscience, through our anxiety, through our feelings of aimlessness. And like hunger, when it is satisfied, our bodies and souls will be immeasurably strengthened, enabling us to lead a more meaningful life.

Your first responsibility is to yourself, for you can hardly hope to civilize the world at large if your own life is out of sync. We are all responsible for our own conduct; you cannot blame anyone else for your decisions or actions. You cannot blame your parents or your teachers, your employers or your leaders. Nor can you blame G-d for making life so difficult. No matter how intimidating any obstacle may seem, G-d would not have placed it in your path without also providing you with the abilities to overcome it.[1] Therefore, it is your responsibility to do so.

This independence is the greatest manifestation of human dignity. You—and no one else—are responsible for what you make of your life. Of course, certain people will always need to be cared for—children, obviously, and adults who are unhealthy or incapacitated. But we must also recognize that every single person, from a special child to a handicapped adult, has deep inner resources that must be cultivated to the fullest. So you are also responsible for the welfare of others and for society as a whole. We have all been given a choice—to see life as it truly is, with each human being connected to the next and the next, all linked in one large cosmic destiny, or to be consumed with self-interest.

A revered rabbi once journeyed to visit a younger rabbi who was known for his religious devotion. The older rabbi was very much impressed with the young man's total immersion in prayer and study, and asked the secret of his unwavering piety. The younger man replied that by concentrating deeply on his studies, he was able to ignore any outside influences that might distract him. Indeed, the older man had noticed that many of the nearby villagers were involved in activities that were quite contrary to piety. He said to the younger man, "When it is very cold, there are two ways to warm yourself. One is by putting on a fur coat, the other is by lighting a fire. The difference is that the fur coat warms only the person wearing it, while the fire warms anyone who comes near."

Each of us has been given distinct talents and abilities, and it is our responsibility to share them in a positive way. A leader must lead, a teacher must teach, a writer must write. A skill that you take for granted may fill an indispensable need for someone else, or may have a far greater impact than you could have imagined. It is your obligation to regularly ask yourself how you can use your unique abilities to improve your world.

True, it might seem possible to look the other way, to insulate yourself and your family from influences that you may consider dangerous or corrupting. But that is not responsible behavior; that is simple protectionism. When we see someone in need, we must respond. When we see injustice, we must cry out. When we see imperfection, we must do everything possible to help perfect the situation.

This does not mean that we should think of ourselves as saviors, sweeping in to rescue people from themselves. It simply means acknowledging that we are not self-contained individuals; that we are all part of a larger community, and are therefore responsible for each other. It means building a fire instead of putting on a fur coat.

No matter how unseemly a person may be, we are responsible for him, and must do everything in our power to help him grow. We have a special responsibility to assist the incarcerated, for instance, giving them every possible opportunity to achieve and grow and rehabilitate.

Sometimes we will see the effect of our help, but often we will not; it doesn't matter. We may feel frustrated and helpless, as if we had been asked to move the entire ocean one spoonful at a time. But it is not only the result that counts; it is your effort, and the sincerity behind the effort, that fulfills your innate need to be responsible. And ultimately, every effort does bear fruit.

WHAT DOES RESPONSIBILITY MEAN IN TODAY'S WORLD?

We are all greatly indebted—to the families who raise us, to the friends who guide us, to the educators who teach us, and to the nations that protect us. It is obvious that we must repay these debts by doing whatever we can to better society. Just think for a moment how different your life would be if no one had exercised the responsibility to care for and educate you.

Never before has there been such an urgent need to reach out, to listen for the cries of those in need. This is a critical generation, with so many people lacking direction in their lives and their relationships. And yet many of us are tempted to say, "How can I possibly think about someone else's problems when I have so many of my own?"

⌘

One night, when a rabbi was deeply engrossed in his studies, his youngest child fell out of his cradle. Even though the rabbi was only in the next room, he heard nothing. But the rabbi's father, who was also studying in his room upstairs, heard the baby crying. He came downstairs, put the baby back in the cradle, and rocked him to sleep. The rabbi remained oblivious throughout it all.

Later, the older man admonished his son: "No matter how lofty your pursuits, you must never fail to hear the cry of a child."

One must never doubt one's ability to help. "What can I *really* accomplish?" we ask ourselves. "Who will listen to *me*?" Every person without exception has been given the abilities to illuminate his or her corner of the world.

As history continues to show us, humanity is a continuum—something that happens in the farthest corner of the planet will eventually affect your life. In earlier generations, we were far more isolated, and may have been able to insulate ourselves and our communities. But that is plainly no longer the case. We interact with each other at every turn, at every level; personal standards influence universal ones, and vice versa.

We cannot afford to remain on the defensive, waiting for a crisis.

Ignorance and aimlessness are not neutral; they are active, destructive forces. Each one of us today must take responsibility for his fellow man. In order to help each other, of course, we must first help ourselves by being properly educated and prepared. But in times of great need, it would be foolish and selfish to wait until we reach a state of total personal perfection before reaching out to help.

You must not fear leaving your comfortable environment for a world that sometimes seems hostile, for as in many matters, the challenge of a new situation draws out a level of determination you never knew you had. After all, your very life originates from G-d uprooting your soul from its comfortable spiritual environment and transplanting it to a foreign, material world.

There is but one condition for fulfilling your responsibilities—that you are connected to a divine and absolute code of ethics and morality. If you depend on your own subjective views, and let your own personality dictate your actions, you may do more harm than good to yourself and to others.

Besides our responsibility to ourselves and our fellow humans, we are also responsible for the environment around us. The human being is the jewel of creation, but every single thing in our physical world—animal, mineral, and vegetable—has also been charged with divine energy and purpose, and must be treated accordingly. The environment is sacred and no man has a right to destroy it; we are invited to take advantage of its elements only as they relate to our mission on earth. So yes, we raise animals and vegetables for sustenance, we cut down forests to build houses and schools, and we extract fossil fuel from the earth to warm ourselves. But unless we are using the environment responsibly, for wholly productive purposes and higher ends, we must protect it as vigilantly as we protect ourselves.

We all live in the same world. If one person is in pain, we should all feel it; if one person succeeds, we should all benefit. Each of us has been given the choice to see this underlying unity or to look the other way and worry only about himself, even at the expense of others. Responsibility is one of the greatest gifts G-d gave us—

the gift of being active participants in the dynamic unfolding of the world's destiny. We must never ignore this gift. In the delicate balance in which the fate of the world hangs, it may be one deed of merit that tips the scale.

No matter how much his family protested that he needed to rest, an elderly scholar refused to shorten his schedule of study and prayer, which lasted twenty-one hours each day. "But why can't you rest even one more hour?" they asked him. "Surely, twenty hours of study is enough!"

"The people of the world are like links in a chain," he explained. "If I were to take off even one hour, it would have an effect on a person in some other country who prays or studies only one hour a day, and he might stop even that hour. And another person who prays only once a week might also stop. And another person who prays but once a year might also stop. So, yes, my one hour may not seem like much, but consider how it might affect these others!"

You can have a positive effect on every person you meet, to an extent far beyond your scope of vision. You might even be saving a life, and each life is an entire world.[2] And because responsibility is one of the most fundamental human needs, fulfilling your responsibilities means saving *your* life as well. Wherever you go, whomever you meet, look for an opportunity to help, to inspire, to lend support.

In this complicated and troubling world, we must always remember to take responsibility for ourselves, each other, and our environment. For besides G-d, we are all that we have. Remember: "If I am not for myself, who is for me? And if I am only for myself, what am I? And if not now, when?"

In 1969, the Rebbe delivered a talk addressing the crisis in the Crown Heights neighborhood of Brooklyn and in other neighborhoods, which were being torn apart by riots, tension, and the flight of many longtime residents. "People living in a neighborhood are responsible for one another," he said, "and cannot just run away, leaving at risk those who cannot afford to move, and harming the local merchants. While it may seem difficult at the moment, by staying together, we will bolster the community, and it will become an example for other communities." The Rebbe encouraged investing in the neighborhood and helped establish schools and community centers. He even suggested that weddings and other celebrations should always take place in the neighborhood—not only to help the economy, but so that the joy of the occasion would inspire the community. "If we remember our responsibility to one another, G-d will bless each of us and the entire community with prosperity and success."

19

GOVERNMENT
E Pluribus Unum:
Out of Many, One

Seek the welfare of the city . . . and pray to G-d for it, for in its
peace, you shall have peace.
—Jeremiah 29:7

The role of government is to balance communal and individual
good. This is only possible when society is governed by the
principles of morality and justice, law and order, under one G-d.
—The Rebbe

---

*I*n 1978, the Rebbe called upon the governments of the world to
provide "an education that places greater emphasis on the promo-
tion of fundamental human rights and obligations of justice and
morality." Congress ultimately designated the Rebbe's birthday
"Education Day U.S.A.," and he received letters of appreciation
from Presidents Carter, Reagan, Bush, and Clinton. In 1990,
George Bush wrote to the Rebbe: "Our nation's moral tradition—
indeed, the development of all Western civilization—has been deeply
influenced by the laws and teachings contained in the Bible. It was

a Biblical view of man, one affirming the dignity and worth of the human person made in the image of the Creator, that inspired the principles upon which the United States is founded."

WHAT IS THE ROLE OF GOVERNMENT?

Over the centuries, the human race has experimented with many forms of government. Imperialist monarchies and despotism once ruled the world, giving way to such political and economic extremes as fascism and democracy, Marxism and capitalism. The twentieth century has been a particularly turbulent one. After two world wars and the rise—and unexpected fall—of communism, we now have the luxury of hindsight to assess and learn from these various systems.

In each case, mankind continues to be plagued by the same basic conflict: individual rights versus the greater good of the community. The role of government is to strike a balance between the two, and yet no political system has been able to perfect this balance.

Human beings are naturally diverse in their beliefs and ambitions. Such differences often produce conflict between individuals and throughout society. Suppressing this diversity would infringe on individual liberties, and is therefore unacceptable; and yet allowing every person unbridled freedom is also unacceptable, for what would prevent one person's interests from harming another person or society?

Most governments have reacted to this paradox by opting for one extreme or the other. Totalitarianism may argue for the good of the whole at the expense of the individual; it maintains that the selfish needs of the individual will ultimately fragment a nation and undermine the common good. Ironically, it is under such regimes that individuals—that is, dictators—assume unprecedented powers. We need no reminder of the untold misery that this form of government, in most cases, has caused the human race.

Democracy, on the other hand, nurtures the very individualism that totalitarianism squelches; it declares that all men were created equal and possess the right to pursue their beliefs without hindrance. Democracy contends that it is better to have motivated free people and risk excessive self-interest than to destroy their drive by suppressing individualism for the common good.

Democracy would appear to be a far better form of government than totalitarianism. But democracy contains an inherent flaw, in that its essential motivating factor is self-interest. Over time, the core values of a community can begin to crumble under the accumulated weight of millions of individual desires and needs. Ultimately, these conflicting interests can erode a society's unified drive for meaningful achievement. Several democracies have struggled mightily with this dilemma, perhaps none more than the United States, the largest democracy in the history of the world. Consider the current battle in dozens of American cities where individuals' freedom of expression has come in conflict with community standards of morality.

Since people are bound to have vastly different beliefs, who should define the standards of morality and justice that must rule *all* the people? At what point does a government intervene to keep an individual from harming himself or others? How do we avoid the abuse of power by government leaders?

The only government that can successfully balance individual and societal needs is a righteous government built on faith in G-d. The underlying flaw of all governments, whether fascistic or democratic, is that they are based on *human* rules. Any government built solely on human judgment is bound to be subject to the prejudice, subjectivity, and arbitrariness of individual humans or groups. But G-d, who created all people equal, also gave them a system of absolute morality and justice.

A society that yearns to be righteous must be built on such ethical values. The very foundation of civilization rests upon the basic principles known as the Seven Noahide Laws given at Sinai:[1]

1. Belief in G-d
2. Respect for and praise of G-d
3. Respect for human life
4. Respect for the family
5. Respect for others' rights and property
6. Creation of a judicial system
7. Respect for all creatures

Without these laws as a bedrock of government, a society will either have despotism, where individuals' lives are compromised and possibly abused, or anarchy, where every person pursues his or her own needs without regard for the law.

So how is it possible to balance individual freedom with the good of society? By looking beyond self-interest and recognizing that we are all part of the same family and community; by recognizing that we are all bound by the same divine laws and entrusted with the same mission in life—to civilize the world in a meaningful and G-dly way.

WHICH COMES FIRST: THE INDIVIDUAL OR SOCIETY?

We are seeing more and more examples of conflict between individual freedom and the needs of society—the question of whether one person should be allowed to help another take his or her own life, for example, or whether the government should alert a community as to the whereabouts of a released prisoner.

Such issues are complicated, and must be resolved case by case. Under any circumstances, we must respect the individual's rights, for the sanctity of a community is built on the sanctity of each individual life; abridging one person's right, therefore, is an attack on the entire community. On the other hand, there are times when one person's self-interest, though it may fall within the boundaries of the law, threatens an entire community.

The resolution of such conflicts depends on an objective view built on divine moral principles. The key lies in recognizing that individuality is *not* an enemy of community and that community is not an enemy of individuality. Consider the human body, "a world in miniature."[2] Every organ, while it participates in any number of shared duties, also has its specific individual functions. What would happen if a particular organ abruptly surrendered its individual functions and applied itself solely toward the communal good of the body? Ultimately, this would be disastrous for both the organ and the organism, for the body is able to function only by integrating *separate* components that perform *individual* tasks.

The same could be said for an individual within a society, a minority group within a nation, or one nation within the community of nations. Freedom of expression, for example, is vital for a healthy and vibrant society, motivating individuals to invest and contribute in a manner that will ultimately benefit the entire community.

A civilized nation needs to be built on a foundation of morality and ethics that is timeless and unconditional. At the same time, a nation's survival is dependent on its constant progress and growth. Just as an individual must balance his or her needs with the good of the community, any one nation must balance its needs with the community of nations.

Since all nations today are part of the same "global village," they are all responsible for one another, and the neglect of one nation ultimately affects all the others. Every nation must be helped, and every nation must be ready to help. It is irresponsible to look the other way when a nation is in need.

WHAT STEPS SHOULD GOVERNMENT TAKE TO ENSURE THE WELFARE OF ITS CITIZENS?

The key, therefore, to balancing individual and communal needs is education. For a government to be truly dedicated to the welfare of its citizens—their physical, emotional, and, above all, spiritual welfare—it must make education its primary objective without which all the other points are moot. A government and its leaders not only must teach citizens how to pursue rational solutions to complex problems but must teach them *how to live*. It must educate them that human conduct must follow the divine laws given to us all by G-d. This is the only guarantee that individual rights will be preserved without compromising the common good.

The United States epitomizes these principles. This is a country, after all, whose founders declared it "one nation under G-d." Sessions of Congress are opened with a religious invocation; the Bible is used to swear in elected officials, and chaplains are appointed in the armed forces. Even this nation's currency—the very icon of materialism—declares "In G-d We Trust."

The majority of this country's early settlers were religious refugees who firmly believed in G-d and the Bible, and were determined to protect their right to do so. This was not an abstract belief in a supreme being who dwelt somewhere in heaven; it was a belief that permeated every aspect of their lives, particularly the education of their children. They understood and appreciated this newfound religious freedom.

These core beliefs are the secret of the nation's endurance. Having built itself on a firm and permanent foundation, the United States has become the most powerful of nations, in a unique position to positively influence every inhabitant on the face of the earth.

And yet we are currently witnessing a sad phenomenon. The spirit of the Constitution has been misinterpreted, with some parties taking "religious freedom" to mean freedom *from* religion. Even a nondenominational "moment of silence" in schools has been opposed. When the founding fathers included "freedom of religion" in the Bill of Rights, they were ensuring the freedom of every person to worship G-d according to his or her own conscience; there can be no doubt that the Constitution was meant to *preserve* religious freedom, not to wean the nation away from G-d.

The principle of separation of church and state should not be misconstrued as a denial of G-d and religion. This separation is necessary so that government cannot impose any *one* religion on all its citizens, but such vigilance must not be carried out at the expense of belief in G-d, which is shared by all denominations.

The United States is now faced with countless social disorders, many of which stem from the lack of belief in and responsibility to G-d and a corresponding lapse in respect for the divine laws of morality. Shouldn't the Constitution be interpreted in a way that *addresses* this national crisis instead of avoiding it?

The only way to ensure that people adhere to a moral order is to instill in them a permanent sense of values. Punishing a person after he has committed a crime, for instance, is attacking not the cause of the problem but its symptom. Clearly, a child who is brought up without fear and respect for G-d in his heart will have no fear or respect for any authority—his parents, his teachers, law enforcement officers. He must learn to accept the concept of a divine moral code that we all must obey. He must realize that the laws of man are rooted in something far more eternal: the Ten Commandments.

We must use every opportunity to cultivate this awareness. The moment of silence at the beginning of each school day is a good example. By no means is this a violation of the separation of church and state, for the child can use the moment however he or she wishes. But by encouraging this moment, we are telling the child that believing in a higher being is fundamental to all education, that knowledge per se is worthless without knowing how to use it for the good of society at large.

After all, there is another motto on U.S. currency besides "In G-d We Trust"; it is "E Pluribus Unum," or "Out of many, one." We must never allow our government to forget that every community is inherently made up of many individuals, and each individual should be encouraged to participate and contribute his individual strengths toward the greater good of the united community.

WHERE IS OUR GOVERNMENT HEADED?

We are now at a point in history where individual rights are largely recognized across the globe, the same globe that until just a few centuries ago was ruled exclusively by tyrants and kings.

Such individual freedom poses its own dilemma. Without the proper guidance, we can become slaves to our own selfish desires, which can lead to discord and, ultimately, anarchy. So the challenge is to harness this freedom, to channel it for good and righteous purposes.

The United States plays a key role in this effort. More than ever before, the civilized world looks to this country as a true superpower whose strength is derived from a commitment to a moral code that invites the many to become one, that cherishes and supports the poor and the weak as much as the rich and the strong. The United States must continue to use its influence to inspire other nations in the areas of education and human rights; if there is one world conscience, America must be the country that voices it. Now is not the time to underestimate this sacred duty.

The United States and all nations must recognize the unprecedented times we are living in. Thanks to technology, the world is more united than ever. And yet, because this nation and many others have deviated from the divine laws that brought us to this point, we are experiencing terrible conflict. The leaders of the world must encourage their constituents to live by G-d's divine laws, which will enable them to use their personal freedom to usher in a true unity between man and man, community and community, nation and nation. Leaders of all communities, cities, states, and countries must come out with a call to all their citizens to follow the universal moral code of the Seven Noahide Laws. They must teach us to share our wealth, our time, and our spirit. By demonstrating responsible and virtuous behavior, by showing themselves to be selfless and genuine, and above all, by accepting the higher authority of G-d in our lives, our leaders can set an example that will help foster love and care between all citizens.

The time has truly come when all nations "shall beat their swords into plowshares and their spears into pruning hooks."[3] The government of every nation must now prepare to do everything possible to finally bring peace to the entire world.

In 1975, on the twenty-fifth anniversary of the death of his father-in-law, the Rebbe recalled how grateful his father-in-law had been to the United States government, which helped save his life on two occasions: in 1927, when the ruthless Russian regime, determined to end his religious activities, had sentenced him to death; and in 1940, when he was saved from the Holocaust. "We are confident that the American tradition of active concern for religious freedom, and for those who are oppressed on racial or other grounds, will be zealously continued," the Rebbe said. "Certainly, those Americans who have been elected to public office will consider it their privilege and duty to show what America and Americans stand for. To be sure, such action is not always universally popular, but do not all deeds of virtue and duty require great courage?"

20

LEADERSHIP
The Art of Selflessness

The purpose and intent [of a true leader] shall be to elevate mankind's faith, and to fill the world with justice.
—Maimonides, Laws of Kings 4:10

Everyone must be a leader.
—The Rebbe

After the passing of his father-in-law, the previous Rebbe, in 1950, the Rebbe was initially reluctant to lead the Lubavitch movement, saying that one needed to have "special strengths" for such a task. A year later, on the first anniversary of his father-in-law's death, he finally accepted and formally assumed leadership.

One of the rare occasions on which he discussed his role as leader was during a celebration of his eighty-third birthday in 1985. "Immodesty is one of the most destructive attributes in human nature," he said. "It is the root of all inappropriate behavior. How can we then allow people to gather here today in honor of one individual?"

The Rebbe explained that the gathering was not meant to honor an individual, but an entire movement toward righteousness. "Therefore, it isn't relevant which individual heads the movement—only the movement itself," he continued. "The success of the movement is dependent on the unity of all its followers, a unity that transcends their differences. However, in order to unite people who are diverse by nature, there needs to be one leader who is a servant to the cause, whose sole role it is to teach and inspire and perpetuate the activities of the movement."

DO WE REALLY NEED LEADERS?

At some point in our lives, we have all had a relationship with someone—a parent, a teacher, or an employer perhaps—who greatly changed the way we looked at life and the world. Someone who had high standards and truly stood for something. Someone who inspired and motivated us. Someone who taught us to set goals and instilled the confidence and spirit to achieve them. Such a person is a true leader.

Today, we are surrounded by people we may call leaders—in government, in business, in education, in the arts. But we are suffering from a scarcity of genuine leadership. Where are these people really leading us, and why?

After witnessing so much deceit and such frequent abuse of power, many people have ceased trusting their leaders. Still, no matter how cynical we may grow, we resign ourselves to the fact that we need someone to keep our various houses in order. Since we are so preoccupied with our own lives, we are willing to elect or appoint officials to manage the affairs of the land.

But is a leader merely a manager? What should we expect from our leaders? And do we really need leaders in the first place?

Yes, we do need leaders. On our own, we may lack the vision, direction, and strength to reach our goals. We all begin our lives in need of guidance—even the most precocious child could not possibly be expected to make certain crucial decisions. Once we become adults, with the capacity to reason for ourselves, most of us are so overwhelmed by the pressures of daily survival that we rarely find the time and energy to focus on life's larger issues. And when we do, our emotions and inherent subjectivity limit our vision and constrict our movement. As the sages write, "A prisoner cannot release himself."[1]

A leader provides a new perspective, inspiring us to expand our narrow field of vision. When we are preoccupied with our self-interests—be they petty or great—a leader sends out a wake-up call, alerting us to seek the true priorities in life.

A sense of urgency is just as important in a leader as a sense of vision. Leadership today is sorely lacking the quality of urgency. Many of our leaders are effective managers, and some are even inspirational; we have CEOs who can direct thousands of employees toward a single objective, and politicians whose rhetoric inspires millions of citizens to support them.

What these leaders *don't* provide is simple—and essential: a vision of life itself. Genuine leadership must give people a long-term vision that imbues their lives with meaning; it must point them in a new direction and show how their every action is an indispensable part of a purposeful whole. It is not enough for our leaders to teach us to be productive or efficient; they need to inspire us to change or improve the world in a productive, meaningful way. And this creates a compelling sense of urgency: to fulfill this vision of life.

WHAT MAKES A TRUE LEADER?

With so many people purporting to be leaders these days, how do we recognize a *true* leader? To answer that question, we must step back and ask: What is it that a leader is really trying to accomplish?

A true leader wants nothing more than to give people pride, to make people stand on their own, as leaders in their own right. Instead of trying to blind us with his or her brilliance, a true leader reflects our own light back to us, so that we may see ourselves anew.

Moses was the quintessential leader. We read in Exodus that he was a shepherd[2]—a rather modest beginning for the man who would speak to G-d. He kept watch as thousands of sheep wandered the fields. Moses noticed that one sheep was missing and went off to look for it, finding it at a distant brook. He waited until the sheep had finished drinking, then he lifted it onto his shoulders and carried it back to the flock.[3]

When G-d saw this, he realized that Moses was a man of reason, empathy, and selfless devotion, a man truly worthy to lead His people. After all, no one was watching Moses; he could easily have thought to himself, Why be concerned with one sheep when there are thousands?

In our secular society, we tend to think of a leader as a person who is well connected, who is powerful or charismatic or wealthy. We judge our leaders by what they *have*. But a true leader should be judged by what he has *not*—ego, arrogance, and self-interest. A true leader sees his work as a selfless service toward a higher purpose. As the sages say, "Leadership is not power and dominance; it is servitude."[4] This does not mean that a leader is weak; he derives great strength from his dedication to a purpose that is greater than himself.

Each generation has its Moses, a leader who inspires absolute trust, who is totally dedicated to fulfilling his unique role. He understands and appreciates each person's role in perfecting this world, and guides him or her accordingly. He rises above any individual perspective to take a global view, seeing how each person and issue fits into the entire scheme of the contemporary world.

A true leader shakes people from their reverie and tells them, "No, you *don't* need to live a life of desperation and confusion. Yes, you *do* have the ability to find meaning in your life, and the unique skills to fulfill that meaning. You are an important link in a chain of generations past; you have a legacy worth preserving and a future worth fighting for."

A true leader shows us that our world is indeed heading somewhere and that we control its movement. That we need not be at the mercy of personal prejudices or the prevailing political wind.

That none of us is subservient to history or nature—that we *are* history and nature. That we can rid the world of war and hate and ignorance, and obliterate the borders separating race from race, rich from poor.

Centuries ago, kings and queens ruled the world, but we are today far removed from the very concept of absolute leadership. Indeed, leadership would seem to contradict our democratic tradition, which has taught us not to subordinate our lives to another human being. But we cannot afford to be so literal-minded. If the ideals of democracy were followed to the extreme, if the public demanded a referendum for even the smallest piece of legislation, society could not function. So our current political makeup is a pragmatic and acceptable compromise, allowing individuals a role in choosing their leaders while holding the leaders responsible to society.

Still, many people have lost faith in contemporary leaders. The solution is not to resign yourself to this sad state of affairs, but to search for and demand a leader of sterling character. The ultimate goal should be to have all the benefits of democracy *and* the benefits of a visionary leader.

It is important, especially today, to distinguish between leadership and demagoguery. A demagogue may inspire people, but his motives are impure and his expectations unrealistic. It is wise to be a bit skeptical when assessing a leader: Is he truly devoted to his mission or just seeking glory? Is he truly interested in the welfare of others or simply building a flock for his own aggrandizement?

A true leader does not seek followers; he wants to teach others how to be leaders. He does not want control; he wants the truth. He does not impose his leadership on others, nor does he take away anyone's autonomy. He inspires by love, not coercion. When it comes time to take credit, he makes himself invisible; but he is the first to arrive at the time of need, and he will never shrink away in fear. He is so passionate about your welfare that when you consult him for guidance, it is like coming face to face with *yourself* for the first time.

After several days of receiving visitors who were seeking his advice, a revered rabbi suddenly locked his door. The hundreds of people who were still waiting outside assumed that he was exhausted and needed to rest. But the rabbi's secretary emerged visibly upset, his eyes red from tears. Several people went to listen at the rabbi's door, and they heard him weeping loudly and praying, reciting chapters from Psalms with extreme urgency. They were very much concerned for his well-being.

It was two days before the rabbi resumed seeing visitors. Finally, he revealed the source of his despair. "When someone comes to me for guidance," he explained, "he reveals to me the inner maladies of his soul. To help him, I must be able to relate to his problem; I must find a reflection of the same failing within myself, and strive to correct it. Two days ago, someone came to me with a problem. I was horrified to hear of the depths to which he had fallen. Try as I might, I could not find within myself anything resembling what he had told me. But this man had come to me, so I knew that there had to be something inside me, however subtle, that could relate to his situation. I finally realized that in some form such a blemish must be embedded deep within me, beyond my conscious reach. The thought shook me to the very core of my being, and moved me to repent and return to G-d from the depths of my heart."

A true leader must be a living example of his teachings. When we see that a leader's personal life embodies his philosophy, we too are inspired to learn and practice that philosophy. Conversely, if we see that a leader does not live by his own words, we cannot trust him.

It is useless for a leader to be a visionary in the abstract; he must be a successful communicator whose vision can be translated into specific, applicable principles—not knowledge for the sake of knowledge, but knowledge that can actually help improve the world.

So a leader must be many things—selfless, devoted, visionary, courageous, and, above all, humble. When G-d chose Moses to lead His people out of bondage in Egypt, Moses replied, "Who am I, that I should go unto Pharaoh?"[5] Indeed, "Moses was humbler than any man on the face of the Earth."[6]

We must recognize the characteristics of a leader—not only so we can weed out the demagogues, but so we can freely embrace a true leader when he does emerge. When people sincerely believe in a leader, they can rise above their petty self-concerns. They become eager to accept his direction and input, and are inspired to accomplish far more than they could have on their own.

By recognizing the characteristics of a true leader, we set a standard for our leaders and, more important, for ourselves. Setting your sights on the summit, even when you have yet to arrive there, is the surest way of completing the journey.

HOW CAN EACH OF US BECOME A LEADER?

It is true that not everyone can be a leader like Moses. But every person, no matter how uneducated or poor, has something to teach the wisest and richest among us. No one is incapable of being a leader in some way, and no one is exempt from the responsibility.

You may think that you were not a "born leader." But why, then, were you created? Each of us has been given unique strengths and abilities; we have the choice to use them selfishly or to share them with others.

Every generation places particular demands on its leaders, and the leadership of every generation is linked to its predecessors. We have just as much to learn from Moses as from the leaders of the twentieth century; although the future may be vast, we can see a great distance when we stand on the shoulders of giants.

Our current generation is so hungry for meaning and direction, for spiritual nourishment, that each of us must serve as a leader. Whatever you have learned, whatever you have been touched by, you must share it with others. You cannot waste time wondering if you are truly equipped to help your fellow man. When someone is drowning, you don't take a life-saving course—you jump in the water and save a life!

So examine the areas in your life where people look to you as a leader—within your family, in your class at school, at work or at play. Ask yourself: Are you doing everything you can to influence them positively? Are you using all your abilities to inspire them intellectually, emotionally, and spiritually? Are you helping them live up to their true potential, so they can become leaders in their own right?

One leader creates another and another, ad infinitum, just as one candle's flame lights another and another, until the once-impenetrable darkness has turned to brilliant light.

❦

In 1951, in the first talk he gave upon assuming leadership of the Lubavitch movement, the Rebbe addressed the very issue of his leadership: "Our faith demands that everyone must do good on his own, and not depend on his Rebbe. Don't deceive yourselves into thinking that I will lead and you will engage only in singing songs and toasting 'L'chaim' and that that will be enough. Each of you has your own load, your own battle. I do not decline from helping, but nothing—even heaven—can replace personal responsibility."

21

WOMEN AND MEN
Uniting Forces

Man and woman are like two fires. When they
have G-d between them, they unite; when they don't,
they consume each other.
—Talmud, Sotah 17a

After thousands of years of male dominance, we now stand at the
beginning of the feminine era, when women will rise to their
true prominence, and the entire world will recognize
the harmony between man and woman.
—The Rebbe

The Rebbe, in anticipation of the modern feminist movement, developed a comprehensive approach for defining the responsibility of women today. In 1952–53, he founded the Lubavitch Women's Organization, which encouraged and celebrated the feminine voice. Efforts included the establishment of classes, workshops, publications, and social programs. Several times a year, the Rebbe would speak exclusively to the women of the community, encouraging them to take an active role in education and the perpetuation of higher values. Such pursuits were more than the women's inalienable rights, he *believed—they were the women's duty. And in 1975, the Rebbe called for a campaign encouraging Jewish women and girls to light Shabbos candles every Friday afternoon. He taught that the prevalent spiritual darkness must be countered with as much light as possible. "And imagine how much light is added to the world every Friday," he said, "when women and girls worldwide light these millions of candles."*

Are Women and Men Equal?

One of the most trenchant and volatile issues of our time is how men and women relate to one another. After many years of male-dominated hierarchies, women are determined to be treated fairly and equally in the workplace, in the classroom, in government, and within the family. Indeed, in all of life.

Will the struggle ever end or are men and women destined for perpetual conflict? What are the roots of this strife? And most important, what are the unique roles of man and woman?

These questions are compelling, for how we define ourselves as men and women greatly determines who we are and how we live our lives. How we identify with our gender lies at the very core of a person's essence.

Contemporary society is just beginning to delve into the true distinctions between men and women. Besides the obvious physiological differences, there are also differences in the way men and women think, speak, and behave. Some of this is due to social conditioning, but some can also be traced to the inherent characteristics of each gender.

Great is the challenge today for men and women to be internally honest about their relationship with their particular gender. Increasingly, the boundary has been obfuscated. Ostensibly, men and women are alike. But are they? There is a mass identity crisis abrew:

Each gender, in an earnest attempt for equality, has sacrificed its own uniqueness. In school, at work, and in the community, men and women have become nearly fully integrated; as a result, questions abound about their similarities and differences. Trying to conform to society and especially the work marketplace, men and women often behave in ways that suppress their natures. In order to protect themselves, they may be overaggressive; in order to please everyone, they may be unduly passive.

Our perception of gender roles has been shaped and distorted by many years of social programming, manipulation, and abuse. Many men have used their strength to dominate women and abuse their positions of authority. And women, eager to make their own mark on society, have grown increasingly frustrated. In a backlash effort, some women have become equally aggressive in asserting themselves.

How can we untangle this mess and reveal the true man and true woman that lie beneath the distortions? First we need to understand how and why G-d created man and woman.

The question many people ask is this: Did G-d create man and woman as equals? This is the equivalent of asking whether an engineer built two parts of a machine equally—the parts may be utterly different from one another, but without either one, the machine would either cease to function or malfunction. As the sages state, "G-d did not create anything in vain."[1] So we must recognize that man and woman were created by design as two equal beings, yet each with a distinct role to play toward one unified goal.

In order to understand the essential nature of man and woman, we must put aside limited human subjectivity and peer through G-d's eyes. All human beings, men and women, were created for the same purpose—to fuse body and soul in order to make themselves and their world a better and holier place. In their service to G-d, there is absolutely no distinction between a man and a woman; the difference lies only in the manner in which their service manifests itself.

Men and women have been given different tools with which to fulfill their common goal. Indeed, their physiological, emotional, and psychological differences are a result of their divergent spiritual mandates as instructed by G-d. Were each of us destined to fulfill exactly the same role in life, there would be no need for so many forms of expression.

G-d created the human race as one entity and then divided them into two—"a single individual with two faces."[2] Just as each person is composed of two elements, the body and soul, which we must learn to fully integrate, man and woman are the two elements of humankind.

The unity between man and woman is most profoundly experienced in the framework of marriage, through which both a man and a woman, each in his or her own way, can achieve the fullest potential for growth by learning to transcend their own individuality. Man and woman are drawn to each other because they each yearn to connect with their other half, the partner with whom they were originally joined before they were divided into two. Paradoxically, through the merging of one's self with another, a person has the capacity to reach his or her most personal essence, his or her real individuality.

WHAT ARE THE ROLES OF MAN AND WOMAN?

In order to appreciate the harmony between men and women, we must appreciate their sameness in serving G-d. When men and women humbly recognize and join in their shared purpose, with an understanding that through their sameness, self-actualization of the most personal form will follow, they can develop mutual respect for one another—as *true* equals. When they serve only their own needs, there is room for discord between them.

But the question remains: Why did G-d need to create man *and* woman, and what is the particular role of each?

Man and woman represent two forms of divine energy; they are the male and female elements of a single soul. Indeed, every aspect of the entire universe is distinguished by these two dimensions.

G-d is neither masculine nor feminine, but has two forms of emanation: the masculine form, which is more aggressive, and the feminine form, which is more subtle. For a human being to lead a total life, he or she must have both forms of energy: the power of expression and the power of deliberation; the power of strength and the power of subtlety; the power of giving and the power of receiving. And, ideally, these energies are merged seamlessly.

Man and woman encompass both dimensions. In general, though—and in their most spiritually pure form, undistorted by social and cultural pressures—man and woman primarily embody one of these two energies.

Men are physically stronger. By nature, a man is often more aggressive and externally oriented. In dramatic contrast, a woman often embodies the ideal of inner dignity. Society at times mistakes such subtlety and calls it weakness; in truth, it is more formidable than the most aggressive physical force. True human dignity does not holler; it speaks in a strong, steady voice; it resonates from within. The nature of a woman is subtle, not weak. And the nature of a man is aggressive, not brutish.

Feminine energy is who you are and masculine energy is what you do. For man and woman to be complete, then, they must each possess both energies. One's noblest values or ideas become meaningless unless they are actualized. So, too, action without the dictate of an inner voice of truth is also meaningless.

In general, the man's primary role is to utilize his aggressive masculine energy to refine the material world, while the woman's primary role is to utilize her subtle feminine energy to reveal the innate G-dliness in all that exists.

The man "goes out" in search of G-dliness; the woman absorbs G-dliness. The man provides the seed to create life; the woman bears life. The man teaches his children how to live; the woman *is* life. The man gives love; the woman *is* love.

This is not to say that only man can refine the outside world or that only woman can reveal innate goodness. Indeed, experience has proved that in "conquering" and creating change in the world, the feminine approach can often be more effective than the masculine approach, which often hinges on confrontation. So the man must access his sensitivity and subtlety, while a woman must access her assertion when necessary.

The answer is not for men and women to try to be alike—nor, for that matter, for men to be like other men and women like other women. All men and women must be *themselves*, realizing that G-d has given to each of us unique abilities with which to pursue our goals, and that our primary responsibility is to take full advantage of these abilities.

G-d asks of man to understand himself in context of his maleness, which incorporates his "feminine self," and asks of woman to understand herself in context of her femininity, which incorporates her "male self." And, above all, we are ultimately each responsible, as a freestanding human being, to G-d and society.

In order to unite forces in a wholesome and constructive fashion, men and women must first learn to appreciate their true selves and their true differences. This includes a certain modesty and mutual respect in their manner of dress, conduct, and communication, as well as recognizing that a physical union between man and woman is possible only within the divine union of marriage. It is no coincidence that a good marriage also requires both the feminine and masculine dimensions, so that a couple cooperates to build a strong union while having the introspective faith to face life's inevitable vicissitudes.

ᏫᎻᏫ

A husband and wife came to a rabbi with a disagreement. The husband argued that a woman is greater than a man for her capacity to carry out so many responsibilities at home and at work, for enduring the pain of childbirth, for dealing patiently with her children, and—most of all— for tolerating her husband. His wife argued that a man is greater than a woman, for besides having to work hard to provide for his family and serve as their protector, he must tolerate his wife's frequent complaints and requests, even after a long day of work.

"You are both right!" replied the rabbi. "The wife of such a righteous husband is definitely righteous herself, and the husband of such a blessed wife is clearly blessed himself."

WHAT ARE THE FORCES DIVIDING MEN AND WOMEN TODAY?

It is a great challenge to achieve the proper blend of masculine and feminine energy. We live in a time when the material world supersedes the world of the sublime in many people's eyes. When ego and power prevail, style takes precedence over substance, form over spirit; the true and healthy balance between man and woman becomes distorted. Their distinct energies, rather than being integrated toward a unified goal, become amplified and serve only to separate them.

When we place more emphasis on the material than the spiritual, the masculine and feminine energies begin to diverge, and the male aggressive energy is inclined to dominate. When we value external power and control over the hearth and family, when we value aggressive business tactics over sensitivity and wisdom, we are placing a higher premium on a man, or rather, on the parts of the man that find this form of expression natural and comfortable. We thus create an environment where masculine energy dominates and is valued most.

Inevitably, both man and woman suffer from this distortion of priorities, but it is women who feel its brunt, for a woman's primary strengths lie in the sublime and the sensitive. Some dismiss or underestimate these strengths, misinterpreting them as vulnerability; this distortion, and men's subsequent abuse of the distortion, is the most compelling reason for today's feminism. And, indeed, it is warranted.

Though feminism rightfully calls for the stop of male domination, and for equal rights for women, it is vital to get to the root of this distortion—that our focus in life, as man *or* woman, must not be to satisfy our own ego or needs, but to serve G-d.

True women's liberation does not mean seeking equality within a masculine world; it means liberating the divine feminine aspects of a woman's personality and using them for the benefit of all humankind. Women need to clamor for their rights because the world insists on it for its cosmic well-being.

But many women, just as many men, have succumbed to the growth of materialistic values at the expense of spiritual ones. The women's movement has accomplished much tangible good, yet it has stunted its own potential by failing to address the root problem. The feminist fight for equality and validation on masculine terms ultimately fuels the power struggle between men and women. Instead of using their distinctive traits toward a united goal, they often simply fight for domination, fostering deep resentment.

The only healthy response to such a standoff is to reintroduce spiritual values into our lives—to reintroduce humility, to learn to recognize and appreciate the innate personalities of men and women, to see them as complementary halves of the same whole serving one G-d.

This is not to say we should abolish careers and forfeit the opportunities presented by contemporary life; rather, we must refocus our priorities. Instead of seeing the workplace as the core of your existence, instead of seeing money as the richest reward, you must see who you really are: a man or a woman created equally by G-d to use your particular strengths to improve the world. For some, this might mean considering a career that enables them to enhance their family life rather than compromise it. For others, it might mean taking time from work to pursue their own spiritual growth, community work, or humanitarian efforts. Some people may find themselves happier and more fulfilled dedicating themselves to educating their children at home, a trend that is intensifying of late.

As we become more spiritually oriented, our appreciation for the responsibilities of building a home life will continue to grow. After all, building a home—transforming this material world into a G-dly home—is the purpose for which we were created.

But whether you pursue a career outside the home, make your home your career, or fuse the two, it is vital to reassess your priorities in life, and concentrate on your role as a man or a woman under G-d.

Women, because they are more sensitive to spiritual energy, must spearhead this new awareness. This would be the ultimate feminist revolution—to topple the walls that separate spirit from matter, to lead the rebellion to a state in which there is a true harmony between the masculine and feminine energies.

For this to work, men and women must realize their respective equal roles and strive to complement each other in their shared struggle to improve life. In order to correct the abuse of male dominance, men must concentrate on using their dominant qualities for the good. They must use their strength to protect and preserve the feminine character, helping women realize their true potential in exposing G-dliness, which the world so desperately needs today.

We must use the "battle of the sexes" as a catalyst to reach back into our true selves. We must undo the distortion that has blurred the male and female roles as two unique divine energies, and come to understand how every woman and man must fulfill herself or himself. We must always remember that they are two halves of the same soul, and that they complement each other.

So ask yourself this question: Are you being true to your nature or are you contradicting it in order to succeed in the material world? Learn about what it means to be a man or a woman, about masculine and feminine energy. Learn to live up to your potential, to balance these energies to lead a productive and meaningful life—a G-dly life. And finally, learn to appreciate and respect your male or female counterpart.

After so many years of male dominance, we are standing at the threshold of a true feminine era. We are witnessing a return to higher values; we have recognized that materialism cannot make us happy, that an exclusively materialistic life and a meaningful life are in contradistinction to one another. We have seen a resurgence of feminine energy, of the power of the serene.

It is time now for the woman to rise to her true prominence, when the subtle power of the feminine energy is allowed to nourish the overt power of the masculine energy.[3] We have already proved that we can use our strength to slay the demons around us; let us now learn to nurture the G-dliness within.

A couple who was having communication problems came to see the Rebbe. The woman said that her husband was consumed with his work, and that when he finally found time to speak with her, he criticized her and ordered her around. The husband said that his wife had no respect for him and didn't listen to any of his suggestions.

"Why do you think your wife should listen to you?" the Rebbe asked.

"Because a woman must listen to her husband," he replied.

"But why should a woman listen to her husband?" the Rebbe asked.

"Because the man is the master of the house."

"No," said the Rebbe. "The first thing that you as a man must follow is the edict that 'a man should honor his wife more than he does himself.'[4] And then the righteous woman will have a husband she can respect and love. If the man does not fulfill his role, then it is the woman who must respectfully bring it to his attention."

22

SCIENCE AND
TECHNOLOGY

Discovering the Divine
Within Nature

*Everything G-d created in His world He created
to express His glory.*
—Ethics of the Fathers 6:11

*Technology taps the divine forces present in nature from
the moment of creation.*
—The Rebbe

In the early 1950s, a couple and their young daughter had a private audience with the Rebbe. After the wife and husband had consulted with him on various issues, the Rebbe turned to the six-year-old girl and asked if she had any questions. Her parents tried to quiet her as she began to speak, so as not to take up the Rebbe's valuable time. But the Rebbe encouraged her to go ahead. The little girl, with a concerned look on her face, asked the Rebbe whether he thought that atomic energy was good or bad. "In your kitchen at home, there is a knife," the Rebbe said. "Is the knife good or bad?" The little girl replied, "It depends what it is used for.

If it is used to cut food, then it is good. If it is used to hurt someone, then it is bad."

"That is a good and true answer," the Rebbe told her, *"and the same could be said for atomic energy or any other technology that man has developed."*

TECHNOLOGY: VICE OR VIRTUE?

We live in a highly scientific world. Virtually every moment of our day—whether we are at home, at work, or in transit—is affected by modern technology. The computer age and the information revolution have given all of us enormous power and the ability to reach virtually anyone anywhere, at any time. Yes, technology allows us to live more comfortably and work more efficiently, but do we understand how it makes our lives more meaningful?

As we begin to glimpse its far-reaching implications, the technological revolution can indeed overwhelm us. To truly appreciate and benefit from this revolution, we must first understand what it means to our personal and global destinies.

On its own, science is morally neutral; it attempts to give us an objective view of our physical universe and its natural forces, but it does not draw a conclusion as to how we should use these forces. It does not deal with good and evil or with questions of ethics. At its best, science acknowledges its own boundaries, recognizing that it is neither the basis nor the code for moral doctrine.

Technology, like all forces in our lives, can be used either constructively or destructively. Developments such as television, computers, and lasers and discoveries in nuclear energy, medicine, and biology—these are all instances of tapping and understanding G-dly forces that are manifested in nature. Man has been charged with tapping these resources to refine and civilize the world, to transform our material surroundings into a proper home for spirituality and G-dliness.

Remember, G-d did not create bread; He created the sun and land and water and seeds of grain. We must plant the seeds, harvest the wheat, grind it into flour, mix it with water, and bake it. Only then do we have bread to eat. Couldn't G-d have just as easily given us whole bread, already made? Of course, but we are partners in the universe; our lives are an expression of free will, not a predetermined script. It is up to each of us to either use the earth to make bread or let it lie fallow.

It is the same with all of technology. G-d has created powerful forces throughout nature for us to utilize. We can choose to ac-knowledge the hand inside the glove, understanding where the power truly comes from, and use these forces as tools to lead a more meaningful life. Or we can choose to be distracted by the glove, to see technology only as a means unto itself, using it for indulgent, selfish, perhaps even destructive purposes.

WHY IS IT IMPORTANT TO UNDERSTAND TECHNOLOGY?

As Maimonides wrote, "By contemplating G-d's grand creations, one comes to recognize G-d's great wisdom, which evokes deep love for G-d and a desire to bond with Him."[1] Much of the tech-nology discovered in this century, particularly in the area relating to the subatomic structure of matter, has given us a comprehension of the dynamic unity that bonds the entire universe and man.

Even for a person who doesn't understand how a microchip or an electromagnet works, the resulting technology is an obvious tes-tament to an unprecedented level of unity in our universe. Modern communications allow us to connect instantaneously with practically anyone around the world. Modern transportation enables us to reach places in just a few hours that only a hundred years ago might have been months away. Computers allow us to process billions of pieces of information in a few seconds, performing tasks that used to be utterly impossible.

Yes, all of this technology saves enormous amounts of time and energy and creates countless new business opportunities. But such advantages should only be considered by-products of technology, whose true purpose is to unite the world and make it a more fertile ground for a unified spiritual life. This is the answer to understanding the technological revolution and where it is taking us.

The sweeping technological changes that have taken place during the past several generations are in keeping with the prediction some two thousand years ago in the Zohar,[2] a classical text of mysticism, stating that in the year 1840, there would be an outburst of "lower wisdom," or advancements in understanding the physical universe, and an increase in "sublime wisdom," or spirituality, which would begin to usher true unity into the world, leading toward the final redemption.

The increase in both types of wisdom—wisdom of the mind and wisdom of the soul—has surely come to pass; where we have fallen short is in integrating these spheres of knowledge. Only by balancing the scientific with the spiritual can we transform the dream of an ideal future into a functional blueprint for society, for true communication can begin only when human minds and souls interact. With communication comes understanding; with understanding comes compassion; and with compassion comes a natural movement toward universalism.

So the current technological revolution is in fact the hand of G-d at work; it is meant to help us make G-d a reality in our lives. And as time goes on and new discoveries are made, we will see more and more how science reflects and parallels the truths of G-d, thereby revealing the intrinsic unity in the entire universe.

The divine purpose of the present information revolution, for instance, which gives an individual unprecedented power and opportunity, is to allow us to share knowledge—spiritual knowledge—with each other, empowering and unifying individuals everywhere. We need to utilize today's interactive technology not just for business or leisure but to interlink as people—to create a welcome environment for the interaction of our souls, our hearts, our visions.

Understanding science and technology as divine tools for our personal and spiritual growth is also critical for our well-being. History has taught us that it is not enough for a society to be scientifically or intellectually sophisticated; "wisdom," "knowledge," and "enlightenment" can all too easily be perverted by the equally human qualities of arrogance and brutality. Only when infused with an external standard of goodness, with the standard of a virtuous life as dictated by G-d, can wisdom truly achieve a higher plane.

This has never been more true than today. We are experiencing an explosion of technology that places undreamt-of power in human hands. Biotechnology, for example, has given us access to the levers of creation—the ability to develop powerful new medical treatments, for instance. Or, conversely, the power to hurt or destroy. In this century alone, we have seen stark testimony to the destructive capabilities of various technologies. But even when technology is not used destructively, it is often simply wasted or left wanting.

Every day, our load of manual labor is lightened. We have more effective machines to do the work that used to take up so much of our time. Do we take advantage of these hours by spending more time with our children and with those in need? Do we volunteer to teach a class or help out a neighbor? Or do we simply reach for the next new button that will make our lives that much more convenient and comfortable? We all feel the need to better our lives, but we must balance the wonders of technology by responding to the spiritual demands of our soul's potential.

These demands are beginning to resonate throughout our society. Parents, for instance, are pleased that their children are learning computer skills at school, but wary that such occupational training is not complemented by more *human*, more compassionate training. It is well and good to learn to program a computer, but unless a student also acquires a sense of discipline and integrity, he or she might use that skill to wreak havoc. The best students—and the best teachers—recognize that there is much to be learned by inspecting the failure of cultures before ours. In doing so, it becomes painfully clear that no amount of wisdom or technology can overcome a value system that does not do enough to discourage selfishness or evil.

With all our human capacity for technological advancement, we must never forget our higher objective. We must strive to enhance our scientific search for truth by constantly expanding our spiritual search for the divine.

CAN WE RECONCILE SCIENCE AND RELIGION?

Our spiritual search, though, is sometimes impeded by various barriers. The scientific revolution, for instance, caused some people to abandon their faith in G-d, rejecting their beliefs in the face of newfound scientific "truths." Others clung stubbornly to their convictions, refusing to recognize the discoveries of science. This battle peaked in the nineteenth century, when science presented itself as an almighty new "religion." Despite a certain degree of enlightenment and various attempts to reconcile, for some people there still exists today a rift between science and religion, as though some parts of life are controlled by G-d and others by the laws of science and nature.

This compartmentalized attitude, however, is wrong. Since G-d created the universe and the natural laws that govern it, there can be no schism between the creator and His creation. The natural laws of the universe can hardly contradict the blueprint from which they were made! So science is ultimately the human study of G-d's mind, the search to understand the laws that G-d installed to run the physical universe.

Science today is learning to recognize its true place. Whereas scientific conclusions were in the past considered natural "laws," with all the rigid implications of that word, modern science no longer holds such a dogmatic view. Contemporary scientists now accept the fundamental indeterminism of nature;[3] Heisenberg's "uncertainty principle," for instance—the unpredictability of both the position and velocity of subatomic particles—is understood as being intrinsic to the entire universe. This uncertainty does not point to a limitation in our ability to measure, but to an inherent characteristic of nature; the modern scientist, that is, no longer expects to find absolute *truth* in science.[4]

This is not meant to cast aspersions on science or to discredit the scientific method. On the contrary—scientific accomplishments have dramatically bettered human life. For science to be most effective, however, it must be viewed in perspective; we must accept that science on its own is a search, not an absolute system; it is *neutral*, a set of theories that we can put to good or bad use.

The wisdom and will of G-d,[5] on the other hand, is absolute and specific, teaching how man should act to the fullest advantage of himself and the community at large. Unlike science, G-d's wisdom *is* absolute truth; it is not limited by cause and effect, and it is decidedly not neutral.

There are two approaches, then, in the search for truth—the human search via science and the search via G-d. There is no question that the universe is guided by a certain logic. At the outset, man begins searching for the truth from the "outside in," as it were, trying to understand various phenomena and then piece them together like a jigsaw puzzle to come up with a complete picture. Scientists and philosophers peer through the outer layers of the universe to discover the forces lying within. What we are all actually searching for, whether or not we acknowledge it, is G-d, the hand inside the glove. But if we choose instead to search for the truth from the "inside out," looking directly through the eyes of the creator and abiding by His laws, we begin to gain a more complete understanding of how the world operates and why.

One can therefore say that secular or scientific wisdom deals with *what* the universe is, while spiritual wisdom deals with *why* it is and what it means to one's life. True science and true religion, therefore, are two sides of the same coin. The emphasis is on "true"—not a science that denies G-d or a religion that sees science as its enemy. Both of these attitudes stem from the same flaw: the belief that G-d, who created the natural universe and its laws, cannot coexist with His creation! Any scientific theory that seems to contradict His laws will ultimately be scientifically proven to be unverifiable even by the most diligent scientific exploration.

Because the world has been so categorically affected by science in recent centuries, today's scientists and scholars have a great responsibility. They must teach not only the laws of science but its *role*—what science is and what it is not. So the true challenge of science today is not to refute G-d, but to discover how it reflects and illuminates parts of G-d's mind that have yet to be uncovered. Only then will science fully become part of the search for truth. As scholars in the Middle Ages often counseled: "Love Plato, love Aristotle, but love truth more than all."

WHAT CAN TECHNOLOGY TEACH US ABOUT OURSELVES?

Everything a person sees or hears is meant to teach us a lesson about life. When we look at technology merely as a source of personal comfort or advancement, we are seeing only the end product. When we look at technology as an expression of G-dliness, though, we are better prepared to understand life itself.

From atomic energy, for instance, we realize the power of every individual human being. We now know that even the smallest bit of matter can release a massive amount of energy; so, too, does every person contain enormous power. How is it released? By getting to a person's very core and shaking him from his contented state. It is the human equivalent of nuclear fission or fusion—a person's inner strengths are released when he is acted upon by the proper combination of force and direction, when we help him live according to the laws of G-d and encourage him to help others to do the same.

This creates a chain reaction. Just as the splitting of the first atom triggers other atoms to split, every positive human thrust and every virtuous act creates an energy that can only intensify. On the other hand, the energy released through negative behavior can be controlled, just as an atomic chain reaction can be controlled.

Atomic energy also shows us how the macrocosm of the entire universe is reflected in each of us. In an atom (according to the planetary model), the various particles orbit around the nucleus, while in the human being, the various material aspects also orbit around a nucleus: our soul.

Finally, we see that an atom ultimately *releases* far more energy than the amount of energy required to split it. Not so many years ago, the prospect of producing atomic energy must have seemed painfully complex and expensive, perhaps even futile. And yet it turned out to be highly productive. We may feel similar reservations on a personal level—wouldn't it be much simpler to wander through life without imposing on ourselves the demands and responsibilities of a spiritual life? Perhaps, but then we would waste our own most precious natural resource, leaving our inner potential untapped.

Our sages have described each person as an entire world, and the world as a personality in macrocosm.[6] Indeed, the new developments in science show that the world is a dynamic system of inseparable, interacting components, and that the human observer is an integral part of this system. The universe can no longer be perceived as a series of independent building blocks, for we have discovered that all matter—and, therefore, all people—is inextricably linked.

One of the most important reverberations of this new physics is that the long-accepted idea of scientific objectivity can no longer be upheld. We now understand that the scientist becomes involved in the world that he observes to an extent that influences the properties of the objects he observes.[7] His perceptions of nature, therefore, are intimately connected with his own mind, his own ideas, and his own value system—all of which are sure to inform the scientific "results" he reaches. So any scientist must exercise moral as well as intellectual judgment in his research.

There is much to learn from the technological revolution, as long as we understand its role in our lives and see it as a final step in our dramatic search for unity throughout the universe, in search of redemption. After all, developments in science and technology teach us to be more sensitive to the intangible and the sublime: the forces behind computers, telephones, television, and so on are all invisible, and yet we clearly recognize their awesome power and reach. Similarly, we must come to accept that the driving force behind the entire universe is intangible and sublime, and we must come to experience the transcendent and G-dly in every single thing—beginning, of course, with ourselves.

⟨⟨⟨⟨⟩⟩

A college student once visited the Rebbe. He had heard that the Rebbe was also a master of the sciences. "A scholar must spend many hours studying and reading," the student said. "How does the Rebbe find the time to do so and also keep abreast of scientific developments?"

The Rebbe smiled and replied: "I am not responsible for the rumors that others spread about me. But I will share with you my answer to the same question concerning another religious scholar, in the eighteenth century, who was also known to have mastered science. The universe, having been created by G-d, works according to laws defined by G-d's way of thinking. So, though the understanding of science in all its detail is achieved by intensive study and by mastering the scientific method, when one masters G-d's wisdom, he learns how G-d chooses to think. He can therefore derive the general thrust of true scientific ideas—the fundamental principles and forces G-d uses to run this universe. And most important, he can recognize when a scientific theory is in sync with these principles. This, of course, greatly lessens the time required to study the details of science and the need to slowly build the picture piece by piece."

23

⟨⟩

UPHEAVAL AND CHANGE

Finding Real Security in Uncertain Times

When a calamity strikes the community we must cry out, examine
our lives and correct our ways. To say that the calamity is
merely a natural phenomenon and a chance occurrence is
insensitive and cruel.

—Maimonides, Laws of Fasting 1:1–3

Upheaval—especially on a global scale—heralds a new stage in
life and in history. When life is profoundly disturbed we must not be
tentative and defensive. We must intensify our offensive, foresee what
is coming, and initiate new programs that will better the world. For
every disturbance we must add a new commitment to goodness.

—The Rebbe

⟨⟩

The Rebbe's life was filled with upheaval. Born in 1902 in
Czarist Russia, the Rebbe personally lived through the Russian Revolution and World Wars I and II. He was studying in
Berlin when the Nazis came to power, and in Paris when they oc-

cupied France. After narrowly escaping Europe, he arrived in the United States in 1941, settling in New York, and lived there during the turbulent second half of the twentieth century. When the Rebbe discussed upheavals over the years, a single thread ran through his talks—how to transform chaotic events into forces of positive change. He instructed us to use upheavals to fulfill our mission of integrating G-dliness into our daily lives. The Rebbe saw our generation as one of transition, and all the upheavals of our generation as part of the transition process. "We stand at the threshold of a new world," he said in 1990. "We are concluding an age consumed with materialism, and entering the time of Redemption, an age of heightened spiritual consciousness, where materialism is but a means to the sublime."

How Do We Cope with Upheaval?

Unlike personal tragedy and loss, which affect the lives of individuals and those close to them, upheaval is large-scale disruption that imperils communities, destabilizes nations, or even endangers the entire world. Suddenly the underpinnings of our security—personal safety, economic well-being, our very lives—have been sabotaged.

At such times, when the foundations of our world seem to be collapsing, it is difficult to avoid being overwhelmed by fear and uncertainty. We ask: What is happening? Will the world ever return to normal? How can we prepare for an unknowable, unpredictable future? Can we regain our equilibrium and overcome our feelings of alienation? The questions come faster than the answers, which may not come at all, and we grow disoriented and fearful. We may even become paralyzed, unable to gain a perspective on the events that have overtaken us or to regain control over our fates. In such a difficult situation, what can we do?

To live meaningfully, we must face upheaval directly and not re-treat into fear or denial. Even the most dire experiences are part of life's purpose and mission, and we must struggle to accept them in this spirit. We do not welcome calamities, and may even challenge G-d for allowing them, yet part of our own challenge is to get beyond our anger, fear, and pain in order to unearth possibilities for growth. Even when our way of life appears to be in jeopardy, we must school our-selves to detect in upheaval the seeds of transformation.

Before we can learn from cataclysm, however, we must recover from the shock and restore some sense of safety and security. In times like these we need to seek comfort and strength from the people closest to us—family, friends, and community. The hand we extend to calm and comfort our fellow human beings helps to ease our suffering as well.

⌘

A woman who suffered a great tragedy came to see her Rabbi. The Rabbi said to her: I have no answers for you, but I can cry with you.

The time for analysis and explanation comes later. The first re-sponse to large-scale trauma is communion, offering and receiving strength and solace. Empathy and compassion may appear to be merely ways to shield ourselves from the disorder around us, but they are also the first steps in the process of healing.

HOW CAN WE COMPREHEND UPHEAVAL?

Once we ensure our own safety and the well-being of the peo-ple close to us, we can look beyond the immediate crisis to comprehend the upheaval and what it means for us. When we see the larger picture, it is possible to learn and grow from our experiences. We may find that we resist taking these steps, that we are blocked by a second fear, deeper and more profound than the one associated with the terrible events: a fear of the unknown.

Fear and uncertainty are necessary, even healthy, parts of the growth process. Upheaval on a national or global scale is a sign of change. Just as the great cataclysms recorded in the Bible—the Flood, the Egyptian enslavement, the Exodus—represent stages in a grand, Divinely ordained historical plan, so do the ruptures of the geopolitical fabric in our own times. When we feel disoriented by what has happened—even if at first we experience panic and pain—we are acknowledging the profound changes taking place around us. It is disturbing to find ourselves suspended between a past that has been swept away and an unpredictable, unformed future. At such moments, what we see is destruction and disorder, and we cannot comprehend how today's upheavals are beginning to usher in the future. But they are.

Our sages teach, "Who is wise? The one who sees the birthing"[1]—not just the darkness, but how it leads to light. Growth occurs in three stages: an embryonic state, a void between old and new, and a state of transformation. Upheaval is the middle, chaotic stage. From our human perspective, it may appear as an abyss, but in the larger view, it is the first sign of something new, a birthing. When catastrophic changes create disruptions to the everyday fabric of our lives, we can fall victim to them, or we can seize the opportunity to seek signs of the changes that follow troubled times. What we discover will lead us to an entirely new vision.

⁓

Among the many great upheavals caused by World War I and the Russian Revolution was the devastation of religious life under Soviet rule. Millions of people were killed and others were persecuted and not allowed to live freely. One of the great Rabbis at the time, who openly defied the Soviet authorities, was arrested and sentenced to death, but he was saved miracu-

lously. He later explained that as difficult as a situation might be, we must hold on to our faith and know that these dark times will lead to a new renaissance of Jewish life and to the beginnings of a new world order where peace and freedom will reign. The Rabbi promised that one day soon, we would see in retrospect that these terrible events (like the events that led to the miracle of Purim) were pieces of a bigger puzzle, steps in a process, and that we would ultimately recognize the Divine plan that is leading us to a greater place.

WHAT BRINGS US TRUE SECURITY?

In times of upheaval, we are given the rare opportunity to perceive directly and with certainty what is true and real in our lives. As a result, we notice two crucial things. First, we see through the fragile, ineffectual material comforts we often rely on for our sense of security. Faced with a crisis, we immediately recognize that it is folly to depend on such insubstantial things for our safety and survival. Second, as we glimpse beneath the surface of our material realm, we begin to discern the outlines of a more enduring world, where we can locate pillars powerful enough to support and sustain us. We discover, in other words, the source of a security that is both permanent and eternal.

Our selves—our true selves—consist of two components: a body and a soul. Happiness is possible only when we bridge these dichotomous entities, when we nourish our souls as much as we do our bodies. True security is possible only when our material existence is rooted in and connected with our spiritual life.

This is not an ascetic doctrine, one that encourages us to deny our bodies or the material world. But we must acknowledge that material life is not a self-sufficient end in itself, but a means for spiritual expression, and the body is a vehicle for our soul's journey in this world.

The body and soul, however, are not natural allies; the material and spiritual worlds are often in opposition. In general, the more value we place on material things, the more challenging it is to discover the spiritual. It does not take long to reach the point where we are conscious of nothing but matter: our property, our prosperity, and our professional achievements create a seductive illusion of worth and invincibility. As long as we are living comfortable lives free of disturbance, our illusions can be perpetuated.

The instant disaster strikes, we perceive with terrifying clarity just how mistaken we were to devote our lives to the pursuit of purely material ends. By rediscovering our inner purpose—and reconciling the goals of body and soul—we can get back on course. To do so, each of us must ask, What do I stand for? What are my priorities? What should my purpose be? What would make me feel secure in this world, no matter what happens? The questions we ask in times of upheaval—and the answers we give—are probably the most critical of our lives.

When the world threatens to veer out of control, as it can when disaster strikes, we have an opportunity to glimpse behind its facade of false solidity and take an honest look at ourselves as well. We may find ourselves face-to-face with the existential fear and loneliness that people have long wrestled with: that we are alone in our universe, that life lacks purpose and direction. In overcoming our terror, we answer the challenge to define our true beliefs, who we are, and the values we live by. At such moments, we have an opportunity to discard old patterns of behavior and outfit ourselves with new ones.

FAITH IN TROUBLED TIMES

When times are uncertain and values are in flux, we need, more than ever, our absolute, spiritual foundation. Whether or not we are aware, each of us was sent to this world with a unique purpose. Our calling is an expression of our profound and intimate relationship to the Eternal, to G-d, and it is this mission that anchors our lives. Even in our most difficult moments, our purpose never wavers; this helps us to find our way when all the familiar signposts have vanished.

There is something paradoxical about the capacity of times of upheaval to raise our spiritual consciousness, since catastrophic events can also pose great challenges to faith. Yet the power of faith is undeniable. Sometimes it expresses itself through actions that seem to have nothing to do with faith. Where do people get the determination and willpower to persevere against overwhelming odds? What drives them, in times of crisis, to unfathomable and unexpected acts of heroism? What is the source of our empathy and compassion?

The answer to all these questions is faith—in a higher purpose, a more perfect form of justice than human institutions are capable of. However we refer to it, faith infuses us with the certainty, will, and resolve that good can overcome indifference and evil. The path may be long, but faith helps us to recognize that for all of us life is a process that leads to redemption, a process in which loss leads to renewal, suffering to growth, and death to rebirth.

Faith is a power we cultivate, but it is also a gift that we receive. It is the soul granting us the ability to celebrate life, to reconnect to the Eternal and to our lives' absolute purpose. This power is especially precious when life threatens to become unbearable; it enables us to refuse to become victims, to realize that even if we cannot understand why terrible things happen, we can respond to them with humanity, hope, and the dedication to build a better world.

Life is infinitely more than the here and now of individual existence, it is part of a continuing process that began long before our birth and will continue after we have left the stage of this world. We are therefore not simply products of our immediate circumstances, but part of a complex chain. We have a role in shaping our own lives, as well as the lives of those who come after us. The things and people we fear do not have power over us, because we are creatures of G-d and can access our spirituality when we lack control over our material circumstances. Even if those around us are trembling with fear—even if we ourselves are afraid—we can find strength and courage in this single, simple truth.

❦

In the back of the room a man sat alone, nervous and fearful. Someone approached him and asked, "Why are you so afraid?" He replied, "How can one not be afraid in this world where we don't know what to expect next? Whether it be illness or poverty, there is so much to fear."

The other replied: "A great mystic and sage, the Baal Shem Tov, lost his father at a tender age. On his deathbed the father told his young son, "My child, remember this your entire life: Fear nothing besides G-d." This gave the young boy the strength and confidence to go on in life and become one of the greatest visionaries and spiritual innovators who ever lived. His father's words remained etched in the impressionable mind and heart of the child. He never feared anything—people, the course of nature, all the insecurities that life throws at us. He was in awe of one thing only: G-d. When a young child hears such words, it infuses him with the fortitude to withstand all challenges."

He put his hand on the nervous man's shoulder. "You must always remember," he said, "that no matter what comes your way in this transient world, you have nothing to fear, because you only have to answer to G-d, who transcends all the forces in the world that can frighten a person."

WHAT ACTIONS SHOULD WE TAKE?

To sustain faith and hope, and to perfect the spiritual potential that stirs within us, we must channel faith into action. Neglected, faith can lie dormant in our unconscious. To thrive, it needs to be cultivated. History has shown us the limitations of the material world, and it is up to us to strengthen the eternal pillars upon which the world stands: study of Divine wisdom, prayer, and acts of kindness.

Designate time each day to study Divine wisdom and contemplate the larger questions of life: Why are we here? What is the real purpose of our lives? What provides us with true and permanent security? Open your soul and emotionally connect with G-d. Pray for all who suffer and for your own needs. Pray for the strength to move forward, to rebuild and create a more sensitive world. Give more charity than usual: money, time, and expertise. When we act charitably, we open new passages through which blessings can flow into our world. Seek guidance in the texts studied by our ancestors. One by one, start eliminating the little evils in your life: envy, anger, hate, gossip, slander, and all other pettiness to which we often succumb.

Talk to your children about the disquieting changes going on around us in the world today. Encourage them to share their reactions and express their fears. When you talk to them about change and upheaval, stress that all change—even the normal stages of human and social maturation—is frequently disruptive. Discuss the upheavals around us to explain our own internal changes, and vice versa.

Seek community with other people, especially at times of great stress. Ask older people who have endured difficult trials in their lives to relate their experiences. They help us to see the bigger picture and remind us that there have been upheavals in other times and places, and that afterward people have rebuilt and recovered.

Invite friends into your home, comfort one another, and work together to build a stronger community. When we are together with others, we can dispel the loneliness and isolation that plagues individuals. By reaching outside the walls of our homes, we get beyond our narrow perspectives as well. Gatherings create synergy, a power that is greater than the sum of its parts.

By translating faith into action and drawing strength from community, we can anticipate the future with hope and give ourselves a meaningful role in bringing it into existence. Then the darkness can be seen for what it is—temporary and transformative—and we can begin to regard ourselves as agents of hope. With awareness, faith, and hope we can restore confidence in ourselves and others even in the face of overwhelming adversity. When we allow G-d in, G-d tells us, "I am with you. I will protect you wherever you go."[2] That assurance becomes the source of the light that we see at the end of the tunnel. No matter how daunting the challenge, whatever the enemy or the battle, when we connect to G-d we have the power to overcome and conquer anything and everything.

What shall we do with this power? Strengthening ourselves and our communities is the beginning, but we must not stop there. We carry responsibility for the universe, and how we fulfill that responsibility directly affects our personal security and survival.

To understand this requires that we understand the forces of history, and in moments of upheaval we can at times distinguish the forces that shape our histories. The Bible reveals these forces on an epic scale; contemporary crises of our own times are the modern echoes of those seminal events.

WHERE DO WE STAND NOW?

Every generation is a link in a long historical chain, and the more uncertain our own times are, the more essential it becomes to investigate our histories, the documents of our ancestors, reservoirs of spiritual wisdom and our collective past.

When profound and sometimes violent events occur on the world's stage, we recognize them as potential signs of global—even cosmic—change. But how can we distinguish between a temporary disturbance and the turmoil that signals that something more profound is going on, perhaps even the dawning of a new age?

There are two signs to look for. The first, like the Richter scale that measures the intensity of earthquakes, is easier to read. When an upheaval and its aftershocks affect people across an entire continent or more, unsettling communities and nations, historic changes may follow. The second sign, when the roots of the confrontations we witness reach back through history, is less evident to the naked eye. To recognize these conflicts and locate their wellsprings, we must step back and examine what has come before and the forces, past and present, that have shaped us.

Among the Bible's many profound messages, there is one that is especially timely today: the world will not be at peace until it makes peace with G-d. But this harmony is possible only when we incorporate G-dliness in everything we do.

The struggles to integrate the Divine and the human, matter and spirit, body and soul, the inner and the outer, are as old as history itself. The tension between these opposing but complementary forces lies at the root of all conflict: inner (personal) and outer (social and political).

Our Biblical patriarch Abraham was the first to perceive this struggle and to analyze it. He rejected his idol-worshiping family and society and embarked on a solitary spiritual quest for something more. He turned to sheepherding, in order to spend his time alone, thinking and reflecting about the relationship between human beings and the cosmos. He discovered G-d and embraced faith, but his belief in one G-d offended the pagans around him, and they imprisoned him. To introduce his revolutionary concept of one G-d, Abraham contended with and overcame the resistance of a harsh material world.

His story is our story. Reading and applying the Biblical stories of Abraham and his children illuminates our lives today. Abraham taught what he learned to his children, yet they struggled with his ideas and with one another. These challenges and conflicts have persisted, but the direction of history is a forward one, slowly integrating these opposing forces—religion and secularism, science and religion, faith and materialism.

The battle is not yet over. As in Biblical times, confrontations between nations continue to reverberate throughout the world. Biblical texts describe battles that will be fought in the final days before the world makes its peace with G-d and nations learn to coexist in harmony. The Biblical battles between the children of Abraham—Ishmael, Isaac, Esau, and Jacob—will be replayed on a global scale. Confrontations between the children of Ishmael, Esau, and Jacob—the Arab/Muslim world, the Roman/Christian world, and the Jewish world, respectively—will take place. These wars have many immediate geopolitical causes, but they also reflect the venerable struggle to harmonize spirit and matter.

The Talmud says, "When you see nations confronting each other, prepare yourself for the footsteps of the Messiah."[3] Our sages recognized that large-scale conflicts, especially those that arise between the children of Abraham, are signs of things to come. But the sages assure us that they are preludes to a time when nations will respect one another's differences while uniting under universal, shared principles. One nation under G-d will expand to many nations under one G-d.

Our sages also inform us that the battle is not waged entirely outside ourselves; its final frontier is on the personal plane. It entails integrating our own material and spiritual lives, what we do and who we are. We are not just observers and bystanders of the events happening around us; we and our actions are an integral part of the unfolding story, and we must know that we carry the profound responsibility to help guide the world toward its destination—the final Redemption.

When civilizations collide, we must experience this upheaval as the dawn of a new age of spiritual consciousness, a true age of knowledge, a world without war and destruction, a world filled with Divine knowledge as the waters cover the sea.

WHAT IS OUR ROLE TODAY? TOWARD A MEANINGFUL FUTURE

Our best strategy to counter the uncertainty and fear associated with change and upheaval is to anticipate the future and welcome it. We must channel the strong emotions awakened by the unsettling events into positive action. Beware of apathy and complacency, and be suspicious of nostalgia for the "good old days." Do not attempt to slip back into the comfortable posture of the past. It is time to move forward, and it is our responsibility to keep ourselves and others from falling back. We need to remain alert to our cause, our calling, our higher purpose.

The world is changing. We cannot control the changes, and we cannot stop them from happening. *How*—not whether—to react is the paramount question for us. Have we the courage to use these events as springboards for growth? As we approach our destination, we discern signs of a new era, and we can direct our conscious efforts toward it.

Upheaval is a sign of paradigm change. Do we hear the footsteps? All the characters are in place. The question is: Are we ready?

⟳

During the Persian Gulf War in 1991, the Rebbe cited the Midrash that states: The leader of Persia will attack an Arab nation and will bring destruction to the entire world, and all nations will be outraged and confused . . . and they will say, "Where shall we come and go?" G-d will answer them: "My children, do not be afraid, everything I have done, I have done for you. Why are you afraid? Do not fear, the time of your Redemption has arrived."[4] The Rebbe explained that major changes were taking place in the world, with more changes to come. Revolutionary changes will behoove nations and cultures to confront their roles and make peace with one another under G-d. We must be wise, the Rebbe said, and not be frightened by these global tremors. We must see them as birth pangs of a new world order—a redeemed world where G-d feels at home.

24

OUR GENERATION
Understanding the Time in Which We Live

There will be neither famine nor war, neither envy nor strife, because goodness will flow in abundance and all delightful things will be as available as dust. The occupation of the entire world will be solely to know G-d.

— Maimonides, closing of Code of Law

We are the seventh generation, the one that will actualize G-d's reality on this earth.

—The Rebbe

The Rebbe began his leadership in 1950, just as America began feeling the not-so-gentle stirrings of a new awareness. This would develop into a revolution, with young people raging against the conformity and hypocrisy of their parents; the pursuit of materialism, which might have satisfied previous generations, was simply insufficient.

The Rebbe's leadership would extend over four decades—forty

turbulent years that saw unprecedented and radical change. In this respect, the Rebbe was as prepared as any leader could be, rooted in religious tradition yet thoroughly educated in secular matters. He was also a visionary leader. Throughout these tumultuous decades, he anticipated changes on both the personal and societal levels, consistently offering enlightenment and encouragement toward handling the challenges of these rather daunting times.

Above all, the Rebbe saw this generation as one of final redemption. In his first discourse upon assuming leadership, the Rebbe said: "Our sages explain¹ that Moses was the seventh generation from Abraham. In that generation, the world experienced at Sinai an unprecedented revelation of G-dliness. So, too, our generation is the seventh [of Rebbes]; we have the responsibility coupled with the ability to finish the process of making this world a G-dly place."

HOW CAN WE MAKE SENSE OF THIS DIFFICULT TIME?

To understand ourselves and find meaning in our lives, we must first understand the unique time in which we live. This can be more difficult than it sounds. Because we are so immersed in our everyday lives, we find it hard to step back and cast a clear eye on our chaotic surroundings.

On one hand, we are experiencing breathtaking technological advances. Hardly a day goes by when we don't hear about a new development in medicine or communications or industry. Global affairs are fast changing, too—consider the bloodless fall of communism, which until just a few years ago was considered a great threat to mankind's well-being.

Because of these breakthroughs, the world is ever more united. But on the personal level, there is unprecedented *disunity*. Our value systems lie shattered; each day, another taboo is broken. We are in the midst of a crisis, desperately seeking happiness and fulfillment. It is a sad paradox: The more technological wizardry and material comforts we pile up, the more steeply our values seem to decline. Our spiritual standard of living is being sacrificed in favor of our material standard of living.

The breakdown of the healthy family structure is no longer a new problem—it has extended into a second and third generation—but we are just now feeling its full, brutal force. Unfortunately, the evidence is all around us: physical, psychological, and emotional abuse of every sort. There is a psychological crisis at hand—a *spiritual* crisis. Many are so resigned to this fact that they don't dare hope that things can get better.

How can we possibly make sense of this strange, difficult time? By understanding the spiritual forces behind human progress.

WHY IS THIS GENERATION
DIFFERENT FROM ALL OTHERS?

History is a process, with each generation growing out of the ones that preceded it. Hundreds of years ago, before mass communication and world travel, people were hardly aware of anyone outside their own village. Monarchs ruled with an absolute authority. In the Middle Ages, people's lives were controlled by institutionalized religion and an inflexible society that imposed a profound value system, though often at the expense of individual freedoms.

During the so-called Enlightenment of the early eighteenth century, a new breed of free thinking began to flourish, and democratic ideas began to sweep Europe. Napoleon, following the French Revolution of 1789, espoused the ideals of liberty, equality, and fraternity, promising emancipation to the oppressed.

But this newfound freedom exacted a severe spiritual toll, leading to a state of permissiveness, moral anarchy, and G-dlessness. All too often, "liberty" translated into "license"; set free from the bonds of authority, man often gravitated to his most base desires, abandoning many of the traditions of a healthy, G-d-fearing society.

The Enlightenment, coupled with the scientific revolution and a new liberalism, divided people into two groups: those who embraced science so absolutely that they rejected G-d in favor of atheistic materialism and those who rejected science and reason in favor of religious dogma.

Both groups essentially sought to answer the same question: What is the meaning of our existence and of truth? This conflict would rage on until science—and technology, its child—would render established religion practically irrelevant for many people.

In the mid-twentieth century, this tide began to turn. People began to realize that the technological, political, and cultural advancements of the previous two centuries were hardly a solution to the human condition. The upheaval in the wake of two world wars led many to question whether the path that mankind had chosen would necessarily lead to happiness. Materialism, which had seemed to be the means to a fulfilling existence, suddenly began to look very empty.

As the century wore on, our surroundings grew less and less familiar. Whereas in previous generations people's lives followed clearly mapped-out patterns, nothing seemed certain anymore. Every area of modern life—economics, politics, science, medicine—seemed to be in a state of flux. Since the information explosion, there has been even more change, resulting in a constant revision of our past attitudes.

The only thing that hasn't changed throughout these centuries is mankind itself and our search for meaning and purpose. But as the twentieth century draws to a close, we have learned that we can no longer look for solutions from without—that we must begin to look within ourselves.

Even though we have never been so materially prosperous, we feel a deep unease. Where are we headed? What are we to teach our children? What has become of the world we thought we knew? Do not feel alone if you ponder such questions, for millions of people are feeling the same way.

Why do we feel so restless? Because it has become more and

more obvious that no amount of material comfort can truly satisfy us, that no amount of reason can truly answer our questions about the meaning of life, that the greatest technological discoveries cannot comfort our souls. This realization has created an intense void in men and women around the world. Whenever there is an imbalance between conflicting forces in our lives, a deep inner tension begins to surface. After experiencing major changes in our external world and being faced with the challenges and catastrophes of our century, a new demand for balance beckons us. The shifting reality in which we are living upsets our existing frame of reference, creating unease and restlessness.

We now live in a place that is split between materialism and spirituality. Most of us live in one world or the other, and are unable—or afraid—to straddle the chasm that divides them. If you live primarily in the material world, you might consider the spiritual world too demanding or rigid. If you live primarily in the spiritual world, you might consider the material world too self-serving or rootless. Both attitudes are the result of the same philosophical flaw: the belief that G-d and the universe cannot coexist.

This flaw was the undoing of the two extremes of belief in previous centuries—atheistic materialism and dogmatic religion. We now have the luxury of hindsight to appreciate the shortcomings of this compartmentalization.

The challenge we face today is to truly unite the forces of matter and spirit. This means acknowledging the dichotomy between body and soul within ourselves, and creating a harmony between our material and spiritual drives. Our unique generation offers a unique challenge: to find a language that can reach deeper into the soul, an unconventional language to deal with an unconventional problem, to apply eternal spiritual truths to contemporary life.

ᏬᎻᎬᏬᎧ

A student was sitting in a garden with his grandfather.
"I am getting excellent grades," he said, "and my professors

see a great future for me. And yet I am miserable."

"A happy and wholesome life is like a perfect circle," his grandfather replied, picking up a stone and a small tree branch. He placed the stone on the ground and, using the branch as a compass, drew a perfect circle with the stone at its center.

"When you have a fixed and steady center, then your circle will be perfect," the grandfather said. "However, if the center is constantly shifting, you will never be able to draw a circle. Today, many people receive a good education and establish a successful career, but never establish a spiritual center around which their life's activities orbit. Especially in these turbulent times, one needs such a center.

"When you establish your center, my son, and it is clear, all else will follow."

WHERE IS OUR GENERATION HEADING?

As we approach the end of this millennium, we are all well aware of the sweeping changes that have taken place in the world during the last several generations. The very landscape of our world has been radically altered, and we can anticipate even more revolutionary changes in the coming years.

After mankind's long search for unity and meaning, the world is ready for deep and meaningful change. Clearly, a revolt is under way. Never before has there been such public discussion of unhappiness, such an obsession with therapy and self-help, such a deep hunger for anything or anyone who can soothe our weary souls. Throughout America and the world, people are genuinely searching for spiritual meaning.

When we don't find relevance in what we are being taught, we look elsewhere. The rebellions and transitions of the last decades testify to the disillusionment in old value systems. There is no doubt that much of what we learn today is spiritually irrelevant. We have been trained for material success—by our schools, by television, and by our peers. It is only natural that materialism has become the magnetic north of our moral compass. But this is not the work of some evil force; it is simply a state of default. Darkness is often not an enemy, but simply the absence of light.

So the solution to today's spiritual crisis lies not in slaying some dragon from without, but in battling the disunity within ourselves. This requires a grass-roots awakening. We each need to make a new commitment to kindness. To spread a message of love and cooperation, of moral and spiritual values. A message that this world is changing and we need to actively participate in its change. That we stand poised at departing the age of materialism and entering the age of knowledge; knowledge that unites rather than materialism that divides us. And with today's technology we can reach and unite with people everywhere.

Imagine if all six billion people on this planet chose to be unselfish for one given moment, everyone united in the pursuit of true and meaningful knowledge. Just think what could be accomplished! This is the challenge of our generation. It may seem insurmountable, but remember: This process began long ago and its energy accumulates. History is one generation piled on top of the next, like single bricks that, together, form a mighty fortress. We may think of ourselves as a meager generation, but when we stand on the shoulders of our predecessors, we have the potential to become the mightiest of structures.

The birth of the modern era has meant a triumph of freedom over authority. We have learned that freedom presents various challenges, but we have also been taught that G-d would not place an obstacle in our path unless He provided us with the abilities to overcome that obstacle.

Past generations have abused their freedom, taking advantage of it for personal and selfish gain. It is the challenge of this generation to redefine freedom, to bring about a liberation of the soul, to embrace a life that answers the soul's deepest yearnings and realizes its divine purpose. We have been challenged to introduce to the world a freedom that does not challenge the sovereignty of G-d, but which is its ultimate complement.

Our sages tell us that there will come a day when our earthly reality will be a flawless mirror of its divine source, its architect's vision. We are now on the threshold of that day. There has never been a better time to reach people, for their hearts and souls are thirsting for nourishment, understanding, and love. Instead of using modern technology simply for personal and business means, we must learn to use it to spread inspiration and goodness.

None of us are excluded from the monumental responsibility of learning and teaching what G-d wants of us and our generation. It is up to each of us to open our eyes, our minds, and our hearts to this new awareness.

Every era has its calling. Every generation has its mission. We must recognize that we live in a special time, and that we have been groomed for this moment. You must ask yourself: Am I fulfilling my calling?

⌇⌇⌇

During a festive holiday celebration, the Rebbe suddenly stopped the singing and began to teach a new song, matching the words of a familiar prayer with the melody of "The Marseillaise," the French national anthem. The Rebbe turned to a group of guests from France who had come for the holiday and invited them to sing along; ultimately, the whole crowd joined in. Later, the Rebbe explained that this new song redirected the freedom of the French Revolution toward its true, G-dly end—a revolution of spiritual freedom.

III

G-D

25

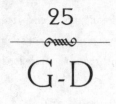

G-D

Absolute Reality

The foundation of all foundations, and the pillar of all wisdom, is to know that there is a First Existence, who brings all existences into being.
—Maimonides, opening to Code of Law

G-d created the universe in a manner in which we perceive our own existence as the intrinsic reality, and G-dliness as something novel and acquired. Our role is to achieve an entirely new level of perception, where G-dliness is the absolute reality and we are the novel creations, channels for divine expression.
—The Rebbe

On the day that he formally assumed leadership of the Lubavitch movement, the Rebbe began his discourse with a verse that states, "I have come into my garden."[1] He explained that G-d, at the beginning of creation, was calling the universe His garden, the place where His essence was first revealed.[2] The Rebbe declared that after all the millennia that G-d's presence had been hidden, and after all the work that had been done to reintroduce G-d into people's lives, the time had come to complete the process so that G-d could once again proclaim, "I have come into My garden" —this time forever.

Throughout his leadership, this would remain the Rebbe's essential theme: the role of the current generation in making G-d a reality in our lives, in making this world a welcome place for Him to dwell.

HOW DO WE DEFINE G-D?

G-d. The very word evokes the widest possible range of opinions and emotions. Some people enthusiastically believe, others emphatically disbelieve, while others argue agnosticism. Who doesn't have a strong opinion about G-d?

People could debate one another about G-d for their entire lives and never come to a conclusion, because they may all define G-d differently. Many who claim to reject G-d are actually rejecting a false definition of G-d; if they were presented with an accurate description, there might be no argument.

⚬⚬⚬

A rabbi was once trying to persuade a self-proclaimed atheist to perform a good deed. In explaining why he considered such deeds to be useless, the atheist said, "You know, rabbi, I do not believe in G-d." The rabbi replied, "The G-d that you do not believe in, I do not believe in either."

When it comes to the word "G-d," we all have some preconceived image. Some people may retain the image from nursery school of a man with a long white beard sitting on a throne in heaven, hurling down lightning bolts when we misbehave. To a child, G-d may simply be someone who is even bigger and mightier than his or her father. Perhaps this is an acceptable image for a young child, but for an adult to think of G-d in such simplistic, corporeal terms is plainly insufficient.

Your own definition of G-d may be based on the opinions and attitudes of people whom you consider to be religious. You might have a negative impression of G-d based on hypocrisy you experienced at home or at school, or you might have warm feelings based on the loving ways of your family, friends, or teachers. Your feelings about G-d have also been affected by the books you have read, the classes you have taken, the music you have heard, and thousands of other influences.

Before attempting any discussion about G-d, therefore, it is vital to peel away the layers of terminology and impressions. But the first question is: Why is it even necessary to define G-d? Why can't everyone have his or her own definition? Because our attitude toward G-d is not a private affair. It affects how we behave at home and in public, how we treat our family and our co-workers, and how we see our role in life.

A person who wishes to lead a meaningful life must ask himself: What is G-d? And why do I need G-d in my life? How you answer these questions will define, more than anything else, who you are and how you live your life, for the question of G-d is at the root of all human behavior.

Any human definition of G-d, though, will be limited by the subjectivity of human comprehension and the boundaries of human knowledge. After all, we have no model other than ourselves against which to measure. So, using ourselves as a template, we try to extrapolate out to G-d. But are we really in a position to be able to define G-d? After all, are we seeking to define a G-d created in the image of man, or a man created in the image of G-d?

Since G-d is the creator, we are created in *His* image. Since G-d is a reality, He must be defined in His terms, not ours, for He also created the laws of logic and reason. Obviously, it is not sensible to assume that we, the creatures, can define our creator. No matter how sophisticated a machine may be, it cannot tell us about the engineer that created it or about the vision and hidden forces that inspired him to create.

And yet, if G-d is totally beyond our comprehension of reality, how can we relate to Him? Before answering that question, we must examine how we try to understand reality itself.

WHAT IS REALITY?

Let us examine the different approaches to defining reality. We must first recognize that reality, like anything else, is defined in part by the instruments we use. Does reality consist only of what we experience on a sensory level, of what we can see or hear or taste or touch or smell? This definition cannot be accurate, for it ignores our intellect and emotions. Is reality, therefore, defined by our abilities to think and feel in addition to our sensory capabilities? This, too, is insufficient, for it precludes the subconscious, which cannot be entirely accessed either cognitively or emotionally.

We can never define total reality, for it encompasses far more than our limited human instruments can observe or experience. Human beings are but a small piece of reality, one part of a much larger whole. The part does not define the whole; the whole defines the part.

Why is it that we have such a large vocabulary when it comes to discussing business or recreation or the weather, but when it comes to talking about our intimate selves, we struggle to express our feelings? Shouldn't it be easier to discuss our innermost emotions than superficial external matters? And yet, the more intimate the feeling, the fewer words we seem to find.

The reason for this paradox is that language is a limited instrument that cannot contain the intensity of deep, intimate expression. To communicate such intimacy, we use other languages—the languages of poetry and music and art, even the language of silence. We can stand before a beautiful painting and feel its effect, but our verbal language may be inadequate to describe that effect.

Similarly, we have insufficient tools to define reality. So how do we know it exists? The same way we know that our intimate side exists even if we cannot touch or define it. We may be unable to define love, for instance, but when you feel a loving embrace, is there any doubt that the emotion is just as real as the embrace itself?

To see the truth, to glimpse reality, we must learn to look at our existence in a new way. By the very limits of nature, ours is an "outside-in" form of observation. What our human instruments are able to observe and experience—sensorially, intellectually, and emotionally—is only an indicator of what lies beneath the surface. We begin by observing the physical phenomena around us, and then use our minds and feelings to strip away the outer layers, trying to comprehend the forces within that make nature behave as it does. If we were able to strip away *all* those layers, we would begin to have a glimpse of reality. As it is, we perceive at best a few outer layers of reality, leaving the inner layers untouched.

If we cannot perceive reality, how can we have any real perception of G-d? Because G-d wants humans to reach for Him, search for Him, and unite with Him. So, through the Bible, G-d chose to define Himself, to allow us to understand and know Him, and then actualize His reality in our lives.

When G-d sent Moses to liberate the Jewish people from Egyptian bondage, Moses asked G-d to describe Himself so that Moses could prove G-d's existence to the people. G-d replied: "I am who I am."[3] By saying so, G-d was describing the essence of His reality—that is, He exists *because* He exists.

Human beings understand existence only as a process of cause and effect; we cannot comprehend or even imagine an existence that is undefined, that has no cause, that is totally unlike our own. Our concept of existence is based upon empirical perception; something exists only after we prove that it exists.

On the other hand, G-d has no cause other than Himself; nothing preceded Him; His being derives from His own self.[4] G-d's existence *must* exist, for it is true reality.

So G-d is an existence that is unlike any existence, "a non-existential existence."[5] It is real because it is real; a reality that exists because it exists: "I am who I am."

Therefore, we cannot define G-d. If a person were to use the human mind to prove, beyond any shadow of a doubt, that G-d exists, it would not be G-d that he discovered; it would only be a product of the human mind. To truly know G-d's "nature," we would have to be like G-d.

~~~

A young child who would grow up to become a great rabbi was once asked, "Where is G-d?" And he responded innocently, "Wherever you let Him in."

To begin to understand G-d, then, we must learn to go beyond our own mind, our own ego, our own tools of perception. Only then will G-d emerge. To look for G-d with our eyes, with our intellect, with our logic, would be like trying to capture the sun's light in our hand. G-d is not definable.

The fact is, then, that we cannot *find* G-d. We must allow G-d to find us by removing any obstacles in our lives that prevent Him from entering—self-centeredness, dishonesty, ignorance, or our very fear of acknowledging something separate and greater than ourselves.

~~~

A philosopher was arguing with a respected rabbi about the existence of G-d. The philosopher felt that although there were some persuasive arguments for proving G-d's existence, there were many equally persuasive ones disproving His existence. After a time, the philosopher grew exasperated. "You are a wise man," he said to the rabbi. "Why is it that you are not moved by all the arguments disputing G-d's existence?"

The rabbi smiled. "I envy you," he said to the philosopher. "Because you are so involved in pondering the existence of G-d, you are always thinking about Him, while I spend

*most of my time thinking about myself." With that, they
parted ways.*

*The philosopher was flattered by the rabbi's remarks, yet
disturbed that his question was never answered. As time
passed and he grew older, the true implication of the rabbi's
words finally dawned on him. "The rabbi actually insulted
me," he reflected. "The reason I spend all my time pondering
G-d's existence is that I am sure that I exist, so the only
question is whether G-d also exists. For the rabbi, G-d's existence is a given, so the eternal question is whether he exists, and if so, why?"*

By understanding G-d as the essence of absolute reality, we
come to the awesome realization "There is none else besides Him."[6]
Or, even more simply, "There is none else."[7]

From the perspective of an absolute reality, there is truly nothing
else. This is the cardinal law of existence: if you place an object of
100 cubic feet inside a space of 100 cubic feet, no other object can
share that space. Likewise, if you have an object of infinite size, no
other object can possibly occupy any space, at any time.

This is the case with G-d. The absolute reality of G-d, while it
extends beyond the conceptual borders of "existence," also fills the
entire expanse of existence as we know it. Which leaves no space
possible for any other existences or realities we may identify—the
objects in our physical universe, the metaphysical truths we contemplate, our very selves. Should we conclude, then, that none of these
things exist? No, for G-d has told us that they do. *But they do not
exist in their own reality;* they exist only as an extension of divine
energy, a created part of an absolute, G-dly reality, a far different
reality than our mind alone can perceive and all our instruments can
experience. To understand and enter this absolute reality, we must
learn to suspend our rigid human perceptions and allow ourselves

to develop new ways to see, think, and believe. And in order to do so, we must first stand in awe of G-d.

WHY DO WE EXIST?

Once we recognize G-d as the absolute reality, we must question human existence. We know now that we exist (because G-d told us so), but we also know that there is nothing to say we *must* exist. G-d's universe would hardly cease to be if any one of us had not been born. Indeed, G-d's absolute reality would not be affected in any way if our entire existence had never occurred.

Our creation, therefore, is G-d's way of *choosing* each of us to exist. None of us is here by accident; we are here because G-d *wants* us to exist. But why?

G-d created the universe and life as we know it to fulfill His vision as a divine architect: "G-d desired to have an abode in the lower worlds."[8] He created the earth, the resources that rest within it, and the human beings who dwell upon it. It is our duty to tap those resources in order to refine and perfect the material world and make it a home for G-d. This is the purpose of human life.

In order for us to achieve this purpose, G-d created this "lowest" world, our world. It is a world in which G-d's reality is initially obscured, where we see human reality as primary. Why did G-d choose to obscure His "authorship"? Because in order for man to truly exist, to make choices in life, we are allowed to experience ourselves as an independent reality. If we had no independence, our existence would be meaningless; we would be like mere puppets on a string.

Instead, G-d created an "agnostic" world, where His reality is not visible. He obscured His presence from us so effectively that we actually perceive *ourselves* as the *only* reality. We may understand that G-d is reality, but we experience G-d's existence as something outside ourselves, as a superimposed reality, whereas in truth, it is G-d who is real, while our existence is "on the outside."

There are layers and layers of comprehension dividing our sensory reality from the absolute reality of G-dly energy. Is this a game that G-d is playing, hiding Himself from human eyes? On the contrary, it is actually a gift, an opportunity for us to grow accustomed to the landscape. Before a child can write, he or she must first learn the alphabet. And before we can understand the brilliant light of G-d's reality, we must first let our eyes grow accustomed to the light that surrounds us. Then we can use our light to peer inside the many layers of a deeper reality.

But if our entire existence is based on the principle that G-d is obscuring His presence, how do we know that we actually exist in *His* eyes? How do we know that we are actually accomplishing anything by perfecting our material world? In the Bible, G-d tells us that He wants us to know Him, but how can we know a G-d that is totally beyond us? And does G-d really care about what we do?

The answer to these questions lies in understanding the mysterious and complex process by which G-d created human existence. G-d, who is Himself undefinable and indescribable, chose to create man and place him in a physical world that is both definable and describable. He also chose to manifest Himself in this world through the laws of logic that He created, through the awesome design of nature and of each human being, and through divine providence. We are allowed to experience these divine attributes so that we can begin to comprehend G-d and have a personal relationship with Him. Then we learn to abstract Him, ultimately realizing that G-d is even beyond anything that we can abstract.

Yes, we do actually exist from G-d's perspective, and G-d does care what we do—not because we *need* to exist or because G-d *needs* to care, but because He *chooses* it to be that way. So His care for us is absolute, nonarbitrary, and noncompromising.

The fact that G-d obscured His presence from us so that we feel that we are an existence unto ourselves does not mean that we do not exist from G-d's perspective. G-d's concealing His presence is not an absence of light; rather it is like a "container" that hides from our eyes that which is within the container. And what is inside the container is G-d's pure light and energy.[9]

On our own, though, we do not exist, for "there is none else besides Him." But "with Him," we exist. What is *not* real is our perception that our existence is all there is. It is not within the scope of human intellect to comprehend how G-d can conceal His presence while allowing us to carry out an independent existence. But this mystery does not limit our relationship to G-d; it actually enhances it, further demonstrating how far removed G-d is from our existence, thus inducing our further awe of Him, and our longing to draw closer to Him and integrate His reality into our lives.

In order to unite with G-d, we must combine both perspectives, G-d's and ours. We must first fully use our minds and hearts to discover and understand G-d as much as we are capable; then we must accept that the human mind is not everything, that some things simply cannot be understood with our limited perception. This acknowledgment allows us to better relate to the very mystery of G-d's existence. We recognize the paradox that G-d is *beyond* reality as we know it, while at the same time *encompassing* reality. That G-d is able to create both the finite and the infinite, the physical and the transcendent—because He is beyond both; He is neither defined nor undefined. By contemplating this mystery, we raise ourselves to an entirely new plane; above all, we come to relate to G-d on *His* terms.

Since G-d does want us to unite with Him, He created an elaborate and elegant process by which we can do so. We begin by probing and asking questions, then emotionally grappling with our existential pain through our search for meaning. We slowly scale the vast mountain of reality, step by step, answering some questions and discovering new ones, continually finding deeper answers until we finally begin relating to and uniting with G-d. We come to realize that we cannot define G-d; we accept that He is beyond all definitions, including the term "beyond all definitions." This is the ultimate unity: In a world of definitions and paradoxes, we recognize G-d, who is beyond all definitions and paradoxes.

Everything in this universe consists of two dimensions, an outer dimension and an inner dimension. Over time, we come to understand this dichotomy within ourselves. We recognize that although the physical body is our more visible, outer dimension, it is our inner dimension—our emotions, our desires and aspirations, our souls—that is far more important.

We must train ourselves to look at the universe in the same way. It is a matter of changing our perspective from "outside-in" to "inside-out." Instead of looking first at the outer layer, then traveling inward, we must learn to see the inner layer as our primary force. And we must cultivate the experience of this layer to the point where we can use it to inform the outer layer.

This is not a simple task, for we spend our entire lives looking at the universe from the outside in. At first, it may seem impossible to get to know a G-d who is so different from us. But G-d gave us the ability to talk about Him, and told us that we must do so. We can find G-d within ourselves, and we can even find the G-d that is well beyond us.

It is our duty, and our greatest challenge, to recognize the difference between human reality and G-dly reality, and to accept the opportunities he has provided to transport ourselves from one realm to the next.

HOW DO WE CONNECT WITH G-D?

To find G-d, we must slowly acclimate ourselves to spiritual growth. We must rise step by step until we can begin to see the universe from a spiritual perspective and, ultimately, from G-d's perspective. This journey completes the circle of our cosmic mission—starting in G-d and ending in G-d, thus fulfilling the vision of our creator.

The first step in this process is to simply acknowledge a reality that is far greater than ourselves, and acknowledge that our reality is not real on its own; it is but an extension of divine energy. The second step is to make this world a comfortable dwelling place for G-d. Ultimately, we unite both realities, ours and G-d's.

We accomplish this by living a material life in service of a spir-

itual goal—by actualizing our soul, our inner layer, to direct our
bodies, our outer layer, toward a higher purpose. A person may
spend 90 percent of his life eating, sleeping, earning a living, rec-
reating, and otherwise tending to his or her material needs. But if
all of this is done in order to devote the remaining 10 percent to
prayer, study, charity, and other G-dly endeavors, then he or she is
actively transforming the very nature of his or her physical reality.

By opening our mind to a new possibility—that our human reality is really but a small part of an all-encompassing reality—we
are able to move beyond the boundaries of human existence. We
begin learning to think like G-d Himself. We learn to embrace faith
and reason, independence *and* unity. Once we have risen above the
limits of human thought, we can incorporate this higher knowledge
in our physical lives—in our logic, our emotions, and, most important, in our conduct. As the sages instruct us, "As G-d is merciful,
you too are to be merciful. As G-d is compassionate, you too are
to be compassionate."[10]

Such G-dly conduct creates a unity between man and G-d,
which is the goal that we were put on earth to achieve. Your very
perspective of the world begins to change; you begin to glimpse the
"light" within the "container." You recognize G-d in everything
around you. When you eat, you understand that you are nourishing
yourself for constructive and G-dly purposes. You realize that every
object has a divine purpose greater than the mere fulfillment of your
own needs. Your table is meant for study, your living room for
meaningful conversations. Your job is no longer just a means to earn
a living, but an opportunity to behave more morally and ethically,
and to introduce G-d into our world. A doctor recognizes the divine
wonder within the human body and an engineer sees in his work a
reflection of divine design and unity.

And finally, you learn to be sensitive to divine providence. You
recognize that everything from the fluttering of a leaf in the wind
to the movement of the galaxies is driven by G-d's hand. Instead of
looking at life from the outside in, you learn to look from the inside

out. The next time you take a business trip or a vacation, do not be preoccupied with the trivial or external aspects of the people you meet or the things you see. Instead, examine your life at a new level of reality, and ask yourself: Why has G-d brought me here? What deeper lesson am I to learn from this encounter?

As you learn to search for the meaning in everything that happens in your life, you will find your life itself becoming more meaningful. Your daily interactions, no matter how trivial, will take on new significance. As you begin to peel away the many layers that obscure G-dly reality, your intellect and sensory perception grow sharper. The *real* world begins to emerge, no longer shrouded in confusion and darkness, but bathed in the light of higher knowledge.

At that point, we achieve an unprecedented feat: while maintaining our existence, we recognize ourselves as a manifestation of G-dliness. In addition, we introduce a new energy into this "lower" world; we help reveal G-d's essence in a universe that originally saw itself as independent and opposed to G-d. We recognize that our world, which feels that it has no cause, could have been brought into existence only by an undefined, undefinable G-d, who has no cause.

To accomplish all this, the divine architect provided a blueprint, a road map that illuminates the world's many winding, dark paths. This road map is the Bible, which provides mankind with the directions to lead a meaningful, productive life. It gives us the insight to see beyond the outer layers of our physical universe and behold the G-dliness within. It shows us the good deeds each person must perform, the means by which we refine our lives and our environment. Every human being has a small corner of the material universe that is to be refined and prepared as a home for G-d, whether he or she is a doctor or a scientist, a clerk or a truck driver, a parent or a teacher. And when the entire universe comes to behave in accordance with the intentions of its creator, we enter into the Messianic Age—the time of redemption and the revelation of G-dliness throughout the universe.

By suspending our egocentric drives and reaching for G-d, we don't become less, we become more. Since we and all of our material pursuits are transient by nature, so too are all of our material rewards and goals. When we connect our lives to a reality that is real and eternal, our every activity and accomplishment becomes more real and eternal. Remember: G-d created each of us with unique abilities. The mission that you have been chosen to fulfill on this earth can be fulfilled by no one but you; it is your responsibility to become aware of your mission and channel all your energies toward it.

Paradoxically, your life becomes meaningful only when you first discover how meaningless it is on its own, in relation to G-d's existence. But ultimately, once you achieve G-d's perspective, you see that your life could not possibly be more meaningful.

We often hear people questioning the existence of G-d. Perhaps you are one of them. It is interesting to note that many people tend to question G-d's existence with far greater rigor than they question many other aspects of their lives. Think about how often you rely on the expertise of others to determine your life decisions. We accept the judgment of doctors and scientists. We accept the advice of people who tell us how to eat and sleep, how to play and work, what to wear and how to behave. How often do you ask to examine the research that went into a doctor's prognosis, or ask to inspect the kitchen of a restaurant where you are eating?

When it comes to G-d, though, we are far more skeptical. Why do we suddenly become so rigorously logical? Is it that we fear the enormous responsibility we are accepting once we embark on our divine mission to lead a meaningful, productive life?

People today are increasingly talking about G-d, about the need to return to a pursuit of higher values and greater awareness of our spiritual mission on earth. All this talk is well intended; now is the time to *do* something about it.

Allow G-d into your life. It doesn't take much. G-d asks each of us only for a slight opening, the eye of a needle, through which He will provide us with the widest entrance to an absolute reality.

Devote just one small corner of your life to G-d, but use that corner
for no other purpose.

We are the generation that will complete the process of bringing
to consciousness G-d's presence in the world. Let us finally raise the
curtain that has shrouded G-d's presence for so long. We are tired
of the masquerade. We have been waiting, and G-d has been waiting. Let us not make Him wait any longer.

*When the Rebbe was a young child, just two and a
half years old, his mother came to check on him one evening
after she had put him to sleep. She was surprised to find
that he was not in his bed. She searched the house but could
not find him. Finally, she thought of looking in a room in
the house that the family used for prayer. To her amazement, the little boy was standing and swaying in prayer.
Indeed, throughout all his years, the Rebbe always carried
his prayer book with him wherever he went.*

26

FAITH AND REASON
To Touch the Divine

I have chosen the path of faith.
—Psalms 119:30

Faith is not the absence of reason; it is a skill in its own right, which, when cultivated, allows us to experience the ultimate.
—The Rebbe

A writer who came to meet the Rebbe suggested that many people seemed to be nonbelievers. The Rebbe disagreed. "People are natural believers. There may be doubts; to question G-d, however, is the first indication that one believes in something. You must have some acceptance of G-d even to question Him."

"But if they believe, why don't they act on it?" the writer asked.

"They are afraid of their faith," the Rebbe replied. "They fear the demands their faith might put upon them, that they might have *to forgo some of their comfort, or compromise some of their ideas. They fear changing their lives."*

WHAT IS FAITH? WHAT IS REASON?

Human beings have many faculties at their disposal. We have a brain to process information, emotions that move us, and intuition that guides us. We have our sensory tools of sight, hearing, smell, taste, and touch. So where does faith fit in?

Many people don't see faith as a basic human faculty; they see it more as the absence of reason. Others are even more cynical, claiming that faith is a sign of weakness, something to resort to when all else fails. In earlier times, this thinking goes, faith was a necessity because man didn't have science to help explain the laws of nature; but in the face of reason and all of man's brilliant accomplishments, we have outgrown our need for faith. Isn't faith just a creation of our imagination meant to deal with issues that we can't comprehend?

And yet we see that people inherently believe in something greater than themselves. This feeling is inside all of us; we only need to know how to access it. We certainly know how to access reason, for we have spent our entire lives cultivating this faculty— in school, at work, and elsewhere. But how do we cultivate faith? Isn't it something you either have or don't?

We are all born with faith. It is neither acquired nor taught; it is our most natural state. A young child, for instance, just has natural faith. Tell him a fantastic tale and, even though he senses it isn't "real," he believes you.

Not that faith is to be confused with childish naiveté, or gullibility, or laziness. Nor is faith the absence of reason. Faith is a powerful, positive force in our lives, no less integral to the human soul than the faculty to think or the faculty to feel. Faith is a faculty that recognizes truths that are infinitely, incomprehensibly greater than ourselves and accepts them as real and relevant.

So why do so many people claim to have no faith? And why do we think that faith and reason contradict each other? Because we misunderstand their roles.

Look again at the child. As he grows older, he accepts less and less at face value. Does this mean he is losing faith? No, only that his faith is being obscured by reason. Not only that, but as he grows older, he realizes that his faith has been continuously abused. After years of experiencing hypocrisy and being lied to, he learns to distrust his own inner beliefs. To protect himself, he begins using his reason alone to process ideas and establish his value system. In effect, he can silence the inner voice telling him that, even though something cannot be grasped with his hand or totally understood with his mind, it may indeed exist.

We must learn to cultivate our natural faith. We cannot allow our reason to drown out the inner voice that tells us what we know to be true with every fiber of our being. A healthy mind recognizes its innate limitations, acknowledging that there are many experiences outside the narrow scope of our own logic.

After all, we learn to incorporate many beliefs into our lives, even if they might initially seem absurd—like black holes in space or the oddities of subatomic particles. While these premises may not be fully understood, we accept them because they help explain different phenomena in our physical world that are otherwise incomprehensible.

But why are we willing to believe in something beyond the means of our own knowledge and yet, when it comes to believing in G-d—and trusting our innate faith—we demand ironclad proof? Why do we have a double standard?

Perhaps the consequences of accepting G-d, and the personal responsibility it demands of us, are so challenging that we would rather find a way to justify our position by questioning or rejecting G-d.

We must overcome the desire to believe in G-d according to our reason alone. Each of us has an interior "judge of truth," an ultimate arbiter that weighs all the information fed to us by our intellect and senses. Sometimes it tells us that our logic should over-rule a misguided feeling. And sometimes it tells us that our rational or skeptical mind should yield to a truth that our faith has embraced.

Our reason, if it is well developed, comes to the obvious con-clusion that reality is far greater than that which we can experience with our senses and our intellect. We come to realize that this reality is not a product of the mind, but that *the mind is a product of this reality*. Reason may lead us to the door of this reality, but we need different tools to enter.

But all this is still not faith, for faith is the pure experience of G-d. Reason may allow us to function in this world and make sense of our lives, but without faith, we would have no basis for life. We could not connect to G-d, the absolute reality, and life would be a random series of logical and illogical events. We would flounder in our search for meaning and find no solace in a turbulent, fragmented world.

Faith is a power that touches you and you alone. It is the humble truth that is as plain as it is real, as quiet as it is forceful. G-d's reality emits wondrous music for us to hear, but the hustle and bustle of the material world often drown out the melody. Faith is the tool with which we can hear the music. Reason may tell us *how* to live; but faith tells us *why* to live. To lead a meaningful life, we must unite our faith and reason.

How Do We Unite Faith and Reason?

Faith and reason are the two faculties we use to experience G-d. It is through faith that we experience the *essence* of G-d; through reason, we experience the *expression* of G-d.

Faith is going beyond our wisdom, our experiences, our accom-plishments, and allowing a higher presence into our lives. No matter how intelligent a person may be, no matter how much he can appreciate the grandeur of the universe and the elegance of the laws that govern it, no matter how sublime are his spiritual ideas and experiences, these thoughts only distract him from experiencing the pure essence of G-d. All the world's grandeur and elegance may be expressions of G-d, but they are not G-d Himself. As creatures of G-d, we have no language to define His essence or to relate to Him on a rational level; the only way we can relate to the essence of G-d is through pure, undiluted faith. And we each have this faith within us; it is the foundation upon which our reason and other faculties rest.

King David begins one of his psalms with the words "a prayer of a pauper."[1] Why does he attribute prayer to a pauper rather than to a person of wealth and sophistication?

⸙

>Two people were invited to see the king. One was a
>wealthy, educated man, the other an illiterate peasant. The
>rich man arrived first. He entered the palace and walked
>through a room filled with a collection of literature, music,
>and art. Aware of the great value of many of the items, he
>became so immersed that he missed his appointment with the
>king. Later, the illiterate peasant arrived. Because he didn't
>appreciate all the books and paintings, he walked right
>through the room, straight into the king's chambers, and
>spent his entire time visiting with the king.

This is not to say that we can function fully on faith alone; it must be fused with reason and integrated into our lives. Once we experience faith, reason becomes a tool to help us *express* the essence of G-d, to imbue our hearts, our minds, and our daily conduct with a pure G-dly faith.

The expression of faith is in the physical deed, not just in the mind. The purest thoughts and feelings do not—indeed, *cannot*—make you perform a good deed. You may understand that a certain choice is right or wrong but feel unable to act; in fact, our hearts and minds tell us to do far more than we ever act upon. Faith is what helps convert a good intention into action.

The simple good deed has no ornaments. It is not flashy or complicated or bold. But it has the power of the essence. Absolute faith—as expressed in the simple deed—establishes a relationship between man and G-d. Without faith, our other faculties are simply tools without vision or direction; with faith, they become means with which we carry out our divine mission.

And yet faith cannot be compartmentalized. You may try to believe in G-d but relegate Him to certain parts of your life or certain times within your day. This makes your faith incomplete. After all, if G-d is the creator of everything that exists, how can your faith be complete when it doesn't affect everything in your life?

By using reason, you can make faith a constant part of your life; all your thoughts, words, and actions will express your faith, and you will come to see G-dliness and divine providence in all that you do. You will come to "know G-d in all your ways."[2]

Faith in G-d is not passive; it does not mean sitting back and accepting events as they happen. When we see danger, faith dictates that we protect ourselves. When we experience pain, faith demands that we cry out and seek relief. When we see need, faith insists not only that we pray to G-d but that we address the need. Faith means relying on G-d and at the same time knowing that G-d created the laws of nature and gave us the capacity to work within those laws to help us achieve what we are praying for.

Surely, a faithful person knows that no matter how much effort he invests, all his blessings originate from G-d. But each one of us must create the "vessel" to contain these blessings. It may rain for ten days in a row, but if a farmer has not plowed and planted his fields, not a single strand of wheat will grow. On the other hand, without G-d's blessing, there is nothing the farmer can do to coax wheat from the earth.

True faith constitutes not only a belief in G-d, but a *trust* that G-d always does what is good and right. True faith does not waver, even if things do not work out as we would have liked. Yes, we may have doubts. Yes, we may feel saddened by the neediness and suffering in the world. Yes, we may want to confront G-d for allowing tragedies. But abandoning your faith in G-d means that you are compromising yourself. When we witness suffering at the hands of other people, we should direct our anger where it belongs—at man. If anything, war and genocide teach us that our faith in man can be misplaced, but never our faith in G-d.

True faith is not the blind faith of ignorance, but the uncompromising belief in the absolute truth. It is a direct connection to G-d's essence, and is therefore neither arbitrary nor conditional. This is what distinguishes true faith from the immature emotion that sometimes calls itself "faith," which dictates that our belief in G-d is dependent on G-d doing things the way *we* want. We know that G-d believes in us; faith is our calling to believe in Him.

HOW DO WE RECONCILE FAITH AND REASON?

Although some people continue to see faith and reason as adversaries, the truth is that reason leads to faith and faith leads to reason.

Using reason, we can contemplate the wonders of G-d's creation and begin to recognize the breadth of His infinite power. But reason also leads us to understand the limit of human knowledge and how much is beyond our scope. As the sages write, "The ultimate knowledge is knowing that you can't know G-d."[3] Such a realization, such a declaration of trust and humility, brings one to the threshold of true faith, for faith is the tool we use to reach the truth that is beyond what we already know. So it is reason, ultimately, that helps lead us to faith.

And faith leads to reason, because faith in G-d impels us to use our reason, every ounce of the intellect and logic G-d gave us, to internalize and integrate our faith. G-d expressly told us that He wants us to *know* Him—to perceive Him with our mind and its finite tools of logic, to embark on a lifelong quest in which we expand the scope of our reason, learning both to fulfill its power and to recognize its limitations.

So faith and reason are a powerful dynamic. We recognize that faith is no mere crutch for the ignorant; it can take us to a place that even the most accomplished mind cannot approach. To be sure, there are two types of faith—the blind, immature faith of a child, who must be guided by others, and the mature faith of someone who has traveled far with his or her mind and heart, finally reaching a threshold that can only be crossed with a leap of faith.

Two young men once visited a small Russian town in midwinter. They tried to find the ritual bath, and learned that it was at the foot of a steep hill. But the slope leading down to the bath, they were told, grew so dangerously slippery in wintertime that no one used it—no one, that is, except for one very special man who went there daily.

The young men were skeptical, and decided to follow this man the next morning. To their surprise, he was very old and feeble. Surely, they thought, he cannot possibly make his way down the slope. But he walked steadily down the icy hill as the young men, trying to follow, slipped and fell. They watched in awe as he entered the bathhouse.

> *Afterward, they respectfully asked the old man how he*
> *had made it down the hill. "When one is connected above,"*
> *he said quietly, "he does not fall below."*

How Can We Have Faith
in Our Generation?

Many people today still have trouble believing in G-d and are plagued with questions. Is this skepticism healthy or not? Is it an honest search for the truth or a justification for self-serving behavior?

At the end of the day, only *you* know how sincerely you are searching for truth. You have only yourself—and G-d—to answer to. If you are genuinely searching, then you have already begun your relationship with G-d. As with all dynamic relationships, this search is a process. We begin from the limited perspective of our own existence, climbing upward step by step until we come to understand that G-d is the absolute reality of which we are an extension—and not vice versa.

For some, the first step might be to discover whether you are indeed ready to listen and grow, whether you are willing to accept the responsibility of faith. The next step is dealing with your doubts concerning G-d's existence. You must attempt to unite your faith with reason, for only your reason can truly recognize the limitations of the mind and its role in the process of searching for G-d.

Then we must allow our inner, sublime tools to speak. We know there is a G-d just as we know we have a soul—not because we can see or touch it, but because we can *feel* it. We feel the soul's effects. We sense its hunger for meaning, its thirst for knowledge, and we feel its satisfaction when we nourish it. Similarly, we feel elevated when we have G-d in our lives. We feel purpose and direction; we feel there is meaning in everything we do.

This entire process needs fuel—knowledge about G-d and ourselves. We must study the Bible, G-d's blueprint for creation. We must learn to actualize our faith through charity and good deeds. Through our virtue and generosity we strengthen the connection between our material reality and the absolute reality that is G-d.

Above all, we must look anew at the tools we are using to try to reveal sanctity in our lives. We simply cannot limit ourselves to conventional sensory means to relate to something that is supersensory.

Searching for G-d in these times can appear to be especially difficult, for many people today are unfamiliar with faith—what it is and how to cultivate it. Born into a time when material priorities have displaced the spiritual, many know little about G-d and what G-d wants of us. People have free time on their hands and often don't know how to fill it meaningfully. It seems very difficult to find where to turn for direction, since everybody—from parents to educators to politicians—appears to be equally uninformed.

And yet people everywhere continue searching for meaning, searching for G-d. This is a tribute to the deepest faith of all. It is during such periods of spiritual darkness that the deepest faith simmers. We must recognize that there are two kinds of darkness. One is when we realize it is dark, and yearn to see; the other, when the darkness has been so intense and so long-lived that we have resigned ourselves to it. The first step in escaping the darkness is *acknowledging* it; only then can you begin to reach out for the light.

In this climate of spiritual darkness, we all have the ability and responsibility to let our faith shine forth and then integrate it into our daily lives. Talk about your faith with family and friends. Cultivate it through study and prayer. Actualize it through good deeds and charity.

For a moment, stop what you are doing. Let your mind be silent, and allow yourself to hear the small, still voice of G-d. When you set yourself free, you will realize that your faith is much closer to the surface than you had imagined.

Remember: Regardless of anything else, G-d's absolute reality exists. The only question is how you will respond, how true to

yourself you will be in searching for it. In the meantime, G-d is
waiting for you.

〰️

*In 1941, the Rebbe and his wife were living in Paris
during the Nazi occupation. After many desperate phone
calls and letters from New York, Rabbi Yosef Yitzchak
Schneersohn, the Rebbe's father-in-law, helped the couple
obtain the necessary papers and boat tickets to sail via Por-
tugal to the United States.*

*Just before boarding the ship, the Rebbe received a tele-
gram from his father-in-law: "Do not journey on this ship,"
he had written. Even though the Nazis knew of their identity
and location, and even though there was no guarantee that
they would be able to obtain tickets for another ship, the
Rebbe canceled their reservations immediately. Later, it was
discovered that the ship the couple had planned to sail on
had been sunk by a German U-boat, with no survivors.
The Rebbe and his wife took a later ship and arrived safely
in New York on June 23, 1941.*

27

UNITY
The Rapport Between
Man and G-d

G-d is one.
—Deuteronomy 4:6

Everything we do must be directed toward discovering the underlying
unity within.
—The Rebbe

A fundamental aspect of the Rebbe's intellectual approach was to
establish a unity between apparently unrelated areas of
thought by uncovering their conceptual roots. In his discourses, he
created a tapestry of philosophy, psychology, and sociology, showing the intimate connections between the revealed and the hidden,
between the practical and the mystical. He would often begin a talk
with a literal interpretation of a Biblical passage, then show its
philosophical and psychological implications, trace the idea back to
its original concept, demonstrate how it is mirrored in the human
psyche, and finally offer a practical application of this idea in the
daily business of life. Creating such unity, the Rebbe stressed, from

the most sublime philosophical point to the most tangible actualization, is vital in the quest for a meaningful life.

WHY DO WE NEED UNITY IN OUR LIVES?

Human nature is drawn to unity. Look at a child who is given a pile of blocks of various colors or shapes—he or she naturally tries to group each block with the others that resemble it. We are all constantly searching for the connections between the various objects and forces around us, trying to make sense of their relationships. When we are not able to do so, when we cannot achieve symmetry or order, we feel confused and unsettled.

What do we mean when we say we are searching for "meaning" in our lives? What we really yearn for is to make order out of disorder, to gain insight into the unknown forces that determine all movement and behavior. But *why* are we so drawn to unity and so disturbed by chaos?

Because all the different creatures and forces of the universe were created by *one* G-d. Therefore the underlying element of our world is a single comprehensive unity, a seamless all-embracing equanimity. So even when we see disunity on the surface, we can sense a unity within, and our souls reach for it. A leaf, a twig, and a piece of bark may look nothing alike, but there is no question that they are all part of the same tree. In fact, their very existence is possible only as long as they are unified with the tree itself.

Life itself is really a search for unity. A scientist searches to discover the unifying laws that govern the seemingly diverse forces of nature. A psychologist tries to trace the myriad elements of external human behavior back to a few underlying needs inside the human psyche. An engineer combines thousands of individual parts to form one machine. But all these forms of searching for unity are actually a means to a higher end: the search for G-d and the ultimate unity.

Our own personal search for unity is directed toward this same higher end. We have been charged with the responsibility of taking all the elements of our material world—our families, our work, our daily concerns—and channeling them toward G-d, the one true unifying element both within and outside ourselves. To discover unity and meaning in our own lives, we must first understand the unity of G-d; and by searching for G-d, and for the soul within our physical bodies, we begin to make sense of the millions of threads that make up the beautiful tapestry of life. This recognition enhances our lives immeasurably, for it invests deep meaning in every single action and thought.

This is why we crave unity, and why we must search for it. We are destined to unite our body and soul, our thoughts and our deeds, our faith and our reason. Leading a unified life means leading a life of harmony, a life in which we have brought G-d into our every moment.

WHAT IS UNITY?

Unity is often confused with sameness. We may think that if everyone thought and acted the same, we would have perfect harmony. But unity is a *process*, whereas sameness is just a state of being. The same musical notes played again and again would be monotonous or irritating, but many different notes, each played differently, create a beautiful composition.

It could be said that unity is literally as simple as one, two, three. One is the presence of an individual unit, independent but alone. Two is a duality, two distinct entities. And three introduces a third dimension that can combine or contain the two entities, producing a greater unity. So unity can take two seemingly disparate elements and, while recognizing the unique qualities in each, create a whole that is far greater than the sum of its parts. Unity is the harmony within diversity.

There are countless examples of unity all around us. Our human body, for instance, is one unified whole made up of millions of diverse elements—genes, cells, limbs, organs, and systems—all of which are nourished by different foods, liquids, vitamins, minerals, and unseen forces that we have only just begun to understand.

The challenge of unity is to recognize the strengths of these different elements and bring them together without annihilating any one element's individuality. Consider the love between two people: each person must be willing to bond while respecting the other's individual needs and qualities.

The same is true in our relationship with G-d. We humans must achieve a unity with the divine without compromising ourselves or G-d. But how can we integrate our independent, earthly reality with G-d's all-encompassing, absolute reality without obliterating one or the other? Isn't divine unity antithetical to the extraordinary diversity of our physical universe?

This seeming paradox is exactly what G-d intended. He endowed our earthly reality with a seemingly independent existence that appears to mask G-d's absolute reality, with the distinct objective that we would ultimately use our free will to access our innate desire to unite with G-dliness. As our eyes and hearts and minds grow more knowledgeable about our physical reality, we begin to see, like scientists or engineers, that there is indeed an unshakable and divine unity that underlies and gives meaning to everything we do.

The idea of divine unity goes far beyond the concept that there is only one G-d; it also precludes any *existence* apart from Him.[1] Everything we can know or see or feel emanates from this single unity.

How Does G-d Reveal Unity?

Because G-d wants us to become unified with him, and not just subjugated by him, He gave us the ability to achieve true unity with our divine source. And he allowed us to contemplate this awesome dynamic. Yes, we inhabit a finite reality which, by definition and nature, precludes contact with anything truly infinite or transcendent. But in creating us, G-d also imbued within us channels of awareness that allow us to breach the outer fragmented layers of our physical world, the "container," and glimpse the pure essence of G-d's unifying "light" within. How does G-d choose to reveal this light?

Consider a teacher and his student. The teacher knows that the student has a less developed intellect, and that if he presents a concept on the level of his own comprehension, the student will only be confused. To introduce a new idea to the student, he condenses it and uses metaphors or parables to bring it within the student's grasp.

Sometimes, when the teacher is at a far higher level than the student, it may be necessary to completely set aside the original concept. It may not be enough for the teacher to condense the concept; instead, he must find a new frame of reference, reaching for examples and metaphors that the student can understand, even though they are far removed from the original concept. The teacher must make a radical jump from one world of comprehension to another, and then allow a ray of light to stream through, containing condensed information and drawing a connection.

Using metaphors is not meant to separate the teacher and the student, but to bring them together in a unity that does not compromise either of them. For the teacher, the complexity of the concept itself remains intact in his mind even though he had expressed it in a simpler metaphor; he perceives it from the "inside out." The student, meanwhile, gains access to a new concept in a language that he is capable of understanding; he begins to relate to the concept from the "outside in." The "inward" journey from metaphor to concept has begun. The concept grows and becomes integrated in the student's mind until he or she ultimately understands the original concept just as it exists in the mind of the teacher.

We can use this relationship between student and teacher as a metaphor to understand our own relationship with G-d. G-d could have chosen to conceal everything, never extending to us a stream of metaphors through which we could learn His ways. He could have allowed us to coexist as independent beings, separated from His omnipresence. But where would that leave us? Yes, we would exist, but we would have no insight into the significance of our existence. Even worse, we would have no desire to seek the meaning of our existence; we would remain locked into our own limited perspective, with no need to unite with something higher than ourselves.

Instead, by creating our world so that the outermost layers peel away to reveal successively more abstract and spiritual layers, G-d provided us with an opportunity to understand our creator. Just like the student, we gain knowledge of our universe step by step, metaphor by metaphor. Our perception of the "light" continues to be heightened as our "containers" continue to be widened, as we approach ever nearer to the perspective of the creator, our divine guide and teacher: G-d.

Just as the relationship between a teacher and a student requires a delicate balance of closeness and respect, of love and awe, we must strive for a similar balance in our relationship with G-d. This creates a healthy tension, forcing us to separate the finite from the infinite, to differentiate between our limited worldly reality and G-d's absolute reality. The very act of recognizing this separation allows us to begin integrating the two realities. Not only do we feel that G-d is *with* us every moment, but we also recognize that G-d *created* and transcends every moment. Finally, we come to the ultimate realization that "there is none else"[2] besides G-d.

HOW DO WE ACHIEVE UNITY?

To allow us to unite with Him, G-d has provided an elaborate trail of metaphors, like stepping-stones across a wide river. These steps function like a mediator or a translator. A translator does not add any new ideas to a conversation—that is not his role—but he unites two parties in communication. An intermediary does not settle a dispute, but he creates a bridge, a line of communication, that enables the two sides to achieve a common understanding. In a student-teacher relationship, the teacher is both source and mediator. The teacher's metaphor is the intermediary, allowing an abstract concept to be translated into one that can be grasped. The teacher's goal is to create a series of stepping-stones to accommodate the student's intellectual stride, leading him deeper and deeper into the concept. The metaphor, then, is equal parts "light," the teacher's concept, and "container," language that makes the ideas accessible to the student.

In describing the wisdom of King Solomon, the verse states, "And he grew wiser than all men . . . and he spoke three thousand metaphors."[3] At first glance, we might think that this description of Solomon's abilities reflects his fertile imagination rather than any great wisdom. But the metaphor is far more than an entertaining way to convey an idea; it is the translation of a concept into a lower level of intellectual discourse. The greatness of Solomon's wisdom lay in the fact that he could take the most profound, sublime thoughts and bring them to life for minds far less developed—three thousand steps less developed—than his own. This, in turn, enables the recipients to retrace the steps, one by one, until they can achieve the original high level of discourse.

Solomon's wisdom is itself a metaphor for the sort of wisdom that went into G-d's creation of our physical world. After the radical "jump" from a nonexistential reality to an existential one, G-d began creating all existences in their most spiritual, sublime forms. He then caused them to develop, in many stages, ultimately producing our physical world, the most tangible embodiment of G-d's created realities. Every material element or force is actually a physical manifestation of a higher, more spiritual one; water, for example, is the physical embodiment of love and kindness, while fire represents the physical dimension of power.

But as the properties of the world become more tangible, they also become farther removed from their divine source. With each progressive step downward, more of each object's divine "light" is concealed while more of its "container" is revealed, just as the essence of a complex idea may be diluted as it is translated into the concrete and specific words of speech or writing.

In our universe, this process has reached the point where everyone is able to experience the "containers" but very few can glimpse even a hint of the "light" within. We can see or read the words on paper, but we don't always sense the idea they represent.

And yet this is precisely what G-d wants: that our "dark" and "lowly" world obscure its connection to the divine, so that man, out of his own free will, would choose to peel back the successive layers of the container to reveal the light. And to facilitate that process, G-d created different steps along the way, a ladder by which man can climb ever upward and unite with his creator.

⁖

A man visited a rabbi to complain how difficult his life was, with problems at home and work. He said that no matter how hard he tried to work out these problems, he made no progress.

The rabbi suggested that the Biblical verse about Jacob's dream would provide an answer. He explained, "Jacob dreamed that a ladder was standing upon the ground and its top reached up toward heaven. G-d's angels were ascending and descending on it. Suddenly Jacob saw G-d standing over-him . . . and G-d said, 'I am with you.'"⁴ The rabbi paused and looked at the man. "Why were the angels first going upward and then downward, when angels come from heaven?" he asked. "Because a person must first build a ladder climbing upward from his material life toward spirituality. Then his actions sanctify his entire life, creating 'angels' that climb upward. And when they return downward, G-d will appear with them and respond to your prayers."

There is a danger, however, to this cosmic metaphorical structure. Just as a student may see the metaphor as an end in itself, failing to realize that it is only a representation of a far deeper idea, we too may fall short, believing the trivial elements of our material world to be ends in themselves. The master teacher, therefore, will allow a word, a gesture, or an inflection to slip through the layers of metaphor, giving the alert student an occasional glimmer of the more sublime concept that lies within.

Similarly, G-d did not create our existence as an "airtight" reality. Even a person who is totally focused on the material world will catch a glimpse of a greater reality, for G-d always allows at least a pinpoint of light to escape its container. Unexpectedly, we might have a certain experience that rings a bell of a higher truth in our ears. It is up to each of us to recognize and act upon that bell, to find the means to unite with the divine.

To this end, we have the Bible—the ultimate metaphor,[5] for it is G-d's pure wisdom manifested in language that we are allowed to comprehend. By studying the Bible, we unite with G-d's wisdom, and by performing the commandments as instructed therein, we actualize G-d's will. This is the means by which we take the first solid steps toward a unity with G-dliness, by which we can cross the divide between our limited reality and G-d's infinite reality. The first step is to acknowledge the *need* for such unity, which means understanding how the two realities came into being.

Light, with all its paradoxical qualities, is our best metaphor for understanding the process of creation. We speak of "enlightenment" that dispels the darkness of ignorance, of a "ray of hope" penetrating the blackness of despair, of a "divine light" that bathes a soul in virtue.

By contemplating the paradox of light—that it is clearly real and yet appears to have no substance or shape—we can approach an even greater paradox: the unity of our physical universe with the "universe" of G-dliness. The mysterious qualities of light illustrate the main truth of our physical universe: that an existence must be defined not only in terms of its own being, but as a means to illuminate a higher truth. Light becomes both a pure expression of G-dliness and the metaphor that, through our reason and other faculties, allows us to experience the ways of G-d.

This divine light begins as a pure light reflecting G-d's essence, and then manifests itself as two forms of energy: an infinite light and a finite light, a light that can be confined in a finite existence. Even as this second light is compressed into the containers that define our existence, it retains its supernal transcendent quality, always reflecting the essence of its source.

From G-d's perspective, the container and the light are two forms of the same divine energy. But from our perspective, they appear to be distinct, even opposing forces. Within ourselves, we see this difference as the split between body and soul. This tension can only be relieved by reuniting the light with the container, by reuniting our body and soul, and that requires introducing a third dimension: G-d.

When the soul unites with the body, it is finally empowered with the ability to carry out its mission in the physical world. Since each element in our universe reflects another shade of the divine, when we unite our own body and soul, we create a unity that begins to spread throughout the entire world. This is the challenge that faces each of us: to reunite with G-d, first by recognizing the transcendent soul within our own bodies, then by recognizing that G-d is above and beyond us, and finally by integrating G-d into our lives.

As we raise our sensitivity to the spiritual forces within us, we learn to love and blend with others in a way that does not compromise anyone. Together with appreciating the differences between people, we learn to see the common threads that tie us together. Instead of looking at the world selfishly, we learn to see more deeply within ourselves and discover the light within, which in turn allows us to bring out the harmony in the diverse sprawl of humankind.

This unity carries over into everything we do. The food we eat becomes fuel to help the soul carry out its divine mission. The people we meet become opportunities to perform good deeds. By looking at each action and material object as a stepping-stone toward a more spiritual place, we move ever closer to the underlying source of our world, to revealing the light within the containers.

Thus we unite with G-dliness on both our terms and His. You practice virtue and kindness in a way that emulates G-d's virtue and kindness. You use your mind to express G-d's wisdom. Everything you do becomes a metaphor for revealing G-d's light. And *that* is true unity.

HOW CAN WE UNITE WITH G-D IN OUR GENERATION?

History itself is testimony to man's search for unity. With the explosion of knowledge in the last few centuries and the proliferation of technology that has followed, we have become more and more familiar with the inner workings of our material world. Indeed, the world has grown so small that we now call it a "global village." Science has enabled us to begin comprehending the unity within the laws of nature, and technology has allowed us to create a unity with one another across the globe.

And yet we are plagued by disunity within. Marriages fail. We still treat each other cruelly. We do not always care for our needy. This is because of the dichotomy that still exists between ourselves and G-d, because we have not yet arrived at peace with our creator and the higher ideals and values that such a relationship demands. Because we have not yet come in total concert with the ultimate unity underlying all: G-d.

Not so long ago, it was accepted as scientific fact that the world was controlled by hundreds of independent forces and elements. But with advancements in science, it was determined that the atom was the principal building block of all matter, and that matter and energy are actually the same substance, only in different forms. In the same way, by peeling back successive layers of the container of our physical world, we can begin to glimpse a unity within. The "light" and the "container" are being slowly revealed as one and the same.

Isn't it time, then, to peel back a few more layers? Today we have the opportunity to integrate our reality and G-d's reality, to see how they are really one. We are all in a position to achieve the ultimate reality: peace between body and soul. Between our material drives and transcendent yearnings. Between ourselves and G-d. Never before have we had a better opportunity to communicate so easily and form a unity between man and man, community and community, nation and nation. Finally, in our generation, we can conclude the process that was begun at the outset of history: bringing peace and unity to all mankind.

Have you ever wondered where heaven meets earth? The entire process of creation was meant to challenge us with fulfilling this task, with bridging the divide between our reality and G-d's reality. By creating unity in your life, you generate a domino effect that ripples through the entire cosmic order, uniting forces that have been wrestling with each other for thousands of years. And this is the most gratifying experience of all. Our lives become truly meaningful when we know that it is our duty to marry heaven and earth, to fuse the human and the divine. So where does heaven meet earth? Right at your doorstep.

During many of his discourses, broadcast around the world via cable and satellite relays, the Rebbe would strongly encourage the use of modern communications to unite mankind. He explained how people across the globe, normally divided by space and time, are suddenly unified, creating an opportunity for them to study together, pray together, and resolve to do more good deeds, thereby forming a universal wave of togetherness. "One might think, What can I possibly accomplish sitting in this tiny corner on this huge planet of billions of people?" the Rebbe said. "Today, we see how one person lighting a candle in his tiny corner can illuminate the entire world."

28

PHILOSOPHY AND PRACTICALITY
To Know and to Do

Just as the wise person is distinguished by his knowledge, so too must he be distinguished by his actions, behavior, and conduct.
—Maimonides, *Laws of Knowledge* 5:1

When you strip away all the layers and reach the bare bone of the essence, you are then able to apply the most sublime concept to practical life.
—The Rebbe

Every talk the Rebbe ever gave, whether it was a discussion of the most profound spiritual matter or an analysis of current events, ended with the question "And so, what is the practical implication of this discussion?" And then the Rebbe would go on to explain the concrete applications of his talk. "What value does all the theoretical talk have if it cannot be applied to real life?" he would often say.

WHY DO WE THINK ONE THING AND DO ANOTHER?

We live in a world where there is a great gulf between what people think and what they do. We constantly see that people's behavior does not reflect their beliefs, or at least what they profess to believe. Often parents encourage their children to follow a particular set of rules even if the parents themselves do not.

Such a segregation of knowledge and action is unacceptable and false. A way of life means *one* way, not two; someone whose deeds do not reflect his or her thoughts is going in two directions at once. To live a meaningful life, we must learn to direct our thoughts, speech, and deeds toward one end.

The Bible teaches mankind how to lead a meaningful life. It is a life that requires harmony between knowledge and behavior, in which every event, from the most sublime to the most mundane, is permeated with meaning and purpose.

Why is it that we demand consistency from everything around us, but tolerate inconsistency in our own behavior? Perhaps we are not as honest when it comes to ourselves, or perhaps it is because we simply find it easier to do as we please without considering the consequences. But you must ask yourself: "How can I expect to find peace if my life is divided between what I believe and what I do?"

When you see yourself as a self-contained individual with no clear purpose in life, you may be controlled by conflicting thoughts and desires. Were we to see life through the eyes of its creator, though, we would see thought and action for what they truly are: two sides of the same reality. Just as a book is the combination of ideas and the words used to express these ideas, our lives are the combination of our thoughts and our actions.

When we introduce G-d into our lives, we recognize this unity. We recognize that knowledge teaches us how to behave and that our behavior is the way to actualize our knowledge. So for a person to be complete and righteous, he must master both knowledge and action.

But which is more important? In one instance, the sages state that "learning is greater, because learning brings to deed";[1] however, they also write that "the essential thing is not learning, but doing."[2]

Action without knowledge not only is directionless, but can be dangerous. Knowledge without action, on the other hand, is fruitless.[3] An architect can plan for years, draw blueprints, and hire builders, but if the building is never erected, all the preparation amounts to nothing. In our material world, the bottom line is action.

The relationship between knowledge and action is like the relationship between the soul and the body. Without the soul, the body would be lifeless, and without the body, the soul would be unable to carry out even its best intentions. But together, the body and soul form one healthy unit. Similarly, your knowledge infuses your conduct with vitality, direction, and meaning.

Thought is the most sublime form of human expression, while the deed is the most concrete. In our society, most people are in one of two groups—the thinkers or the doers, the creative or the practical, the naive or the sophisticated. Such a split is unhealthy; a wholesome person, no matter how lofty or brilliant his or her thoughts may be, must ground them in deed, and even the simplest deed must be directed by knowledge.

In education, therefore, we need to concentrate on both the cognitive and the behavioral. A student must learn a rational value system that will influence his behavior, but he must also learn a certain behavioral discipline, just as soldiers are disciplined to react instinctively in threatening situations. The cognitive also allows a student to be skeptical of the information he is being taught, to challenge it before absorbing and integrating it into his behavior. Since young children cannot be expected to determine good behavior from bad on their own, they must be taught appropriate behavior until it becomes second nature. There is no such thing as a neutral education; either a child assumes healthy habits or unhealthy ones. Once his cognitive abilities develop, he can be taught the rationale behind the value system he learned.

HOW DO KNOWLEDGE AND ACTION AFFECT EACH OTHER?

Knowledge and action, even though they are on different sides of one reality, are hardly adversaries. In fact, they are the perfect complement to each other.

Knowledge directs action by teaching us exactly what to do, showing us which tools to use, and infusing our actions with enthusiasm and personal relevance. Action contributes to knowledge by providing a touchstone, the measure by which we judge the truth of an idea. Science, after all, is built not just on theory but on experimentation; when a theory will have a practical application, you test it all the more intensely, knowing that it will affect actual lives.

So knowledge is stronger when it is translated into action, and action is stronger when it is suffused with knowledge. We can only achieve such integration by recognizing that we were created by one G-d with one purpose, which is to achieve this harmony between thought and deed, between body and soul. But why do we sometimes find it so hard to actualize our ideas?

Because that is precisely the purpose of our creation—that we harness the forces that pull us in every direction. We were given the free will to meet this challenge, to unify our hearts and minds, our thoughts and deeds, in order to create a unity within ourselves that will carry over into the rest of the world.

But wouldn't it have been simpler if G-d had only required that we *know* Him, instead of having to actualize that knowledge? Why must the deed be so essential?

The answer lies in understanding the very reason for our existence. "G-d desired to have an abode in the lower worlds."[4] The reason there can be a dichotomy between human thought and action is that G-d created a dichotomy in the cosmic order of divine expression, between the spiritual and the material. While G-d's wisdom and sublime dimensions predominate in the spiritual realms, the *essence* of G-d is expressed in this "lower" world, the world of action.

The material world is the final loop of G-d's complex cosmic circle, the last section that must be completed to achieve true unity. And because this world is the most tangible, finite portion of His creation, the divine essence is expressed in tangible and finite terms—and that is human action. The deed is the exclusive property of the material world and the physical body.

Were we to limit ourselves to study, to accumulating knowledge without implementing it, we would never realize the intention of our entire existence. The most brilliant thoughts and virtuous intentions cannot on their own perform a single act of charity; they cannot reach out to another person with love. They cannot change this world.

In order to blend thought and action in a truly profound and lasting way, there must be some degree of regularity. Even the strongest inspiration can quickly evaporate unless it is translated into an actual experience. Every deed must be accompanied by a certain measure of mental preparation and focus. But even if a person does not yet connect the thought and the deed, he or she must still behave morally, because ultimately it is the behavior—not the thought—that realizes G-d's purpose.

HOW DO WE BALANCE PHILOSOPHY
AND PRACTICALITY?

But aren't knowledge and action in conflict with each other? After all, knowledge involves the development of self, while action may mean putting aside self-oriented instincts for the task at hand. So when we have a free hour, how should we use it? How does a person cross over this difficult divide from the sublime world of thought to the material world of deed?

By recognizing why you were put here in the first place—to serve your creator. Personal growth is necessary but not an end in itself. When we humbly acknowledge our role in life, and recognize that the world does not revolve around our ego, we put aside our vanity and act responsibly. We realize that each of us is integral in shaping the world but that none of us has the power—or the responsibility—to do it alone.

⚬

A rabbi was approached by a businessman who had a legal dispute that could be settled in one of two jurisdictions. He wanted to know which judge would render the fairer verdict. One judge was known for his vast knowledge of the law and his brilliant interpretations; the other was known for his humility.

"It seems obvious that the judge with the vast knowledge would be more fair," the man said.

The rabbi disagreed. "Surely, a judge must have the appropriate knowledge and experience. But it is more important to rely on someone who will honestly consider all the arguments, someone who has the humility to eliminate his own state of thinking while he dispassionately considers each side."

We certainly should not serve G-d out of ignorant devotion, but with the power of a well-developed intellect. We have been given minds and hearts, free will and a faculty for pleasure; surely we were not meant to submit blindly to a robotlike servitude.

But the moral person must strive to unite his daily conduct with his convictions, to live up to the standards that he would like others to adhere to. If one's ideals are not reflected in his behavior, the integrity of the ideal itself must be questioned. If a philosophy is not applied, its truths become dubious, for without representation on a practical level, the philosophy—like the architect's unconsummated plan—is empty. If a person is arrogant to others or lacks sensitivity or simple manners, then his wisdom has no value. The goal of a truly wise person is to transform and integrate his wisdom by bringing it to the reality of daily life, in the way he thinks, speaks, and behaves, even the way he walks the street and eats his meals.

How Do We Apply This Unity?

True unity means applying our philosophy on the personal and psychological levels, connecting every aspect of our lives to G-d. By achieving this unity between our ideology and our actions, we will arrive at the point where we do not need to look in books to know what is right; it will become part of our very fabric. Our instincts and actions will be in tune with our souls and with G-d.

We must know what we do and do what we know. We must be role models—not only for our children, but for our friends and associates. *Carry out* your every good thought. *Use* your intelligence to solve actual problems. *Express* your love by stretching out a helping hand. *Give* your money and time to charity. A small talent that is put to use is far more valuable than a great talent that is wasted.

Think about your ideology, and ask yourself: How much of it do I live up to? When considering any plan of action, ask yourself: What difference will it make? Tomorrow morning, before you engage in any intellectual inquiry, do a good deed. Simply do it, and you will see how it enriches your outlook on life, for this is a two-way street—just as the ideology feeds the deed, the deed fortifies the ideology. Indeed, it creates ideology.

And remember, the essential thing is the deed, for a deed has the power of the divine. Your act makes G-d act. In its simplicity, a good deed is mightier than the greatest ideas ever concocted.

There is no better time to act, to unite your thoughts and deeds, than now.

⌒∭⌒

Shortly before the Six Day War, the Rebbe initiated a "tefillin campaign" to create awareness and encourage the donning of phylacteries by those obligated every weekday morning during morning prayers. Israeli General Ariel Sharon visited the Rebbe soon after and asked why he had suggested the act of donning tefillin instead of a simple prayer.

"Let me ask you," the Rebbe said, "why is it that, before soldiers are sent to battle, they go through rigorous training and various military exercises?"

"Obviously," the general responded, "because otherwise they would not know how to fight."

"But isn't it enough for soldiers to study military strategy? Why do they have to go through actual exercises?"

"It is quite understandable that you cannot compare theory with actual practice," replied the general.

"The same is true here," said the Rebbe. "Saying a prayer and having good thoughts are like studying strategy without training. When one does an act that binds his mind and heart and all his activities to G-d, then he is truly ready to go out to face the 'battles' of life with an actualized faith in G-d."

29

GOOD AND EVIL
Light and Shadows

A person must see himself and the world as equally balanced on two ends of the scale; by doing one good deed, he tips the scale and brings for himself and the entire world redemption and salvation.

—Maimonides, *Laws of Repentance* 3:4

Evil is simply the absence of good; it has no real existence of its own, and is dispelled in the light of goodness.

—The Rebbe

A visiting writer once asked the Rebbe a question that many visitors would often ask: How could a good G-d create a world where evil exists?

The Rebbe explained that evil has no real existence. It is only a potential state of being that appears to have a real existence so that man might have free choice. The Rebbe suggested that the writer think about a knife. "On its own, a knife is surely not evil, although there are occasions on which it could be used for an evil purpose," the Rebbe said. "When a doctor uses the same knife for surgery, though, it serves a good purpose. G-d allows us to choose how we will use the knife. To believe that evil has its own, positive *existence is to incorrectly believe that there are two divine powers rather than one."*

DO GOOD AND EVIL REALLY EXIST?

In the history of the world, many battles have been fought. But perhaps the greatest battle of all is the one between good and evil. Between decency and depravity, between selflessness and selfishness, between peace and violence.

We are all confronted with this battle, and we strive to be the best we can. We try to dedicate our lives to good works and we place great value on acts of charity and philanthropy. Above all, we teach our children to be virtuous and morally sound.

But where do our ethical standards come from? What is right and what is wrong? What is good and what is evil?

We live in a time when there seems to be no easy answer to these questions. Behavior that might be considered unacceptable to one group may be fine with another. Yesterday's taboos can become today's everyday activities. There seems to be no universally accepted model of right and wrong; schools that were once a source of objective values have often become ideological battlegrounds where values are neutralized so as not to discriminate against the feelings of any individual or group.

What we are often left with is a diluted form of moral relativism: Anything is acceptable as long as it doesn't overtly hurt someone else. But is this standard high enough? In the name of "live and let live," have we compromised our most basic sense of right and wrong? Ask yourself this simple question: Does such moral ambiguity ring true in your heart and soul?

This leads to an even broader question, which some people may have grown too timid to pose: Is there a real and absolute wrong and right? If not, why do human beings naturally feel positive about certain things and repelled by others? Even young children share this trait, an inner sense of right and wrong that is as strong as the sense of sight or hearing.

To lead a truthful and meaningful life, we must define good and evil and we must have an absolute value system that guides our conduct. Otherwise, our standards will remain arbitrary. We may even wonder why we should bother to dedicate our lives to the pursuit of goodness. When we teach our children right from wrong, we must be able to tell them—and ourselves—why such a distinction is necessary, and absolute.

In the Bible, G-d provided mankind with a set of absolute laws and instructions, which define right and wrong and good and evil.

From G-d's perspective, good and evil are forces that are, respectively, constructive and destructive. And they are defined as absolutely as the system they govern. Just as healthy food nourishes the body and poison harms it, goodness is essential for the soul's health and evil hurts it.

So G-d's instructions—which are manifest in our innate sense of right and wrong—are not merely a suggestion or even a command regarding how we should conduct our lives. Rather, it is a case of G-d, the creator and architect of life, providing an instruction manual that details how to treat our body and soul so they function at their best.

Goodness, therefore, is not just a moral obligation; it is essential nourishment for your body and soul. Similarly, hurting another person is unacceptable not only because you have no right to do so, but because you are also damaging yourself.

Looking at good and evil in this light also explains reward and punishment, which is essentially a system of cause and effect, a cosmic immune system. By committing good acts, you are further connecting yourself to G-d, thereby energizing your own soul; a wicked act, meanwhile, disconnects you from G-d and weakens your soul.

Virtuous behavior is an affair not just between men, but between man and G-d. War breaks out in the heart of man when the human soul becomes disconnected from God, the source of goodness. Why can men hate and destroy each other? Because their egos can wish to deny that all of humanity comes from the same source, and should therefore be striving toward the same goal. Doing good means rising above your own needs, connecting with G-d, and extending this unity to your fellow man.

WHY DO GOOD AND EVIL EXIST?

We all struggle to fathom how a good and righteous G-d could allow so much suffering and could permit such atrocities in the world. The age-old question inevitably arises: Why did G-d create evil, and how can we reconcile it with His goodness?

To answer this, we must take one step back and ask a far more basic question: Why did G-d create life? For without life, there would be no evil and no pain.

G-d created our material world because He wanted us to refine it and make it His home. In order to achieve this, we must first perceive ourselves as an independent reality. So each of us was granted free will, the ability to choose between selflessness and selfishness, and between good and evil, to follow G-d's instructions or not to. This freedom is the greatest gift G-d gave us. Without it, there would be no point to life.

G-d does not want evil; He wants us to do only good. Nor does G-d ever commit evil; only man commits evil. But in order for man to be a true partner in life, he must have the autonomy to choose. Even though G-d cannot bear the pain when one man causes another to suffer, it would be even more painful to take back the free will He has given us.

So we have the potential to do either good or evil. And by overcoming the temptation to do evil, the temptation to advance ourselves at any cost, we reach a far higher plane than we otherwise could have. The greater the challenge, the more strength it draws out from us. And just as a light in the night seems brighter and is more appreciated than the same light by day, an act of kindness shines with all the more intensity when compared to the wrong-doing we could have committed instead. There is a certain risk in G-d's having granted us such a choice, but risk is inherent in growth. For a child to learn to walk, he or she must be allowed to fall.

This explains why there is a *potential* for evil, but how can evil exist in the face of a good and omnipresent G-d? This takes us back to the method that G-d used to create our physical reality. In order to allow us our independence, G-d concealed His presence, challenging us to see beyond the "container," the physical world in which we live, to find the G-dly "light" within.

 ⚬⚬⚬

A student approached a rabbi with a question: "How can we reconcile evil with G-d's omnipresent goodness?" he asked.

"In relation to this world, G-d is like a father who hides himself from his child," the rabbi replied. "The father is encouraging the child to demonstrate his ingenuity in finding him, which will ultimately intensify the love and closeness between them. The father, wanting to truly challenge the child to draw out his deepest strengths, hides himself very well—so well, in fact, that the child finally gives up the search, forgets his father, and goes off to something else. Meanwhile, his father remains in his hiding place, sadly waiting for his child to return. Similarly, G-d concealed Himself from us to bring out our deepest abilities and resources in our search for Him. It is G-d's concealment in the material world—which is intended to create a truly profound search for goodness—that allows for the potential of evil."

G-d's concealment in our material world allows us the free will either to seek Him out or ignore Him. If G-d's presence were obvious to us, we would have neither the inclination nor the opportunity to do evil. But then we wouldn't have the challenge—or the awesome satisfaction—of doing good, either.

Evil, in other words, is the challenge of life gone awry. When we become oblivious to the challenge or ignore it, like the child who stops searching for his father, we allow G-d's concealment to leave room—after many levels of condensation and mutation—for potential evil. When we see only the "container" and not the "light" within, when we selfishly pursue only our material interests and ignore our spirituality, this self-interest can allow evil to flourish.

But one cannot say that G-d chooses evil or sustains it. Wickedness is committed *against* G-d's will, for His intention is not to remain concealed but to be revealed, and it pains Him when we cease looking for Him.

Since evil is against G-d's will, it has no legitimacy of its own; it is only a result of our being deceived by G-d's concealment and not seeing it as a means to G-d's revelation. Consider that evil is darkness while goodness is light: Just as darkness is merely the absence of light, evil is merely the absence of goodness. And just as darkness can be dispelled by introducing even a small amount of light, evil can be dispelled by introducing even a small amount of goodness.

So when we are deceived by G-d's concealed state and succumb to it by committing evil, we are giving substance that is really like a shadow, with no substance of its own. Thus, by refraining from evil conduct, we are actively negating evil, destroying its illusory power and thereby revealing its true purpose. As the sages say of evil, "Its destruction is its repair."[1]

A person must do everything in his power to avoid committing any sin; it is not permissible to sin with the intention of later repenting.[2] But if he does succumb to temptation, he always has within him the power to repent, to release the positive spark from within the darkness of the sin while destroying the evil of the sin itself. The person who commits evil and repents may actually gain a greater appreciation for G-d, for the intense light of goodness is all the greater when we see it in close contrast to the sheer darkness of evil.

ARE WE NATURALLY INCLINED TOWARD GOOD OR EVIL?

Some thinkers contend that good and evil are two equal powers, and some would even argue that evil is the more powerful of the two. They consider man's nature as essentially selfish and morality as a superimposed condition to allow us to coexist in peace. Most people, the argument goes, are controlled by their evil inclinations, and the world at its root is an uncaring or even wicked place.

The Bible teaches us that this is unequivocally wrong. There is only one G-d and G-d is good; therefore, all of G-d's creations, including man and our world, are essentially good. In our hearts, we all have a natural propensity for justice and virtue, and are repulsed by injustice and abuse. We maintain a deep hope and faith that things will be better than they are.

The fact that we live in a world where, often, "the wicked prosper" and where selfishness prevails is a result of our giving priority to the material world and disregarding the spiritual. After Adam and Eve sinned, a dichotomy was created between matter and spirit. Instead of being seen as a "container" for spiritual divine "light" within, the world began to be seen as an independent, self-contained reality. This distortion allows room for evil; but whereas goodness is a real and tangible virtue, evil has no power on its own.

The fact that the wicked prosper, then, is not a reality on its own, but a result of limiting our vision to the one-dimensional material world, or our failure to recognize the container as concealed light for us to reveal. Rather than battling evil, we should concentrate on cultivating the goodness within ourselves and others. After all, since evil has no independent existence, focusing on it only gives it more opportunity to grow. The best and most effective response and solution to evil is to attack not only its symptoms, but its cause: G-d's concealed presence. By introducing G-d into our lives, through selfless acts of goodness, we destroy evil at its root.

When teaching a child, or when you see a friend succumbing to selfishness, it may be tempting to reprimand him, to frighten him by warning of the terrible consequences that will surely befall him if he continues his behavior. But the positive approach is ultimately more successful. Tell the person about the goodness within him, of his pure soul and great potential; show what a great injustice he is committing by not living up to this potential. Such advice will foster confidence and pride, while a grave warning demoralizes a person and closes up his soul.

⌀⌀⌀

A rabbi once entered a rural synagogue and heard a preacher rebuking his congregation. The peasants were wailing in guilt as they heard of the terrible punishment that awaited them for their bad deeds.

Afterward, the rabbi approached the preacher. "There are two ways to prevent a thief from pursuing his vocation," he said. "One is by imprisoning him so he cannot go out and rob. But this doesn't really correct the problem, because the thief remains a thief, and he will likely steal again once released. The second way is to rehabilitate the thief by teaching him how inappropriate it is for him to live this way. Teach him a respectable vocation and evoke in him a sense of pride and dignity that it is beneath him to stoop to being a thief. In the long term, it is always better to inspire rather than criticize, to encourage rather than demoralize."

HOW DO WE HANDLE THE PAIN THAT EVIL CAUSES?

We have all seen the consequences of evil. We may come to understand that such suffering strengthens a human being, that there is no greater satisfaction than overcoming adversity, but such revelations do not satisfy the suffering heart. Inevitably, we ask: Why must it be this way? Abraham cried out to G-d, "Shall the whole world's judge not act justly?"[3] and his cry has reverberated through a hundred generations of tear-soaked history.

All the explanations in the world cannot address the pain of suffering. Even the most logical reason is, at best, only theoretical; the heart will never reconcile itself to pain. On the other hand, faith in G-d is not dependent on answers to philosophical queries; no amount of intellectual prodding can dent the person of faith, because faith is built on an inner sense of what is true and real, which is far stronger than logic alone and far beyond the pain of evil.

The paradox of faith dictates that we both challenge G-d and accept what He does, for we recognize that G-d's reality is far beyond our own and that ultimately we cannot understand His mysterious ways.[4] This paradox has been plaguing the thinking believer since the beginning of time. While the mind struggles to rationalize, the heart learns to love. While the mind tries to categorize a series of conflicting events, the heart tolerates contradiction. Outrage and devotion, judgment and acceptance, pain and pleasure—a heart that loves has room for them all.

So yes, we question and challenge G-d. And yes, we pray and demand that He do away with evil and suffering. And yet we realize that *only G-d knows* why such suffering is permitted, why tragedy and agony are allowed. The only true answer for the heart is silence. After all is said and done, there are no words to explain the pain we feel from evil, and no words can erase it.

But we must also remember that G-d has given each of us a purpose in life—to commit and encourage acts of goodness, to use our time, energy, and knowledge to tear through the layers of the "container" and reveal G-d's light within. Despite the lack of a satisfactory answer to the question of evil, one can—and must—carry on a meaningful life, promote justice and kindness, and, indeed, help create a better world, one in which there is no nourishment for evil, where there is no room in man's heart for any inhumanity whatsoever.

How then should one react to a devastating calamity like the Holocaust, for instance? We, of course, have no answers to such utterly senseless evil, and we must challenge G-d for allowing it. However, at the same time, this experience must be interpreted as the ultimate challenge, which we must meet with complete resolve and determination. We must not allow tragedy to immobilize us, but rather inspire it to motivate us to intensify ever more our commitment to the forces of good. Regardless of how long it will take the world to repent for the Holocaust, we must each say that I, for one, will not slacken my determination to carry out my purpose, to make this world a fitting home for G-d and the rest of humanity.

So what is the best way to deal with evil and the pain it causes? Faith leads us to the most fascinating—and pragmatic—conclusion: We should not get stuck, in our hearts or minds, on trying to resolve this question, for we will never answer it adequately. Instead of wasting our time dwelling on the negative, we should be concentrating on all the good that we can accomplish.

We have the ability to counter the forces of evil by shining the light of goodness on them. And we have the certitude that good will prevail. This confidence goes beyond common optimism. Because goodness is the natural state of the world and humankind, its effect is eternal and cumulative. All of man's good works throughout the ages are building blocks, leading up to a final triumph of goodness in the world. Moral relapses are not flaws, but by-products of this process. It is to be expected that when the forces of goodness show strength, the forces from where evil originates will endeavor to retaliate, and that they will make their final stand just on the verge of their total collapse.

After so many years of goodness and virtue, after all the blood and tears shed by so many wonderful people in their fight for what is good and right, the world is virtually saturated with positive spiritual energy. The goodness is lying just beneath the surface, straining to burst through. The next step is ours. By doing one more good deed—and we do not know which one it is—we will tip the scale, releasing centuries' worth of radiance, bathing the entire world in the light of knowledge and the goodness of G-d.

In 1977, *after the Rebbe suffered a serious heart attack, a doctor was drawing his blood. "What is it that draws the blood from the veins?" the Rebbe asked. "The needle itself or the vacuum of the syringe?" The doctor answered that it was the vacuum.*

"That reminds me of a troubled man who once came to see me," the Rebbe said to his secretary, who was standing nearby. "He complained that he was 'empty' and unfit for anything. I told him that, in fact, the opposite was true— that an empty vessel can draw in with much greater intensity than a vessel that is full, so he is actually in an excellent position to produce much good and holiness."

It was a holiday, a day on which the Rebbe traditionally delivered a joyful sermon. "Since I will not be able to speak," he said to his secretary, "I ask you to repeat what I just said. Just as the vacuum draws in more forcefully than something that is filled, at the gathering tonight, even though the person usually sitting in my chair will be absent, the holiday spirit should not be dampened. On the contrary— the vacuum will evoke all good things from heaven."

30

᠙᠊᠊᠊᠙

MIRACLES
Seeing the Extraordinary
Within the Ordinary

The difference between a miracle and a natural event is only in
frequency.
—The Baal Shem Tov

Miracles are all around us; we must open our eyes to see them.
—The Rebbe

᠙᠊᠊᠊᠙

A group of college students had a private audience with the
Rebbe. One student asked the Rebbe if he could perform miracles.

"This physical, natural world," he explained, "is not a separate
entity from the higher, spiritual world—rather, it evolved from it.
And so, when someone connects himself to the spiritual world, to
G-d, he can affect things in this physical world in a way that
cannot be anticipated. Every person is given the choice whether or
not to connect himself to the spiritual world.

"We must make the right choice," the Rebbe continued, "and
use all our strength to live virtuously, to introduce harmony to

everyone we meet, to encourage others to increase goodness and defeat evil—in effect, to make the world a better place."

The Rebbe concluded: "So, in essence, by inspiring students like yourselves to go out into the world and perform good works, yes, we can perform miracles."

WHAT IS A MIRACLE?

D o you believe in miracles? To answer this question, we must define what we mean by "miracle."

The word is used so often, sometimes for such trivial events, that it has become a cliché. On a superficial level, some people consider a miracle to be simply an unexpected event or a wonderful surprise; for others, however, a miracle is the belief that G-d has intervened supernaturally in their lives. People may disagree on whether events in their lives are indeed miraculous or can be explained naturally. Some see miracles as a true affirmation of G-d's presence in their lives; a more skeptical person might think of a miracle as an unrealistic hope, something one clings to in the face of life's harsh realities.

The question of miracles is really a question of how we understand G-d and the role He plays in our lives. By analyzing the anatomy of a miracle and understanding your feelings about miracles, you can learn much that will help you find deeper meaning in your life.

So what do we mean by "miracle"? If we agree that a miracle is a beneficent occurrence that cannot be explained by the laws of nature, then we must first ask the question: What is a natural event? Why wouldn't any natural event that awes and excites us be considered a miracle?

Truth be told, we don't really understand the "laws" of nature. Yes, nature operates according to a design that we have come to accept as normal. But while this makes life more predictable and, therefore, more comfortable, it doesn't necessarily make it any more *understandable.* When we know, for instance, that the sun will rise tomorrow morning, we feel a sense of order and control; but we still have no idea as to why nature was created this way. Just because we label something "natural" doesn't mean that we understand it any better than we understand a "miracle."

The difference between a miracle and an act of nature is only in frequency.[1] Imagine that the sun were to rise only once in our lifetime. Everyone would rush out to see it, proclaiming it a most miraculous event. But since we experience a sunrise every day, we see it as just another ordinary part of our lives.

This is an inherent human trait—we become so accustomed to something that, no matter how extraordinary it may be, we take it for granted. We constantly need a new rush of excitement to arouse our interest. Someone will say, "If I only saw a miracle, then I would believe, then I would change my life!" What are we waiting for— the parting of the sea? Miracles are happening around us every moment. Life itself is a miracle; consider the sheer wonder of human birth. In fact, we do often refer to birth as a miracle; why, then, do we so easily forget that every person on earth is the product of a miracle?

Since we are so distracted by the daily struggle to survive, by our responsibilities and obligations, we tend to ignore the miracles around us. The very noise of life drowns out the underlying sound of what should be most real to us. It is not that we don't believe in miracles; we simply stop taking the time to appreciate them. To see a miracle means to appreciate the uncommon within the common, the extraordinary within the ordinary.

〰️

Several travelers were warming themselves by a fire in a roadside inn. They began to praise their respective rabbis. One man said that for fifteen years, he and his wife had been unable to have children; less than a year after they were blessed by their rabbi, they had a newborn daughter. Another man related how his rabbi's blessing had brought home his wayward son. A third man related that his rabbi had blessed an important business venture in which he invested several thousand dollars and lost every penny.

"So what's the miracle?" he was asked.

"The miracle," the man replied, "was that I remained faithful to G-d and to my rabbi."

When you can recognize the extraordinary within the ordinary, supernatural occurrences are not that impressive to you. Your faith—and life—is not dependent on such miracles, for you have a mature relationship with a reality that is higher than yourself, and you realize that the ultimate miracle is our very existence.

Just contemplate the awesome design and balance within any one family of the animal, vegetable, or mineral kingdom, to say nothing of the beauty of the human body or the elegance of the solar system. The divine miracle of nature is not to be found in its once-in-a-lifetime events, but in its relentless regularity.[2] Whereas every creation of man is ephemeral, every part of nature is boundless, permanent, and inexplicable—in a word, miraculous.[3]

DO MIRACLES REALLY HAPPEN?

Because so many of us take for granted the many wonders before our eyes, G-d does on occasion perform miracles to shake us from our reverie, to elevate us to a higher plane of awareness. Sometimes a miracle occurs to rescue us from a dire situation. Since G-d created the universe and its laws of nature, it would follow that He can alter or suspend these laws as He sees fit.[4]

But such miracles are infrequent, especially today. "G-d doesn't perform miracles in vain,"[5] our sages tell us, and "we ought not to rely on a miracle."[6] Why is this the case? Because this world was created with a natural order so that we could civilize it and make it a dwelling place for G-d; this is accomplished not by going beyond nature but by imbuing nature with that which is beyond. A miracle momentarily opens the door between the natural world that surrounds us and the spiritual world within; G-d's intention is not to supersede the laws of nature, but to give us a greater appreciation and awareness of our daily, natural lives.

There are two types of miracles—one that openly defies the laws of nature, and one that manifests itself within these laws, initially giving off the appearance of a totally natural event. We have read and heard much of the first type of miracle—the parting of the Red Sea, for instance, or when someone makes a full recovery from an illness that doctors had considered terminal. The second type of miracle is no less wondrous—the bloodless fall of communism, for instance, or the world's retreat from the brink of nuclear war.

So there are, in essence, three levels of miracles: those that are clearly visible and indisputable, those that take on a natural shape but are clearly miraculous, and the miracle of nature itself. Why these three levels? To unite this natural world with G-d. This requires three elements: the language of the lower, natural world; the language of G-d; and an intermediary, something that serves to translate the miraculous language of G-d into our natural world.

The miracle of nature is by far the most common—and the easiest to overlook—for it is constantly occurring around us and inside us. But imagine that you stepped into the modern world from the eighteenth or nineteenth century. Look at the computer that can organize such massive amounts of data or the artificial heart with which a surgeon can save a person's life: Would there be a shred of doubt in your mind that these were miracles? And yet they were produced not by some overt supernatural intervention, but by the very hand of man, using the skills G-d gave him to operate within the laws of nature.

Living a meaningful life means finding meaning in *everything* you do and encounter, beginning with the natural world. The effects of nature color your entire being; you are bound by the demands that nature puts on your body—the need to eat, to sleep, to seek safety and shelter.

The solution is not to surrender to the laws of nature or view them as boundaries that constrict our creativity and drive; instead we must see them as a divine blueprint, which in and of itself is full of miracles. Yes, nature poses a formidable challenge. How convenient it would be, for instance, if humans could fly. But consider the feelings of unfettered release we felt when the first airplane took to the air, or, even more miraculously, when we first reached outer space. Using nature's blueprint—the wings of a bird—we re-created the first miracle of flight for ourselves. And yet, only a few short decades after we held space exploration in such awe, we already take if for granted.

All our significant experiences in life remain wanting if we ultimately find no deeper meaning in them, if we are not able to go beyond the natural order to which we so often feel prisoner. How can we break away from the formidable grip of nature? By understanding exactly what nature is and what it is not; by recognizing that the laws of nature were not placed before us like a barrier, but given to us by G-d so we could reveal the extraordinary within the ordinary.

To do so, we must learn to look at the world with fresh eyes, to observe the beauty of nature and stand in awe of its designer. Nature is one of our best teachers; there is something to be learned from every aspect, no matter how humble. In a bee's honeycomb, we see pure efficiency; in the pull of the tides, we see the cyclical nature of time; in the root system of a tree, we see the instinct for self-nourishment.

We must learn to look more closely at our daily experiences. You will soon see patterns developing; it will become obvious that your footsteps are being guided by divine providence—when you meet someone, when you take a trip, when a new business opportunity presents itself. Every moment in your life contains the opportunity for a miracle; it is up to you to stay receptive, to reveal the sublime within the everyday.

WHAT SHOULD WE
LEARN FROM MIRACLES?

In just the last few years, we have experienced countless miracles based on new technologies and further advances in science. To be sure, these revolutionary developments can all be explained rationally, and yet, when we examine the larger picture, we see a pattern developing: Mankind is coming ever closer to a deeper and deeper unity.

The world continues to grow smaller, thanks to developments in communication and travel. Technological advancements give us more time and energy to pursue nobler goals. Many of the physical obstacles that impeded spiritual and personal growth in previous generations have fallen away.

Consider the collapse of the Iron Curtain and the crumbling of communism. Yes, after years of oppression and corruption, it may have seemed inevitable that the Soviet Union would fall, and yet who could have predicted that it would happen so suddenly and so peacefully? The world is consistently evolving toward unity, toward recognizing the divine rights of all mankind.

Every field, from science and medicine to business and communications, is experiencing major breakthroughs at breathtaking speed. We must see such developments for what they are—not merely random events to be used for self-serving goals, but individual steps toward a path of righteousness, a path leading upward toward a life of meaning and redemption.

Yes, we can explain away many events, even "miraculous" ones. But then again, a good mind can explain away anything. Just as you have a choice in everything you do, you can use your mind to either seek out the miracles in life or deny them. Only you can know the degree of sincerity with which you are trying to understand your life and instill it with meaning.

If you look honestly at your life, you will recognize the miracles within nature and the miracle of nature itself. You will recognize the divine providence in all your activities. You will learn to appreciate the miracles of your own life—the successes you've had and the very miracle of life. Thank G-d for these miracles; don't take them for granted.

And finally, you will realize that the world around you is experiencing miracles within miracles, a revolution from within. It is time to acknowledge that the world is hurtling toward redemption—and that it is your choice and your choice alone whether to be a part of it.

⁓

A man had driven some distance to attend a gathering with the Rebbe, and he stood in line along with several thousand others.

"I don't come just for the inspiration," he explained to the person in front of him. "I've heard of numerous miraculous incidents at these occasions."

Upon reaching the Rebbe, each person in line held out a cup, into which the Rebbe would pour some wine. When the man finally reached the Rebbe, he held out the cup in his left hand, but the Rebbe motioned for him to hold it in his right.

The man made no move to change hands, and the Rebbe did not pour the wine. An attendant urged the man, "Please hold the cup in your right hand."

With obvious trepidation, he extended his right hand. He looked on in disbelief as the Rebbe filled his cup. The people behind him were annoyed with the delay, but he wholeheartedly forgave them. How could they have known that his right hand had been paralyzed?

31

ⁿ‿ⁿ

REDEMPTION
Toward the Meaningful Life

The world will be filled with the knowledge of G-d,
as the waters cover the sea.
—Isaiah 11:9

The final redemption is no longer a dream of a distant future,
but an imminent reality.
—The Rebbe

ⁿ‿ⁿ

W hen the Rebbe assumed leadership of the Lubavitch movement, in 1951, he declared that the long process of human
history was finally coming to fruition. "This generation is the final
generation of exile," he said, "and the first generation of redemption—
personal redemption and universal redemption, leading to the perfection of society and a world filled with the awareness of G-d. Everything now depends on us."

This had been the major theme of the Rebbe's life. He once
wrote in a letter, "From the day that I went to school and even
prior to that, the vision of the future redemption began to take form
in my imagination—a redemption of great magnitude and grandeur,

*through which the purpose of suffering, the harsh decrees and anni-
hilations of exile will be understood."*

WHY REDEMPTION?

Imagine that you have lived your entire life in a dark tunnel. Your parents and grandparents lived there too, and so did *their* parents and grandparents. You have grown accustomed to the darkness and developed the necessary skills to survive. You move through life, sometimes staggering in the dark, at other times feeling your way along. You are totally resigned to the fact that this is what life is, and that it will continue to be so.

But you have been told or have read in some ancient books that long ago, your ancestors lived in a very different, well-lighted place. You have heard that there is indeed a light at the end of this tunnel, that you don't necessarily have to spend your entire life in darkness. However, you are skeptical—after all, this darkness is the only life you know. After so many generations have lived in this tunnel, can you really believe some old tale about the possibility of a life on the outside? And besides, you have learned to cope here, to make yourself comfortable in the darkness, so why would you want to risk changing things?

And yet, something inside tells you that the darkness is just not right for your life. No matter how accustomed you have become to it, you still feel restless and insecure. You realize that although the darkness may be a *part* of life, it is not life itself.

As we stumble along and feel our way through life, we have all wondered whether we will ever find true happiness. Will we ever find peace within ourselves and lead a truly meaningful life, or are we destined to a life fraught with fear and confusion? Will virtue and kindness really prevail? If not, how can we justify to ourselves and our children the need to adhere to moral and ethical principles? After all, even though human nature craves a higher purpose, what is the point of working so hard to live a virtuous life if it is not leading anywhere?

The answer to all these questions is just one word: *redemption*. Redemption is the light at the end of the tunnel. Redemption is G-d telling us that the reason for which He created the universe will indeed be realized—that goodness *will* prevail and that our lives *can* be meaningful. Redemption is both an integral part of G-d's plan and an integral part of human life. Without redemption, our lives would indeed be meaningless—a never-ending tunnel of darkness, with little awareness of an alternative existence and no hope of ever reaching the light.

REDEMPTION FROM WHAT?

But what exactly do we need redemption from? From being trapped in the darkness of the material world, which obscures our search for meaning. From a listless and aimless life. From our doubts and fears.

G-d created each of us with a divine spark that, when cultivated, allows us to illuminate the darkness and move forward. How does one cultivate this spark? By recognizing the strength within your soul. By rising above your ego and acknowledging an absolute force that is far greater than yourself. By being a giving person and leading a virtuous life. And above all, by realizing that amidst the darkness there is indeed a light to be found, which will instill every act of virtue with infinite meaning.

Redemption is not an event that happens at the end of our life on earth; it is a cumulative process that begins at the outset of our lives, and every act of goodness brings us one step closer to completing the process. Redemption means an end to darkness and confusion; it means a time of harmony.

Is redemption a miracle? No. It is the way things were always meant to be. But how can we be sure we will be redeemed? After all, when we look around, the world seems quite far from redemption. Selfishness and darkness abound.

The answer, of course, is that G-d told us it would be so. Ask yourself a simple question: Why do you strive to live a meaningful life? Why aren't you comfortable living only for yourself, thinking of nothing but your own needs and desires?

We are driven by a paradox, a force created by the pull of two opposites: our body, which represents the material universe, and our soul, which represents the spiritual universe. Everything about our existence is marked by this dichotomy. We live in a world that is imperfect and yet we search for perfection. We live a life full of pain and difficulty and yet we strive for peace and harmony.

The same is true on a collective and global scale. From the beginning of time, people have invested their hearts and minds to make life a little bit better. We have created new political and economic systems, we have pursued education and enlightenment, we have developed industry and enterprise—all in search of a more perfect society. Notwithstanding the extreme differences among races, nations, and beliefs, people across the globe—six billion and counting—are looking for a better life.

In a word, we are all looking for redemption. Do not be intimidated by the word; "redemption" is not necessarily a religious or spiritual matter. Redemption means freedom—freedom from the boundaries that confine the human spirit. To be redeemed means to be freed from a tyrannical regime; to be freed from a dangerous habit or an abusive situation; to be freed from the fear within ourselves and the confusion that clouds our vision.

So we are all looking for redemption, whether we use that word or not. Some of us experience brief bursts of freedom, but more often than not, we resign ourselves to lives without such light or clarity. The chains of our existence seem too formidable. We are in a state of confinement, of exile; the shackles of the material world confine us in darkness.

So how do you free yourself? By acknowledging that you were created by G-d—in G-d's image—and are therefore inherently good. By realizing that you come from a higher place than this limited world; that your mission on earth is not merely to use the material world for your own satisfaction, but to refine and civilize it through virtuous acts.

Yes, it can be difficult to find meaning in this dark world. Believing in G-d and experiencing G-d is a process that takes much effort. But the first step is a simple one: Before you can escape the darkness, you must acknowledge it. Before you can leave your state of exile, you must realize that you indeed dwell there.

On a sweltering summer day, an old man went down into a cool cellar for some relief. The moment he entered, he was blinded by the darkness. "Don't worry," said another man in the cellar, "it is natural that when you go from light to darkness, you're unable to see. But soon enough, your eyes will grow accustomed to it, and you will hardly notice that it is dark."

"My dear friend," replied the old man, turning to leave, "that is exactly what I am afraid of. Darkness is darkness; the danger is convincing yourself that it is light."

HOW WILL REDEMPTION COME ABOUT?

Will redemption radically alter our lives? Yes and no. The physical world around us will not change; rather, we will change. Maimonides states explicitly that no miracle must occur; redemption will not be an apocalyptic or supernatural event. The era of redemption (or "the Messianic Age"), says Maimonides, will be a time when we are all absorbed in "knowing G-d."[1]

This means, in part, that people will perceive G-d in all their experiences. Whether a doctor or a businessperson or a parent, we will all see our material pursuits through the filter of spirituality—not as an end in themselves, but as a means to a higher end. Just as a hungry person naturally craves food, we will naturally crave goodness; we will intuit what is right and wrong and act accordingly. No longer will there be a dichotomy between our hearts and minds, our bodies and souls, our internal and external feelings. We will all come to recognize that every detail of this universe is the work of G-d.

The final redemption will come about in a manner similar to the redemption and exodus from Egypt. Just as Moses was sent by G-d to lead the liberation from Egypt, a Messiah—"Moshiach"—will lead the entire world into the final redemption.

Why the need for a leader? Because even though we each have a divine spark within us, the darkness of the material world is overpowering. G-d sends us a selfless leader, therefore, who can rise above the material distractions, who is sensitive to the needs of a generation, and who has the ability to communicate the message of G-dliness to our complicated, confused society. And who, through his actions and teaching, inspires us to study G-d's wisdom and live according to His laws. All the nations of the world will be motivated to serve G-d together, to fulfill their obligations by following the moral and divine commandments as set down in the Bible.[2]

WHERE DO WE STAND NOW?

After thousands of years of living in the tunnel and traveling through its darkness, we now stand on the threshold of the era of redemption. Revolutionary changes are taking place on all fronts—on a personal level and on a global scale, in technology, in politics, and in the human spirit.

The values of freedom, tolerance, and generosity are spreading throughout the community of nations. Family has become important again, as people seek to build meaningful relationships that go beyond their careers or material desires. Throughout America and the world, people are genuinely searching for spiritual meaning, to find the very essence of their being. There is a greater commitment to inner change and personal growth; instead of blaming others, people are beginning to realize that they must take responsibility for their own lives, and are endeavoring to do so.

So the world may be ready for redemption, but how do we prepare for it? By opening our eyes and understanding the unique time in which we live. By acknowledging that the events that unfold each day are part of the process leading toward the meaningful life of redemption. By learning about G-d and spirituality so that we may live according to His will.

This isn't always easy. As we wrestle with an uneasy past and an unfamiliar future, it may seem more comforting to cling to the lives we know. But the thirst for redemption is coupled with another trait that all humans share: hope. Hope for health and prosperity. Hope for justice and virtue. Hope for freedom from the darkness.

Because the challenge is so large, you must start small. Take an inspiring class or go to a lecture. Learn about G-d and redemption—the purpose of creation. Remember, the first step in escaping the darkness is acknowledging that it *is* darkness. Familiarize yourself with these ideas at your own pace, and you will begin to see a larger picture taking shape in your mind. Pause for a moment to reflect on the true priorities in your life. Make your home a loving environment; make your office a place where generosity and compassion replace selfishness and aggression. And above all, share these ideas with your family and friends.

If one person can resolve to make these changes, then ten can. And if ten can, so can one hundred, and on and on. After all, we are intrinsically good; we naturally want to lead better, more productive, more meaningful lives. Commit yourself today and exhort others to do the same.

After traveling for so long in the dark and winding tunnel of life, we are now approaching its end, and we are beginning to feel and see the warm, bright light shining in. Now, then, is not the time to hesitate; it is not the time to be skeptical or selfish. Even the smallest things—a kind word, a dollar to charity, a few minutes of prayer—are immeasurably significant. We must do anything we can to direct even one ray of light into the darkness. Our journey is about to end; we are set to reach our destination, our rendezvous with G-d. The next move is yours.

‿◦◦◦‿

On April 11, 1991, eleven months before he fell ill, the Rebbe delivered an impassioned speech. It was an unusually strongly worded message, and the anguished voice in which he delivered it shocked and roused his followers to intensify their efforts to prepare themselves and the world at large for the redemption.

"How is it that Moshiach has still not come?" the Rebbe said. "Why is our world still a place in which evil and suffering prevail? Why is it acceptable that redemption should not come tonight, nor tomorrow, nor the day after? You must do all that you can to bring our righteous redeemer, immediately! It is not sufficient to mouth slogans. It is up to each and every one of you to bring the ultimate redemption with your actions. It is in your hands to bring about the harmonious, perfect world of Moshiach."

EPILOGUE

<hr>

The Rebbe as the Messiah?

This book presents the teachings and wisdom of the Rebbe, Rabbi Menachem Mendel Schneerson. The Rebbe would have asked you to read closely and objectively, and apply these teachings to your life by becoming a more conscious and compassionate person, by improving yourself and your world, by being your best.

And yet there is one distraction that is obfuscating these essential issues. The focus of much of the attention paid to the Rebbe, rather than being on the study and application of his teachings to bring about redemption, has shifted almost exclusively to the question of whether the Rebbe himself is the Messiah. Without ignoring the fact that this interest reflects the deep human yearning for transcendence, this longing can be fully appreciated only when it is placed in context of the all-encompassing quest for redemption and our active participation in being its vehicle. Since this book proffers the Rebbe's unadulterated ideas without personal commentary or editorial opinion, I believe that this issue should be addressed here by asking: How would the Rebbe have answered the question of whether or not he is the Messiah?

The approach must be based on objective truth, and not be determined by opinion, emotion, or partisan interest. The Rebbe taught that the Torah, the Bible, is the template of objective, absolute truth; therefore, we must search for the answers that the Torah provides, rather than trying to manipulate its truths to accommodate our beliefs.

In the Torah G-d says that redemption will come for all mankind and that it will be led by a Messiah, a global leader with a universal message and the ability to transmit that message so that it resonates within every person on earth.

The Rebbe clearly stated that we have now reached the threshold of redemption, and we must all do our part in anticipating and preparing ourselves for this era, through study and good deeds. Central to the Rebbe's teachings is the acknowledgment that G-d has empowered each of us with the abilities to achieve our mission on earth, to attain a state of inner redemption, and to recognize the leader who will usher in universal redemption. No person can dictate who the Messiah is; only by studying and understanding G-d's words in Torah about the Messiah can we realize who meets these criteria.

The Rebbe taught passionately of autonomy in the course of a spiritual quest. He never required anyone to accept his authority—as a Messiah or, for that matter, even as a Rebbe. He selflessly offered his teachings to anyone who cared to listen and respond. He was not interested in perpetuating his name. The Rebbe often said that when his message was being shared with others, it should be done so in a manner that was most beneficial to the recipient. If it was better to mention the Rebbe's name within the message, so be it; if that would somehow alienate the listener, the message should not include his name. Self-aggrandizement was antithetical to the Rebbe's person.

So is the Rebbe the Messiah? You must answer this question for yourself. Remember, though, that whatever your answer is, it must incorporate your obligation to the all-inclusive objective, motivating you to perfect yourself and the world around you, inspiring you to bring redemption to yourself and everyone you meet, and to anticipate the redemption of the entire world.

ON A PERSONAL NOTE

I initially titled this book *Reality* because, for myself, "reality" is the one word that embodies the Rebbe. And the Rebbe is, in one word, reality. When speaking to, listening to, or reading the words of the Rebbe, one became transfixed by something that was truly real. No superficiality, no vanity, no gossip. There was a constant sense of urgency, a sense that our actions truly matter, that people really matter—that you and I, and everything we do, is of vital importance. And in a climate of cynicism and selfishness, it was more than revitalizing to experience a taste of such reality.

I believe that beneath the surface, many of us are just plain complacent. The pressures of society have convinced us that any one person hardly matters—that we will live and die and, ultimately, the world will remain unchanged. More than anything, the Rebbe taught that such an attitude is simply wrong. Like a good teacher, he communicated this through his actions as well as his words—through his ability to speak heart to heart well into the early morning hours; through his sensitivity to our frailties and insecurities; through his patience as a teacher in repeating an idea over and over until it was absorbed; through his unending pleas with G-d to alleviate human pain and suffering. In all these ways, the Rebbe embodied an unyielding commitment to virtue and an unwavering confidence in the human spirit. In our mercurial world, such confidence creates a security that can never be shaken; it gives a person something truly meaningful to live for.

I miss the Rebbe. I cry for the Rebbe, a true man of G-d. In my heart and mind, he still speaks for hours upon hours, his countenance shining, sharing a taste of reality with us. And I am committed to sharing the Rebbe with everyone with whom I come in contact. There is no doubt in my mind that the Rebbe and his message will prevail. Reality always does; such is its nature.

ACKNOWLEDGMENTS

———— ❧ ————

For this book to become a reality, it was necessary to render a pro-found and intimate knowledge of the Rebbe's teachings in a language that would be accessible for contemporary men and women—a task that could hardly have been accomplished by any one person.

The material in this book has benefited from the tutelage and guidance of many senior rabbis and scholars, and especially the scribes and editors of the Rebbe's talks, who have committed their lives to elucidating his teachings. These people are too numerous to name, but mention should be made of those to whom I am most indebted, teachers and colleagues who shared in the challenge of re-creating on paper the Rebbe's *farbrengens*. First and foremost, Rabbi Yoel Kahan, who from the beginning of the Rebbe's leadership in 1950 headed the team of "oral scribes," pioneering the method of transmitting the Rebbe's teachings. Also, Rabbis Leibel Altein, Nachman Shapiro, Dovid Feldman, Sholom Charitonow, Dovid Oli-dort, Aaron Leib Raskin, and Yosef Yitzchak Jacobson. I am also thankful to the members of Vaad L'Hafotzas Sichos (the Committee to Disseminate the Rebbe's Talks), headed by Rabbis Zalman Chanin and Sholom Jacobson; and "Sichos in English," headed by Rabbi Yonah Avtzon, and his chief writer Eliyahu Tauger, for allowing me the use of various materials. And, of course, the secretariat of the Rebbe, the late Rabbis Chaim M. A. Chadokov and Nissan Mindel, and Rabbis Yehudah Leib Groner, Yehudah Krinsky, Benyomin Klein, and Sholom Mendel Simpson.

On the other end of the spectrum, there are those who helped provide the vehicle by which the material could be presented to a mainstream audience.

I extend my special appreciation to Stephen Dubner, a young

journalist with heart and soul, without whose hard work and many talents this book would not have been possible. I would like to warmly thank Claire Wachtel, my editor at William Morrow, whose direction and encouragement—and patience—charted the course all along. In addition, Liz Perle McKenna, Will Schwalbe, and the entire staff at William Morrow, who so enthusiastically embraced this project. Especially my literary agent, Richard Pine, whose perspicacity was instrumental in the process and whose ongoing support moved it forward.

For their advice, counsel, and recommendations, I would like to thank Hirsh Goldberg, Ashley Lazarus, Zvi Almog, Michael Almog, Norbert Lempert, and Barbara Gamzu. For reviewing drafts of the manuscript and giving me invaluable comments, I thank Yermiyahu Branover, Naftoli Lowenthal, Simcha Gottleib, and Molly Chernotzky. And especially Naomi Perlman and Roy Pinchot for their exceptional input.

For this special edition, I want to especially acknowledge Howard Cohn and Peg Tyre for their invaluable assistance.

Special mention should be made of the thousands of the Rebbe's emissaries worldwide who carry on his work. They are the Rebbe's physically functioning voice, hands, and feet, spreading his teachings and implementing his directives; they travel to all corners of the earth, offering every person material aid and a means by which to quench their thirst for spiritual direction. I thank these emissaries for their help and inspiration, especially Rabbis Abraham Shemtov, Sholom Ber Lipskar, and Eli Cohen.

And I would like to thank my employer, The Meaningful Life Center, also known as Vaad Hanochos Hatmimim (the Committee to Produce and Publish Students' Transcripts of the Rebbe's Talks), and its staff, namely Chaim Abrahams, Baruch Jacobson, Menachem Shagalow, Zev Cadaner, Rochel Chana Schilder, Shoshanna Levin, and Neria Cohen. And particularly Yanki Tauber, the editor of *Week in Review*, a weekly publication presenting the Rebbe's teachings. And also our supporters: Berel Weiss, the Namdar family, Leibel and Yossi Simpson, and Rachel and Sarah Weinkrantz.

The proceeds from this book are going to a special Meaningful Life Center fund dedicated to publishing more of the Rebbe's works, perpetuating his teachings, and making them available to wide audiences, continuing to draw on the vast reservoir of material that has yet to be presented to the English-reading public.

BIOGRAPHY
Rabbi Menachem Mendel Schneerson
(1902-1994)

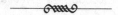

Rabbi Menachem Mendel Schneerson, the leader—"the Rebbe"—of the Lubavitch movement of Chassidic Judaism for forty-four years, was a paradoxical man. While he barely set foot outside his neighborhood during his entire leadership, his influence was felt worldwide. While he was considered one of the world's foremost religious scholars, he was also recognized as a brilliant scholar in mathematics and science. While he appeared to be an Old World leader whose community was somewhat cloistered, he was thoroughly knowledgeable about the modern world and reached out enthusiastically to society at large, to Jew and non-Jew alike, encouraging the pursuit of virtuousness, education, and unity.

Menachem Mendel Schneerson was born on April 18, 1902 (the eleventh day of Nissan, 5662), in Nikolayev, a town in the southern Ukraine. His father, Rabbi Levi Yitzchak Schneerson, was a renowned scholar; his mother, Rebbetzin Chana Schneerson, was an aristocratic woman from a prestigious rabbinic family. He had two younger brothers, Dovber and Yisroel Aryeh Leib. When Menachem Mendel was five years old, the family moved to Yekaterinoslav, now Dnepropetrovsk, where his father was appointed chief rabbi.

From early childhood, Menachem Mendel displayed prodigious mental acuity, leaving school for private tutoring. By the time he reached his bar mitzvah, he was considered a Torah prodigy, and during his teenage years, he immersed himself in the intricacies of

Torah study. In 1923, he met Rabbi Yosef Yitzchak Schneersohn—
then the Lubavitcher Rebbe—who drew him into his inner circle
giving him various responsibilities; five years later, in Warsaw, he
married the Rebbe's second-eldest daughter, Chaya Mushka (1901–
1988).

A short while later, the couple moved to Berlin, where Rabbi
Menachem Mendel had already begun studying mathematics and
science at the University of Berlin. Because of the Nazi rise, the
young rabbi and his wife left Berlin in 1933 for Paris, and he continued his studies at the Sorbonne. Primarily, however, he immersed
himself in prayer and religious study, and was referred to by his
father-in-law on various matters, including the preparation of Lubavitch publications. He also served as his father-in-law's private
secretary and traveled on his behalf to visit various Jewish leaders
in Europe.

When the Nazis occupied Paris, the couple was forced to escape
the city. On June 23, 1941, they arrived by boat in New York,
where Rabbi Yosef Yitzchak Schneersohn appointed his son-in-law
head of Lubavitch's educational arm, as well as the movement's
social-service organization and its publishing house.

In 1950, Rabbi Yosef Yitzchak passed away. Although Rabbi
Menachem Mendel was the obvious successor, he was initially reluctant to accept the mantle of leadership. A year later he formally
assumed the title of Rebbe, explaining to members of the movement
that while he would be devoted to his work as leader, each man
and woman was ultimately responsible for his or her own actions,
and for his or her own pursuit of G-dliness.

The ensuing forty-four years of the Rebbe's leadership saw Lubavitch grow from a small movement nearly devastated by the
Holocaust to a worldwide community of more than 200,000 members. The Rebbe, recognizing the unique needs of the current generation and anticipating the societal upheaval of the coming
decades, began to establish education and outreach centers, offering
social-service programs and humanitarian aid to all people, regardless of religious affiliation or background. He established a corps of

Lubavitch emissaries (*shluchim*) and sent them out to build Chabad-Lubavitch centers worldwide, to serve the spiritual and material needs of the local communities. Today, there are more than fourteen hundred Chabad-Lubavitch institutions in thirty-five countries on six continents.

By blending his intense religious and secular training with deep compassion and insight, the Rebbe quietly became a leader to whom other leaders—those in politics, business, and religion—turned for advice. Beginning in 1986, he would personally greet thousands of visitors each Sunday, distributing dollar bills that were meant to encourage the giving of charity; many people saved these dollar bills as a memento of their visit with the Rebbe, a testament to being moved by his presence.

In 1992, at the age of ninety, the Rebbe suffered a stroke; he passed away two years later, on June 12, 1994. Earlier, a bill was introduced in the U.S. House of Representatives by Congressmen Charles Schumer, John Lewis, Newt Gingrich, and Jerry Lewis to bestow on the Rebbe the Congressional Gold Medal. The bill passed both Houses by unanimous consent, honoring the Rebbe for his "outstanding and lasting contributions toward improvements in world education, morality, and acts of charity."

REFERENCES AND
NOTES

1. *Body and Soul*
1. Proverbs 20:27.
2. Genesis 2:7.
3. *Ibid.*, 2:25.
4. *Ibid.*, 3:7.
5. *Ibid.*, 25:27.
6. Ethics of the Fathers 5:20.
7. Zohar II:14a.

2. *Birth*
1. Talmud, Ohalot 7:6; *ibid.*, Sanhedrin 72b and Rashi's commentary there. See also Nachmanides on Talmud, Shabbat 107b and Niddah 44b; Meiri on Talmud, Shabbat 107b and Sanhedrin 72b.

The issue of abortion is often misrepresented as hinging solely on the question of whether a fetus is a "life," in which case its destruction is "murder," or not, in which case it is merely a question of "a woman exercising control over her own body." But there exist other moral wrongs aside from murder.

According to the Torah, abortion is *not* murder in its ultimate sense, and is therefore justified (and obligatory) if the pregnancy poses a danger to the mother's life. But it *is* the destruction of life, both of a living extension of the mother and of the potential for a full-fledged "soul." The issue of "women's rights" and individual freedom is not pertinent here: no human being, man or woman, has the right to destroy his own life and body or any part thereof, and society has the responsibility of preventing such acts and cultivating the love and sanctity of life.

2. Talmud, Eruvin 13b.
3. Jerusalem Talmud, Yevomot 1:6.
4. Ethics of the Fathers 2:9.

3. Childhood
1. Maimonides, Code of Law, *Laws of Repentance* 3:4.

4. Education
1. R. Tam, *Sefer Hayoshor* ch. 13. R. Isaiah Hurwitz, *Shaloh* 69a.
2. Talmud, Sotah 47a.
3. Talmud, Taanit 7a.

5. Youth
1. Deuteronomy 32:7.

6. Marriage
1. Genesis 1:27.
2. Midrash Rabbah, Bereishit 8:1.
3. Talmud, Sotah 17a.
4. Genesis 1:28.

7. Love
1. Leviticus 19:18.
2. See Tanya, ch. 32.
3. Talmud, Shabbat 31a.
4. Psalms 89:3.
5. Ethics of the Fathers 1:12.
6. Talmud, Berachot 10a.

8. Intimacy
1. Genesis 2:24.
2. *Ibid.*, 1:28.
3. *Ibid.*, 2:25.
4. *Ibid.*, 3:7.

9. Home and Family
1. Proverbs 27:19.
2. *Ibid.*, 14:1.
3. Genesis 21:12.

10. Health and Fitness
1. Talmud, Bava Kamma 85a.
2. Exodus 15:26.

11. Work and Productivity
1. Talmud, Sanhedrin 99b, based on Job 5:7, cited at the beginning of the chapter.

2. Jerusalem Talmud, Orlah 1:3. See Talmud, Bava Metzia 38a.
3. Talmud, Megillah 6b.
4. Midrash Mechilta, Exodus (portion of Yitro) 19:5, cited in Rashi on verse.

12. *Charity and Wealth*
1. Proverbs 21:21.
2. Midrash Tanchuma, Mishpatim 9, citing Psalms 61:8.
3. Midrash Rabbah, Vayikra 34:8.
4. Tanya, ch. 37.
5. Deuteronomy 8:18.
6. Tanya, *Iggeret HaTeshuvah* ch. 3 (p. 93a). *Iggeret HaKodesh* ch. 10 (p. 115b).
7. Talmud, Taanit 9a.
8. Torah Or, Bereishit 1b.

13. *Aging and Retirement*
1. Psalms 84:8.
2. Leviticus 19:32. Talmud, Kidushin 32b.

14. *Death and Grieving*
1. Talmud, Taanit 5b.
2. Maimonides, Code of Law, *Laws of the Mourner* 13:11–12.
3. *Ibid.*, 13:12.
4. Isaiah 25:8.

15. *Pain and Suffering*
1. Job 29:18.
2. Talmud, Berachot 60b.
3. *Ibid.*, 54a.

16. *Fear and Anxiety*
1. Opening of the Code of Jewish Law (Shulchan Aruch).
2. Talmud, Berachot 55b.
3. *Ibid.*, 28b.
4. Midrash Rabbah, Bamidbar 12:3.
5. Talmud, Yoma 75a.

17. *A Day of Life*
1. Talmud, Sukkah 5a.

18. *Responsibility*
1. Midrash Rabbah, Bamidbar 12:3.
2. Talmud, Sanhedrin 37a.

19. Government

1. Maimonides, Code of Law, *Laws of Kings* 8:10–11.
2. Midrash Tanchuma, Pekudei 3.
3. Isaiah 2:4.

20. *Leadership*

1. Talmud, Berachot 5b.
2. Exodus 3:1.
3. Midrash Rabbah, Shmot 2:2.
4. Talmud, Horiot 10b. As G-d told Moses: "I have given you greatness only for them" (*ibid.*, Berachot 32a).
5. Exodus 3:11.
6. Numbers 12:3.

21. *Women and Men*

1. Talmud, Shabbat 77b.
2. Midrash Rabbah, Bereishit 8:1.
3. R. Schneur Zalman of Liadi, *Torah Or* 45a-b. *Likkutei Torah*, Shir Hashirim 48b.
4. Talmud, Yevomot 62b. Maimonides, Code of Law, *Laws of Women* 15:19.

22. *Science and Technology*

1. Maimonides, Code of Law, *Laws of the Fundamental Principles of the Torah* 4:12.
2. Zohar I:117a.
3. The Rebbe was once asked his opinion about the statement attributed to Einstein (upon hearing the indeterminism propounded by quantum theory): "G-d doesn't play dice with the universe." The Rebbe replied that Einstein was incorrect since G-d is not bound by the laws of nature which He created. This, interestingly, parallels Niels Bohr's supposed response to Einstein's comment, "Don't tell G-d what to do."
4. In 1934, Karl Popper, the Austrian-British philosopher of science, propounded the idea that a scientific hypothesis must be falsifiable. What makes it scientific is the fact that is can conceivably be proved wrong. For example, the statement "G-d exists" is not a scientific hypothesis because it is not susceptible to disproof. He writes in *The Logic of Scientific Discovery* (1959), "Science is not a system of certain, or well-established, statements; nor is it a system which steadily advances towards a state of finality. Our science is not knowledge: it can never claim to have attained truth, or even a substitute for it, such as probability.... *We do not know: we can only guess.* And our guesses are guided

by the unscientific, the metaphysical (though biologically explicable) faith in laws, in regularities we can uncover/discover. . . . The old scientific ideal of *episteme*—of absolutely certain, demonstrable knowledge —has proved to be an idol. The demand for scientific objectivity makes it inevitable that every scientific statement must remain *tentative for ever*. . . ."

Just as Heisenberg showed that in subatomic physics laws are at best probabilities, and Popper showed how this is true in general sci-entific theory, Gö del demonstrated the same in mathematics. Gö del's Theorem proves that there exist meaningful mathematical statements that are neither provable nor disprovable, now or ever. That is, not simply because human thought or knowledge is insufficiently advanced but because the very nature of logic renders them incapable of resolution, no matter how long the human race survives or how wise it becomes. "No axiomatic system containing arithmetic can demonstrate its own consistency, so we can never know for sure whether our system is consistent. Any such system must have true statements which are unprovable within the system." The Rebbe addresses this point in a prepared talk for a conference of mathematicians. (See his manuscripts ["*reshimos*"], vol. 3, p. 48. Letter of June 5, 1952, *Igrot Kodesh*, vol. 6, p. 145.)

The Hungarian mathematician Eugene Paul Wigner writes in *Communications in Pure and Applied Mathematics* (1960): "All laws of nature are conditional statements which permit a prediction of some future events on the basis of the knowledge of the present. . . . Thus, classical mechanics, which is the best-known prototype of a physical theory, gives the second derivatives of the positional coordinates of all bodies, on the basis of the knowledge of the positions, etc., of these bodies. It gives no information on the existence, the present position, or velocities of these bodies. . . . Even the conditional statements cannot be entirely precise . . . the conditional statements are probability laws which enable us only to place intelligent bets on future properties of the inanimate world, based on the knowledge of the present state. They do not allow us to make categorical statements, not even categorical statements conditional on the present state of world." Quantum physicist Niels Bohr said, "It is wrong to think that the task of physics is to find out how Nature *is*. Physics concerns what we can say about Nature."

5. Tanya, ch. 4.

6. Midrash Tanchuma, Pekudei 3.

7. In Heisenberg's words: "What we observe is not nature itself, but nature exposed to our method of questioning." "Natural science does not simply describe and explain nature; it is part of the interplay of

nature and ourselves" (*Physics and Philosophy*, pp. 58 and 81). The physicist John Wheeler explains: "Nothing is more important about the quantum principle than this, that it destroys the concept of the world as 'sitting out there,' with the observer safely separated from it by a 20-centimeter slab of plate glass. Even to observe so minuscule an object as an electron, he must shatter the glass. He must reach in. He must install his chosen measuring equipment. It is up to him to decide whether he shall measure position or momentum. To install the equipment to measure the one prevents and excludes his installing the equipment to measure the other. Moreover, the measurement changes the state of the electron. The universe will never afterward be the same. To describe what has happened, one has to cross out that old word 'observer' and put in its place the new word 'participator.' In some strange sense, the universe is a participatory universe" (J. Mehra, ed., *The Physicist's Conception of Nature*, p. 244).

23. *Upheaval and Change*
1. Talmud, Tamid 32a.
2. Genesis 28:15.
3. Midrash Rabbah, Bereishit 42:4.
4. Midrash, Yalkut Shemoni, Isaiah remez 499.

24. *Our Generation*
1. Midrash Rabbah, Shir Hashirim 5:1.

25. *G-d*
1. Song of Songs 5:1.
2. Midrash Rabbah, *loc. cit.*
3. Exodus 3:14.
4. See Tanya, *Iggeret HaKodesh*, section 20 (130b).
5. Maimonides, *Guide for the Perplexed*, 1:57, 63.
6. Deuteronomy 4:35.
7. *Ibid.*, 4:39.
8. Midrash Tanchuma, Nasso 16. Tanya, ch. 36.
9. It is important to eliminate any anthropomorphic notions which may be inferred from these concepts and their analogies. They must be understood in nonspatial and noncorporeal terms. It is only that "the Torah speaks in the language of man," in order for humans to be able to have some conception of these ideas. But it must be kept in mind at all times that these terms and concepts need to be stripped of any temporal, spatial and corporeal connotations, for they are all nonascribable to the Divine.

10. Talmud, Shabbat 133b. Sifri on Deuteronomy 11:22. Maimonides, Code of Law, *Laws of Proper Conduct* 1:6.

26. *Faith and Reason*
1. Psalms 102:1.
2. Proverbs 3:6.
3. R. Joseph Albo, *Ikkarim* II:30.

27. *Unity*
1. "There is none else": Deuteronomy 4:39.
2. *Ibid.*
3. I Kings 5:11–12.
4. Genesis 28:12,13,15.
5. I Samuel 24:14. Rashi on Talmud, Makot 10b. See *Or Hatorah Shmot*, p. 152.

28. *Philosophy and Practicality*
1. Talmud, Kidushin 40b.
2. Ethics of the Fathers 1:17.
3. *Ibid.*, 3:17.
4. Midrash Tanchuma, Nasso 16.

29. *Good and Evil*
1. See Mishne, Keilim 2:1. R. Sholom Dovber of Lubavitch, discourse Ner Chanukah 5670.
2. Talmud, Yoma 85b.
3. Genesis 18:25.
4. Isaiah 55:8.

30. *Miracles*
1. R. Israel Baal Shem Tov, *Keser Shem Tov*, ch. 119, 256. See R. Tzvi Ashkanazi, *Chacham Tzvi*, ch. 18.
2. Schroedinger writes (1933): "It is a miracle that in spite of the baffling complexity of the world, certain regularities in nature can be discovered."
3. R. Yitzchak A'ramoh, *Akeidat Yitzchak*, ch. 38.
4. See note 3 in Chapter 22.
5. R. Nissim, *Droshos HaRan*, Drosho 8.
6. Talmud, Pesachim 64b.

31. Redemption
   1. Maimonides, Code of Law, *Laws of Kings*, chs. 11-12.
   2. *Ibid.*, 11:4

SELECTED
BIBLIOGRAPHY
Of the Rebbe's Teachings

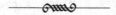

Talks, Letters, and Writings

Sichos, talks, 1950–92 (Yiddish, Hebrew), 100 vols.

Maamorim, Chassidic discourses, 1950–88 (Hebrew), 20 vols.

Sefer Hama'marim-Melukat, selected Chassidic discourses, 6 vols. (Vaad L'Hafotzas Sichos, 1988–92)

Sefer Hasichot, talks 1988–92 (Yiddish, Hebrew), 10 vols. (Vaad L'Hafotzas Sichos)

Likkutei Sichot, selected talks (Yiddish, Hebrew), 39 vols. (Vaad L'Hafotzas Sichos, 1962–95)

Torat Menachem-Hadranim Al HaRambam VehaShas, essays on Maimonides and Talmud, 1980–90 (Hebrew) (Vaad Hanochos B'Lahak, 1992)

Igrot Kodesh, responsa (Yiddish, Hebrew), 1928–65, 24 vols. (Kehot Publication Society, 1987–95)

Letters by the Lubavitcher Rebbe (English), 1950–78 (Vaad L'Hafotzas Sichos, 1979)

Letters to the Lubavitch Women's Organization (English), 1956–80 (Lubavitch Women's Organization, 1981)

Teshuvot Ubi'urim (Hebrew) (Vaad L'Hafotzas Sichos, 1974)

Reshimos, 187 issues (Hebrew) (Kehot Publication Society, 1995)

English Translations and Adaptations

Hayom Yom (From Day to Day), an anthology of Chassidic aphorisms and customs, arranged according to the days of the year (Kehot Publication Society, 1988)

Passover Haggada, with commentary (Vaad L'Hafotzas Sichos, 1983)

Likkutei Sichot, 4 vols. (Vaad L'Hafotzas Sichos,1979–91)

Proceeding Together, the early talks of the Rebbe, in 1950 (Sichos in English, 1995)

Sichos in English, selected talks 1978–92, free English translations, 51 vols. (Sichos in English)

Week in Review, weekly publication (Vaad Hanochos Hatmimim).

The Inside Story: A Chassidic Perspective on Biblical Events, Encounters and Personalities (Vaad Hanochos Hatmimim, 1997)

Torah Studies, selected talks on the weekly Torah portions (Lubavitch Foundation, London, 1986)

The Chassidic Dimension, selected talks on the weekly Torah portions and the festivals (Vaad L'Hafotzas Sichos, 1990)

A Thought for the Week, 12 vols. (Merkos L'inyonei Chinuch, Detroit, 1969–82)

In the Garden of Torah, insights in the weekly Torah Readings, 2 vols. (Sichos in English, 1994–95)

Timeless Patterns in Time, Chassidic Insights into the Cycle of the Jewish Year, 2 vols. (Sichos in English, 1993–94)

In the Paths of Our Fathers, insights in the Ethics of the Fathers (Sichos in English, 1994)

Beyond the Letter of the Law: A Chassidic Companion to the Ethics of the Fathers (Vaad Hanochos Hatmimim, 1995)

A Partner in the Dynamic of Creation, on womanhood (Sichos in English, 1995)

Basi LeGani, Yud Shvat 5711 (1951), first Chassidic discourse (Sichos in English, 1990)

On the Essence of Chassidus, essay (Vaad L'Hafotzas Sichos, 1978)

Sefer HaMinhagim, Chabad-Lubavitch Customs (Sichos in English, 1992)

To Know and to Care, contemporary Chassidic stories about the Rebbe (Sichos in English, 1993)

Please Tell Me What the Rebbe Said, Torah insights, for children (Sichos in English, 1993)

At Our Rebbe's Seder Table, commentary and stories (Sichos in English, 1995)

From Exile to Redemption, Chassidic teachings on the future redemption and the Messiah (Sichos in English, 1992)

I Await His Coming Every Day, analytical studies of Maimonides' rulings on Messiah and the redemption (Sichos in English, 1991)

Sound the Great Shofar, essays on the imminence of the redemption (Sichos in English, 1992)

Seek Out the Welfare of Jerusalem, analytical studies on Maimonides' rulings concerning the construction and the design of the Holy Temple (Sichos in English, 1994)

Anticipating the Redemption, Chassidic discourses concerning the era of redemption (Sichos in English, 1994)

For more information on these and other texts, please visit www.meaningfullife.com, or call or write the author at The Meaningful Life Center, 788 Eastern Parkway, Suite 303, Brooklyn, New York 11213-3409. Telephone: 718-774-6448. Fax: 718-774-7329. E-mail: WisdomReb@aol.com.

About the Author

For fourteen years, RABBI SIMON JACOBSON was responsible for publishing the talks of Rabbi Menachem Mendel Schneerson, the Lubavitcher Rebbe. Rabbi Jacobson is a widely traveled and prolific public speaker, and lives in Brooklyn, New York. He is also the founder of the Meaningful Life Center, which builds bridges between the secular and the spiritual, and helps people discover the deeper meaning of their lives based on the three-thousand-year-old wisdom of the sages.